ABSOLUTE BEGINNER'S GUIDE

TO

Microsoft Office

FrontPage 2003

Jennifer Ackerman Kettell and Kate J. Chase

800 East 96th Street,
Indianapolis, Indiana 46240

Absolute Beginner's Guide to Microsoft Office FrontPage 2003

International Standard Book Number: 0-7897-2966-0

Library of Congress Catalog Card Number: 2003110437

Printed in the United States of America

First Printing: December 2003

06   05   04   03   4   3   2   1

Trademarks

Warning and Disclaimer

Bulk Sales

Que Publishing offers excellent discounts on this book when ordered in quantity for bulk purchases or special sales. For more information, please contact

U.S. Corporate and Government Sales
1-800-382-3419
corpsales@pearsontechgroup.com

For sales outside of the U.S., please contact

International Sales
1-317-428-3341
international@pearsontechgroup.com

Associate Publisher
Greg Wiegand

Acquisitions Editor
Angelina Ward

Development Editor
Howard Jones

Managing Editor
Charlotte Clapp

Project Editor
Sheila Schroeder

Copy Editor
Kate Shoup Welsh

Indexer
Johnna Dinse

Proofreader
Katie Robinson

Technical Editor
Bill Bruns

Publishing Coordinator
Sharry Lee Gregory

Interior Designer
Ann Jones

Cover Designer
Dan Armstrong

Page Layout
Susan Geiselman

Contents at a Glance

Table of Contents

About the Authors

Jennifer Ackerman Kettell has written and contributed to more than a dozen books on Web design, digital photography, and software applications. Her books for Que include *Special Edition Using Dreamweaver MX*, written with Molly E. Holzschlag. For more than 10 years, Jenn was a part of developing and managing some of the most prominent online communities of their time on services such as MSN, Delphi, and Genie. In addition, she has designed Web sites for a wide range of professional, commercial, and nonprofit entities. You can visit Jenn at her Web site, www.gilajenn.com.

Kate J. Chase is the author, co-author, or editor of more than a dozen books on Web design, PC hardware, operating systems, and Windows-based applications. A FrontPage user almost since the product's debut, Kate employs the program to create content and to manage her own professional site at www.kchase.com. Besides writing, Kate has managed thriving technical online and Web communities for such giants as America Online, MSN, and ZD-Net, in addition to consulting on office automation and issues in telecommuting.

Dedication

This book is dedicated to Roberta Ackerman, who's cut from the finest cloth.

Jennifer Ackerman Kettell

This book is dedicated to FrontPage users (such as Terri Stratton) who enjoy the product and constantly discover new levels they can take it to.

Kate J. Chase

Acknowledgments

Thanks to everyone at Que for their contributions to this project, particularly Sharry Gregory, Howard Jones, and Angelina Ward. This book wouldn't have been possible without my co-author, Kate Chase, and I'm grateful for all her hard work. I'm fortunate to have a wonderfully supportive family, and I'd like to thank Greg, Mandy, Zach, and Roberta for their love and commitment. Additional thanks go to Gillian Whitney, Jennifer Montoya, Phil Berman, Carol Berman, Irwyn Berman, and Jeff Rose.

Thanks also to Dr. Mark Yorra, who helped one of the authors through a nasty bout of double pneumonia while writing.

Introduction

During the past 10 years, the Internet has evolved from black text on gray backgrounds written by college professors into living color multimedia designed by everyone from the youngest animé fan to the secretary of the senior gardening club. Billions of pages are added to the Web every day, covering every topic imaginable, weaving a rich tapestry of knowledge and culture previously unimagined. Now it's time to add your thread to the loom.

Deciding to add your voice to the Web can be intimidating. As the Web has evolved from that gray screen and black text, the demands placed upon the site developer have similarly evolved. Web design is now about integrating content with layout to give visual punch to your message—making the site developer assume the role of graphic artist. More recently, Web sites have also reached through the monitor to grab the user and make them an integral part of the Web experience. Message boards, Web logs (blogs), and guest books have given birth to thriving communities—and have forced developers to assume the role of customer-service manager. This dynamic content, including databases, has also turned the Web developer into a programmer as the scripting languages required to invoke such connectivity become more complex.

Of course, not everyone is a graphic artist/customer-service manager/programmer. Fortunately, FrontPage 2003 doesn't expect you to assume such a long-winded job title. Instead, FrontPage takes on these various personae for you, freeing you to return to your primary role: creating the content that forms the meat of your site. FrontPage offers templates and themes to provide the layout and graphics for your site. Some of these templates include dynamic content to enable you to solicit feedback from and communication between your site's visitors. And advanced content such as database connectivity and dynamically updated stock tickers are inserted with wizards and Web components that don't require you to program a single line of code.

Perhaps one of the best features of FrontPage, however, is that it doesn't presume to take on jobs you'd prefer to carry out yourself. If you're the creative type, you can design your own templates, themes, or individual pages. Programmers can write their own scripts. You can even use FrontPage simply as a code editor, writing the HTML yourself. You can have it all, or you can use very little—FrontPage leaves it up to you.

That said, a program as complex as FrontPage certainly has its quirks and its own ways of doing things. That's where this book comes in. *Absolute Beginner's Guide to FrontPage 2003* explains everything you need to get started as a Web designer, from creating your first page to publishing and maintaining a complete site. While you may start as a beginner, you'll find that you're soon delving into those extra roles—and this book will help you take the first steps into those areas, as well.

How This Book Is Organized

This book is organized into five parts, as follows:

- Part I, "Getting Started," familiarizes you with the FrontPage environment and helps you create sites and pages.

- Part II, "Designing Webs and Pages," takes you step-by-step through adding content to your pages—text, links, and graphics. You'll also learn how to use tables and frames to control layout, giving you more flexibility with regards to where your content falls on the page.

- Part III, "Designing Dynamically and Interactively," helps you design a logical navigation structure to help your visitors move throughout your site. You'll also learn how to use Cascading Style Sheets (CSS) to hold all the formatting for your text and layout, enabling you to give your site a whole new look simply by modifying one file. Finally, this section will teach you how to add dynamic and interactive elements such as forms, layers, databases, and other components to bring your site to life.

- Part IV, "Publishing Your Web," talks you through testing your finished site and publishing it on the Web. If you don't already have a Web host to store and serve your pages on the Internet, this section will help you determine your needs and find the right provider, then show you how to upload your files to that provider. Of course, no site is ever truly finished, and so you'll learn how to check up on your site's health and maintain it. In addition, because your site simply joins the billions of others on the Web, it's important to promote it; in this part, you'll learn how to put your best foot forward with search engines and how to market your site.

- Part V, "Coding Your Web," lifts the hood to show you the HTML code underneath your designs. If you're looking to dig directly into the development of your site—getting you the greatest level of control and the most responsibility—you'll get an overview of HTML, style sheets, and scripting and learn how to use FrontPage's HTML coding tools.

By the time you finish reading this book, you should know the basics of designing, developing, and publishing your site. You'll also know how to add the bells and whistles that can help your site stand out from the rest of the pack. Although this book doesn't purport to explain every feature and advanced tool, it will certainly set you on the right path to solid Web design with FrontPage.

Conventions Used in This Book

There's nothing worse than losing track of the message of a book because it's difficult to follow. The layout of this book is fairly straightforward, although there are a few conventions of which you should be aware. There are sidebars in many chapters that provide information about Web design in general, not necessarily specific to FrontPage. We hope you find these design insights to be helpful.

This book also contains information of special importance related to a topic at hand. These elements are formatted as follows:

tip

A *tip* is a bit of advice or insight into how to use a particular feature more efficiently or in an undocumented manner.

note

A *note* provides information that explains or warns of unexpected results or adds necessary context to a seemingly odd requirement.

caution

A *caution* warns of dire results should you take a particular action, such as deleting an element from a page.

PART I

Getting Started

IN THIS CHAPTER

- Getting over the intimidation factor of all those views and options

- Getting the Task Pane and Folders List out of your way--and getting them back when they're really needed.

- Finding additional answers for FrontPage and Web-design questions

- Using Find and Replace to make changes from a small to a grand scale

1

GETTING STARTED WITH FRONTPAGE 2003

Opening FrontPage for the first time is a bit like getting a present from your elderly aunt--you're excited about getting something new, but not quite sure what to do with it. Indeed, the menus, toolbars, task panes, and views are rather confusing and even a bit intimidating at first. They make Web design look incredibly challenging, which is definitely the wrong impression. Once you start looking closely at the FrontPage environment and getting on with the task of developing your first Web site, however, you'll soon find that you're as comfortable in FrontPage as you are with that eight-foot-long, brightly striped scarf you now wear all winter.

Becoming Familiar with the FrontPage Environment

FrontPage is both a Web-design and a site-maintenance tool. Not surprisingly, the features of FrontPage that enable you to perform these interrelated tasks require more than just a lengthy display of menus. If you take a look at FrontPage when you first open it, as shown in Figure 1.1, the workspace consists not only of menus but also of toolbars, a folder list, a task pane, and a variety of view options. The actual design and site management are done in the main window. Development is done using the tools in the toolbars and menus. You access new webs and pages, themes, templates, behaviors, and outside resources using the task pane on the right side of the screen. Finally, the folder list on the left side of the screen helps you keep your bearings.

FIGURE 1.1

The main window of FrontPage puts all of the features and tools within reach.

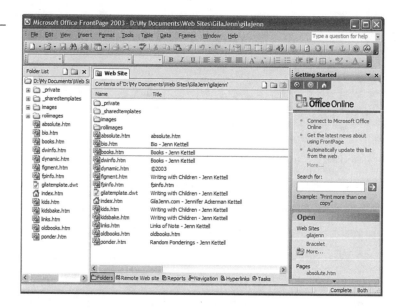

Using the Task Pane

The task pane was introduced in several Microsoft products two years ago in Office XP. Critical tasks such as opening Web sites and pages are performed here. As shown in Figure 1.2, you can also use the task pane when working with layout tables and cells, adding behaviors and layers to a page, displaying search results, and working with databases. The advantage of using a task pane for these tools rather than a dialog box is that you can work in the task pane and the main window concurrently and interactively.

FIGURE 1.2

Switch task
panes by click-
ing the down
arrow to the
right of the title.

The task pane is also the key gateway to accessing external resources and information. Adding clip art to your site? There's a task pane to serve as an interface
between FrontPage and image files on your computer and the Web. Need help using
the drawing tools? The Help task pane can connect you to Microsoft's training and
assistance pages for FrontPage (see the section titled "Finding Help" later in this
chapter). Adding a theme to the site? The Theme task pane accesses the themes
installed on your computer.

As useful as the task pane can be, it also takes up quite a bit of screen real estate. To
hide the task pane from view, click the Close button (the one with an × on it) in the

upper-right corner of the pane, or choose View,
Task Pane (alternatively, press Ctrl+F1). Don't be
afraid to close the pane; it'll return automatically when you choose a menu option or tool
that requires its use.

If having the pane on the right side of the screen
interferes with your sense of order, you can move
it by clicking the textured area to the left of the
pane title (noticeable because the cursor will
change to a four-sided arrow when it rests over
this area) and dragging it to a new location.
Once it's pulled away from the right side of the
screen, the task pane can float freely on the
screen. If you drag it to the left side of the screen,
it will automatically dock to that side. To return

tip

When dragging the task
pane back to its original
location on the right side of
the screen, you may think it's
not going to "grab." Keep
dragging until the left side
of the task pane is almost
over the right edge of the
FrontPage window. It'll find its
way home.

the task pane to its original location, drag it all the way to the right side of the FrontPage window.

Menus and Toolbars

Of course, you don't just want to look at an empty window. The menu bar and toolbars contain the tools, features, and commands necessary to add text and graphics and otherwise develop and maintain your Web site. If you're at all familiar with the current versions of other Microsoft products, you'll know that the menus change seemingly on a whim. Initially, the menu options that Microsoft believes people use the most are visible on each menu; you can access the rest of the menu by clicking the down arrow at the bottom of the menu. As you use FrontPage, however, the menus will change to display the commands *you* use most often while hiding commands that haven't seen much use. Far from simplifying the menus, however, this just makes them more confusing. Fortunately, you can set FrontPage (and the other Microsoft Office 2003 Suite applications) to show the full menu structure. To do so, choose Tools, Customize; in the dialog box that appears, select the Options tab and click the Always Show Full Menus check box to check it.

The toolbars contain the same comments and features listed in the menus, but put them within easier reach. The Standard and Formatting toolbars are open by default. Other toolbars, such as Drawing and Tables, automatically open when you choose those options from the menu. You can also manually view and hide toolbars by right-clicking in the empty space of the toolbar area or choosing View, Toolbars. This is yet another way in which you can view or hide the task pane, as well.

note

The individual toolbars and buttons are covered in relevant chapters so that you can understand their use in the proper context instead of as an obscure reference here.

As with the task pane, toolbars can be moved around. Some toolbars will automatically open as floating bars or dock to the bottom of the screen. To rearrange things, click the textured box on the left side of each toolbar and drag it to your desired location. If you pull a docked toolbar away from the top, bottom, or sides of the screen, it will automatically transform into a floating toolbar. Conversely, dragging a floating toolbar to one of these sides will dock the toolbar in that location. Use the same method to change the order in which toolbars are stacked at the top of the screen, if you wish.

Folder List

The Folder List does exactly what its name implies. When you first open a Web site that you're designing or maintaining in FrontPage, the Folder List might seem redundant next to the Folders view in the main window, but it becomes much more useful when you're actually working on pages. Open files are noted in the Folder List with a pencil over the file icon, as shown in Figure 1.3. The main page (usually named index.htm or default.htm) is displayed with a house icon to show its importance as the foundation of the site. Web sites usually have various folders to hold the images, multimedia, and even other pages; these folders are denoted with a yellow folder icon. Click the plus sign to the left of a folder icon to view the files within it.

FIGURE 1.3

The Folder List helps you navigate the file structure of your site.

The Folder List not only keeps you oriented, it also can be used to open or add new pages and folders. To open a file, double-click it. Perhaps one of the nicest features of the Folder List is the ability to create a new blank page without launching the New task pane. Just click the New Page icon at the top of the list. To add a folder, click the New Folder icon.

FUN WITH FILES

The Folder List is much more useful than it first appears. You can use it not only to create and open files, but also to delete or rename them. You can also open a file in another program directly from the Folder List. You can also use the Folder List to preview a file in your Web browser without opening it first. To see these options, right-click on a file to open the context menu.

The Folder List is another one of those tools that's useful at times, but also hogs its share of the screen. You have two choices in dealing with this. First, you can close it by clicking on the Close (x) button in the upper-right corner of the list (you can always re-open the Folder List by choosing View, Folder List or by pressing Alt+F1). You can also resize the Folder List by moving the cursor over the divider between the Folder List and the main window until it changes to a double-sided arrow bar, and then dragging the border to the left or right.

At the bottom of the Folder List are icons to toggle the view from the Folder List to the Navigation pane. The Navigation pane shows you how your pages are linked together, but only if you've used FrontPage's navigation tools to establish the navigational structure of the Web site.

FOLDERS VERSUS NAVIGATION

The Folder and Navigation Lists and views can be confusing at first. The Folder List and Folder view display the file structure of the Web site, showing what files, folders, and Web pages are contained within it. The Navigation view shows the navigational structure of the Web site itself--that is, how your site visitors will navigate from page to page when your site is published. Just because two pages are listed in the Folder List or view doesn't mean those pages are linked together on your site. Likewise, the linking (navigation) relationship of two pages in your site has no bearing on the location of those pages within the file structure. FrontPage's navigation tools are explained in Chapter 12, "Creating a Navigation Structure."

The Main Window

The most obvious area of the FrontPage screen is the main window. All your actual design and maintenance work is done here, with all the other tools and panes merely serving to make features and files available to get this work done. The appearance of this window changes depending on which view you're using. When you first open a site, the main window will be in Folders view, and it will contain a list of all the files and folders in the Web site. If you double-click one of those HTML files, such as index.htm, the main window will automatically change to Page view. The other views are accessible from the view buttons at the bottom of the main window. These are explained in the "Accessing Other Views" section later in this chapter.

Working in the Page Views

Page view is the workhorse of FrontPage, a place where pages are made, content is created and revised, and images are inserted to dance across the screen (hopefully not so many of those that you'll send your site visitors scrambling for the aspirin). Page view has several key features, as shown in Figure 1.4.

FIGURE 1.4

The tabs at the top of the Page view indicate that several other files are also open. An asterisk indicates that the current file hasn't yet been saved.

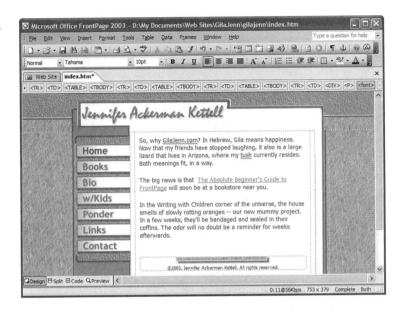

As you open pages, each one is given a tab at the top of the Page view. The Web Site tab, always the first tab on the left, contains the Folders view and provides access to the other views even when pages are open. Click on a tab to bring the respective page or the Web Site view to the forefront.

Pages can be viewed and edited in four different ways, each of which can be selected from the bottom of the main window.

Design view

Most FrontPage developers do the majority of their work in the Design view. Indeed, you can design your pages entirely in this view, adding everything you need using the toolbars, menus, and task panes.

This is commonly referred to as the *WYSIWYG* (short for *What You See Is What You Get*) view, but should more accurately be termed WYSRWYG, as in What You See Resembles What You Get. Remember, this is a working view, and various

note

Unfortunately, FrontPage doesn't make it easy to get your bearings when it comes to view terminology. Page view is a view in and of itself, yet it also has its own different views to control how the page is displayed. It would have been much easier to call the views within the Page view something else, such as screens. You're certainly free to think of them that way if it helps keep things straight.

visual cues to help you in your work will appear here, such as table grids, paragraph marks, and the occasional stray tag. Thus, it's not a truly accurate visual representation of your Web site's final appearance. It's also not useful as a testing environment because interactive buttons, scripts, and behaviors don't function in this view. Hyperlinks can be followed to their target, but only if you Ctrl+Click on them.

tip

If you have several open pages, FrontPage may run out of room to display all the tabs. To see more pages, click the arrows in the upper-right corner of the main window to scroll through the tabs. The Close (x) button can be used to close the current (foremost) page, or choose Windows, Close All Pages to close everything except the Web Site view.

Preview Page View

The Preview Page view provides a more accurate representation of a page. Hyperlinks and rollover buttons work here. As a matter of fact, if you follow a hyperlink to an external site (that is, a Web page outside of your site), the page will open in the Preview Page view if you're currently connected to the Internet.

This view is very useful, but it does have its limitations. You can't modify the page when it's displayed in Preview Page view. Also, keep in mind that Preview Page view only shows how your page will look in Internet Explorer with your current settings. To test your page in Netscape, Opera, or under different resolutions and color displays, you'll need to dig deeper. For more information about testing your site in different environments, see the section "Previewing in Multiple Browsers" in Chapter 19, "Testing Your Web."

Code view

Underlying the text and graphics of a Web site is HTML code. FrontPage automatically generates this code when you're working in the Design view, leaving you free to concentrate on designing your site instead of programming it. If you choose to become familiar with coding HTML, however, you might find that you prefer making quick changes directly to the code rather than using the menus and tools; in FrontPage, you do this in the Code view, shown in Figure 1.5. To learn more about working with HTML in FrontPage, see the section "Using the Code view" in Chapter 11, "Using Code in FrontPage."

Splitting the Page

If you find yourself frequently switching between Design and Code views--or if you're just learning HTML and want to see how elements are coded as they're added--use the Split page to get the best of both worlds. Split page divides the screen into two sections, half code and half design (see Figure 1.6). As you move around in each pane, the other is updated, so you're viewing the same section of the page in both panes. All changes made in the Design view are immediately updated in the Code view. Changes made in the Code view, however, aren't updated in the Design view until you click somewhere in the Design view pane.

FIGURE 1.5

The Code view automatically indents and wraps lines of HTML code to make them easier to navigate and modify.

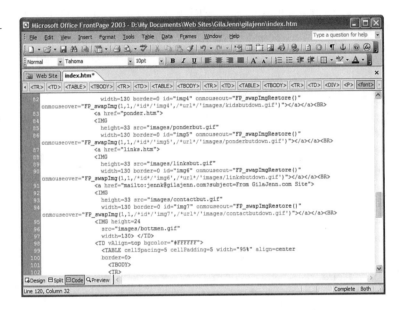

FIGURE 1.6

The Split page lets you work in Code and Design views concurrently, but limits the screen space available for each.

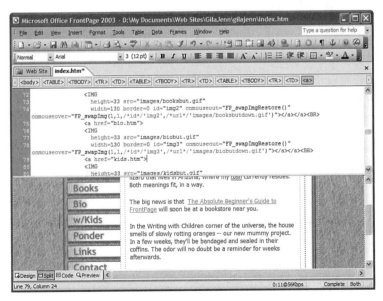

Quick Tag Selector

No matter which view you choose, the Quick Tag Selector is available at the top of each page. The Quick Tag Selector keeps track of your location on a page and lists the tags associated with that position. You can edit a tag using the drop-down menu button that appears when your mouse hovers over it in the Quick Tag Selector. If you're trying to avoid digging into HTML code, this tool is still useful to quickly select tables or paragraphs--just click on a tag and that area is selected in the Design Page or Code view. If just the thought of learning HTML tags makes you turn green, though, you can hide the Quick Tag Selector by choosing View, Quick Tag Selector.

Accessing Other Views

FrontPage reminds you of the need to keep the big picture in mind by opening with the Web Site view. Your site may start as a single page, but it will usually evolve into several or even dozens of pages. And even a single page makes use of graphics and other files. The Web Site views, listed at the bottom of the Web Site tab enable you to work on your entire site.

The Folders View

The Folders view duplicates the list of files and folders contained in the Folder List, but with greater detail. You can sort the list of files in the Folders view by page title, file size or type, modified date, or developer by clicking on the appropriate column heading.

To create a new file or folder, click the buttons on the top right of the Folders view window (shown in Figure 1.1). All the other file-management commands in the Folders view are available from a context menu; right-click a file or folder to open the menu. The context menu for a file contains the following options:

> **caution**
>
> You should do all your file management for your Web site in FrontPage. If you move or rename files in Windows Explorer or another package, you risk corrupting your FrontPage Web site. Be particularly careful about deleting files that appear in Windows Explorer but not in the FrontPage Folders view; FrontPage uses hidden files to store information about your Web site, but doesn't list them in the Folders view by default. To see these hidden files in FrontPage, choose Tools, Web Settings and click the Advanced tab in the Web Settings dialog box. Choose Show Hidden Files and Folders.

- **Open**--Opens the file in Page view. In the case of non-HTML files (such as graphics or multimedia), the file will open in an external editor.
- **Open With**--Opens the file using another package, chosen from the submenu for this option.

- **Open in New Window**--Opens the file in a new window or iteration of FrontPage.
- **New From Existing Page**--Copies the selected page and creates a new page containing the same content.
- **Preview in Browser**--Opens the selected page in your Web browser.
- **Preview in Multiple Browsers**--Opens the selected page in all the browsers you have installed on your computer.
- **Cut**--Moves the selected file(s) onto the Clipboard so that it can be pasted into another folder.
- **Copy**--Copies the selected file(s) onto the Clipboard so that it can be pasted into another folder.
- **Paste**--Pastes the current contents of the Clipboard into the selected location.
- **Set As Home Page**--Sets the selected page as the home page for your Web site. The home page is typically named index.htm or default.htm and is the page that automatically loads when visitors type just your domain name without specifying a particular file.
- **Rename**--Lets you edit the name of the selected file directly in the Folders view. Alternatively, you can click on the filename, pause, and then click the filename again to edit it.
- **Delete**--Deletes the selected file(s). A dialog box asks if you're sure you want to delete the file. If you say yes, the file is not only removed from the Web site, but also from your computer.
- **Publish Selected Files**--Publishes the selected file(s) to your remote site.
- **Don't Publish**--Marks the selected file(s) to be excluded when you publish your site. Toggle this option to include the file in a future Publish session.
- **Properties**--Opens the file's Properties dialog box, which displays information about the selected file and allows you to change the title of the page.

See the section "Setting Up Other Editors" in this chapter to learn how to configure other packages to edit non-HTML files. To learn how to publish a file to a remote site, see the section "Using the Remote Web Site View" in Chapter 21, "Putting Pages on the Internet."

The context menu for a folder contains options specific to folders. You can convert a folder to a Web site or a sub-Web (a separate Web site contained within the current site) to a folder.

The Remote Web Site View

The eventual goal of most Web development is to enable people to visit the completed site on the World Wide Web or an intranet. In FrontPage terms, site development takes place in your local Web site, and you publish to a remote Web site. Communication between the two locations takes place in the Remote Web Site view, shown in Figure 1.7.

FIGURE 1.7

The Remote Web Site view tracks files on both the local and remote Web sites to keep them synchronized and to transfer files between the two locations.

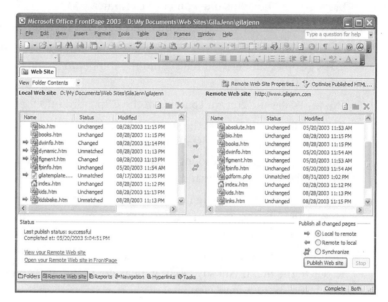

The Reports View

When you're developing a Web site, there are dozens of picayune issues to track, such as lists of hyperlinks to test, page sizes to monitor, and orphaned pages. The Reports view tracks all this information and provides detailed information about each issue in a site summary. For a complete list of reports and the information they track, see the section "Using Reports" in Chapter 22, "Maintaining a Published Web."

The Navigation View

If you establish the navigational structure of your site using link bars, you can view the hierarchy and linking relationships of your pages in Navigation view. To learn how to use Navigation view and create link bars, see the section "Using the Navigation View" in Chapter 12.

The Hyperlinks View

The Hyperlinks view, shown in Figure 1.8, shows the linking relationships of each page and file in your site. You can use it to examine the linking relationships of not only your pages, but also your pictures and external links. Pictures are not shown by default, but you can display them by right-clicking in a blank area of the Hyperlinks view and choosing Hyperlinks to Pictures from the context menu. The context menu also offers options to show page titles rather than filenames and to disable repeated hyperlinks (multiple links between the same two pages).

FIGURE 1.8

The Hyperlinks view uses arrows to show the linking relationship between files. To change the page in the center of the view, right-click on the page you want placed there and choose Move to Center.

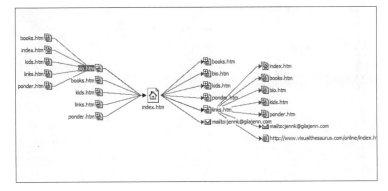

The Tasks View

It's easy to forget little details when you're designing a Web site. You might intend to look up the URL for a site, for example, but get lured away by the dog wanting a walk. The Tasks view lets you give yourself--and others on your design team, if you're working with a group--assignments related to your site. You add tasks by choosing Edit, Tasks or by right-clicking within the Tasks view to open the context menu. Tasks can be associated with the Web site as a whole or with a specific page. To learn how to assign and track tasks, see the section "Creating Tasks" in Chapter 22.

tip

If you choose not to use link bars--and many experienced developers opt out of using proprietary FrontPage tools such as those--the Hyperlinks view serves much the same role as the Navigation view. In fact it's even better because you can see more than just your pages.

Setting Up Other Editors

FrontPage is a full-featured HTML editor. Of course, not all the files associated with your Web site are HTML files. A complete Web site includes graphics, style sheets, and sometimes even multimedia, Adobe Acrobat portable documents (PDF files), and Word documents. Each of these files requires a different program to create and edit them, such as a graphics program to edit GIFs and JPGs, Adobe Acrobat to edit PDFs, and a style sheet editor to edit CSS files.

To configure another editor to modify a file, do the following:

1. Choose Tools, Options.

2. In the Options dialog box, click the Configure Editors tab (see Figure 1.9).

FIGURE 1.9

Configuring editors in FrontPage will spare you from manually hopping from program to program.

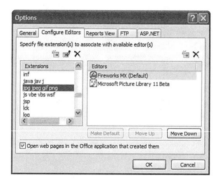

3. Choose a file extension from the list on the left. Any editor(s) currently associated with that extension will appear in the list on the right.

4. Click the New Editor button (Alt+N), the first button on the left above the Editors list, to select a new editor.

5. Choose an editor from the Open With dialog box. Click Browse for More if you need to search your hard disk for the appropriate editor.

6. Click OK to return to the Configure Editors dialog box.

7. Click OK to return to the main window.

caution

There's a quirk in the Configure Editors tool. If you need to configure a file extension that doesn't appear in the Extensions list, you can add it by clicking the New Extension button above the list. The dialog box that opens is the same as the Open With dialog box, except that the Extension field is blank to allow you to enter a new extension. This is all fun and games until someone gets hurt: If the extension already exists, even in combination with another extension, you'll go through the entire process of typing an extension and selecting an editor just to get hit with a warning dialog box saying the procedure can't be completed. How do you avoid this? Scan the Extensions list carefully; you'll find some extensions, such as GIF and JPG, grouped together (in this case, under J but not G).

In some cases, you have multiple editor options. For example, you might have Photoshop Elements and Fireworks installed, both of which can be set as external editors for GIF files. Select one program as the default; the program you set will automatically handle GIF files if you double-click on the file. The other editor is added to the Open With list in the context menu if you right-click the file.

Finding Help

FrontPage can sometimes be a lot to take in. It seems there's always some new aspect of Web design or coding to learn, which you'll then want to incorporate into your Web site. Unfortunately, screaming for help doesn't do much more than annoy the neighbors. A better resource is the index of this book. If you need more information than is provided between these covers, however, there are several other options.

Some of the best help resources are available directly in FrontPage. For example, you can use the Help task pane to search for matches to the search criteria you enter. You can limit the search to the offline help files or the online files at `http://office.microsoft.com`. This Microsoft site also has training and assistance files on a wide range of FrontPage topics, as well as additional themes and templates to spruce up your pages.

For help on more advanced FrontPage development topics, visit the Microsoft Developer Network at `http://msdn.microsoft.com/library/ default.asp?url=/nhp/default.asp?contentid= 28001170`. There, you'll find resources on such topics as using XML and creating advanced menu systems and style sheets.

If Microsoft's resources aren't enough, look beyond the fine folks in Redmond, Washington. FrontPage World (`http://www.frontpageworld.com`), managed by Paul

tip

If you're coming to FrontPage from Dreamweaver or another HTML editor, you might want to access some of the functionality of FrontPage while still doing most of your design work in a more familiar environment. If you associate .htm files with the other editor, you get the best of all worlds. Microsoft touts the compatibility of FrontPage and Dreamweaver code, ensuring an easy transition between the two packages.

tip

The Office Assistant, that animated paper clip equally loved and despised in previous versions of Microsoft products, is still available here, but it displays its results in the same task pane. Feel free to keep it disabled and just use the Help task pane directly.

Colligan, is the Internet's most visited FrontPage-related site. Alternatively, check out Site Builder (http://www.net-sites.com/sitebuilder/frontpage/index.asp), which is managed by Dave Berry, a Microsoft MVP.

THE ABSOLUTE MINIMUM

The trick to using FrontPage is to not let yourself get overwhelmed by all the options. There's no quiz at the end of this book, so relax. Just because you can get your hands dirty in code doesn't mean you need to immediately memorize every HTML tag. It's fun to look at your site in all the different views, but you'll spend most of your time in Page view.

At a bare minimum, you can design a cutting edge, complex site using only the Folders view and the Design view, along with the menu and toolbar options that help you put content onto the page. Throw in a visit to the Remote Sites view to publish your page, and you're done. If you later want to master the intricacies of using the other views to get the best effect, take it on a task-by-task basis, learning only what you need when you need it.

IN THIS CHAPTER

- A little bit of site planning can save a big amount of time.

- Create the Web site first, and the pages will follow.

- You don't have to reinvent the wheel—you can import an existing Web site.

- You can create, open, save, and even delete Web sites and pages with ease.

2

CREATING SITES AND PAGES

It's tempting to jump right in and throw a page onto the screen to start working in FrontPage. Indeed, you'd probably learn quite a bit about the tools and options just by hacking away at them. You'd probably also wind up spending a lot of time making and fixing mistakes, though, and you'd be apt to go through a lot of work just to find that FrontPage doesn't upload your finished creation in the way you expected. Actually building a cohesive site requires embarking on your development journey with a plan and an understanding of how FrontPage handles sites and pages.

Planning a FrontPage Site

FrontPage isn't just a page-design tool, it's also a full-featured site management package. To take full advantage of those features, however, you need to think in terms of designing a site rather than just a page, and that takes planning. Even the smallest, one-page site can benefit from a bit of advance design. As soon as you add a picture to your page, your one-page site has grown to a multifile site—and you're well on your way to losing track of your files (see Figure 2.1). Welcome to the wonderful world of file management, just one aspect of site planning.

FIGURE 2.1

This site might look simple— just a place to promote my books and post deep thoughts— but it actually contains more than a dozen pages, three dozen images, and a style sheet.

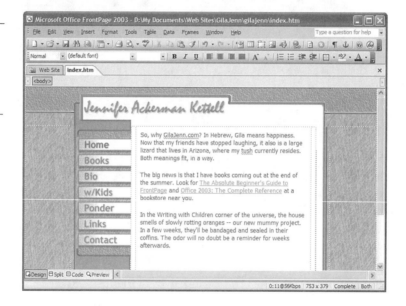

Whenever you create a site, you should think of all the pages and linked files (that is, images, multimedia, external style sheets, and the like) as a unit. This mindset forces you to address issues about navigation—how your visitors are going to get to your site and move from page to page within it. It also lets you save time and resources, because you can copy the same elements throughout the site, resulting in a consistent design.

Approaching Web development on a sitewide basis rather than as individual files and pages isn't just my view of the world order, it's also the FrontPage way of getting things done. In FrontPage, how you create and organize your site is just as important as the site's content. Quite simply, if you take a sitewide approach to FrontPage, you'll be rewarded with a host of options that require more manual labor if you

design each page as a separate entity. These advantages enable you to do the
following:

- Use wizards, templates, and themes to establish a consistent design throughout the site.

- Manage all your pages, graphics, multimedia, and folders in Folders view
and with the folder list.

- Create a to-do list using the Tasks view.

- Automatically update links sitewide just by moving a page or image into
another folder.

- Check and update all the links on your site at once—including links to other
sites on the Web.

- Use navigation tools and link bars to design a consistent structure that can be
easily updated on a sitewide basis.

- Upload your entire site at the touch of a button, and keep your local and
remote sites in synch.

Let's take a few steps backward, though. The consideration you give to your project
before opening FrontPage is just as important as the actual development. This consideration starts not with sketching your first of many design ideas, but understanding the purpose of your site, your audience, their browser limitations, and security.

Pre-Site Insight

The first thing you want to know about your site is its point. What is it going to say?
Do you want to display photos of your family or sell bracelets? You should also
establish goals for your site. Goals aren't the same as the site's purpose. If you want
to share your poetry, your goal could be either to simply share it with the world or to
invite critique using a feedback form. If you want to sell bracelets, your goal is probably to make money.

Having a purpose and goal helps set some ground rules for your site. Obviously, if
you're trying to sell friendship bracelets to teens, you won't put pictures of your
Great Aunt Pearl's 100th birthday party on the same site. Also, friendship bracelets
are generally colorful, funky, and trendy. A dull site with black text on a plain white
background just isn't going to cut it (see Figure 2.2).

Hand-in-hand with the goal and purpose of your site is your target audience. Is your
audience trendy, geeky, young, old, singles, parents, or seniors? Ask yourself the
same questions about you. There are times when you want your personality to shine
through and times when you want to bury it. The personality of a site aimed at selling Italian charm bracelets to an upscale adult market will be different from one

selling five-dollar friendship bracelets to teens. Meanwhile, if you're the harried parent of a colicky infant, you probably don't want your own personality to show through in either case—but that would change if instead of selling bracelets, your site was a forum for new mothers.

FIGURE 2.2

The colors, fonts, and graphics you choose for your site can completely change how it's perceived. If you are selling friendship bracelets, which design looks more in touch with that audience?

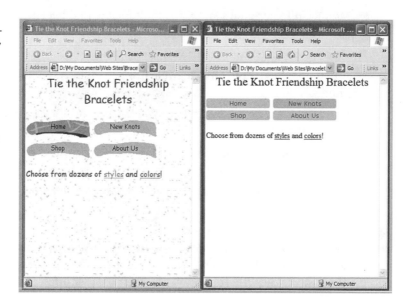

With these insights in mind, you're finally ready to get to work.

Creating Empty Sites

FrontPage offers two methods for developing your site. A *disk-based* Web site is stored on your local hard disk. This allows you to design and develop your site even before you choose a *remote hosting server*—the place where the final site will be stored to make it available to visitors.

To create a new Web site, do the following:

1. Choose File, New. This opens the New task pane, as shown in Figure 2.3.

2. Click the More Web Site Templates link to open the Web Site Templates dialog box (Figure 2.4).

3. Unless you specify another location, new sites are created in the My Documents folder in a new folder called My Web Sites. It's best to create each Web site in a unique folder. If you're happy with the default folder, simply

add the name of the new site folder to the end of it (as in, My Web Sites\Bracelets). You can also use the Browse button to locate and specify a different folder.

4. Click the site template you want to use. The One Page Web Site creates a new site with a blank page named index.htm. The Empty Web Site template creates a new site, but doesn't create any pages within it.

5. Click OK (alternatively, you can double-click on the site template in step 4).

FIGURE 2.3

The New task pane can be used to create both pages and Web sites. Be sure to select from the New Web Site options to create an entire site rather than individual pages.

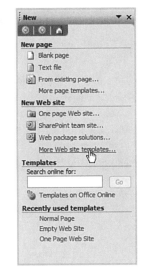

FIGURE 2.4

The Web Site Templates dialog box lists both site templates and wizards. Usually, you'll select either One Page Web Site or Empty Web Site.

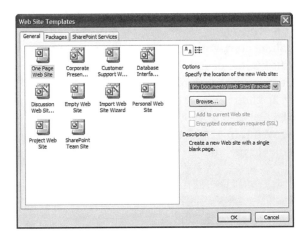

After you create the site, the task pane automatically closes, leaving you in the Folders view of your new site. The new site contains an images folder, which you should use to store the pictures you insert into your pages in order to keep them separate from the HTML pages themselves. The _private folder is used by FrontPage to store information it needs about your site in order to track your pages and files. If you chose the One Page Web Site, you'll also see the index.htm file in the list.

WHY NOT WORK ON THE WEB?

When you specify a location for your new site, it's possible to specify an Internet address—your remote hosting server—and create the site directly on the Web. The advantage of this is that you can test FrontPage-specific Web components and databases in their live environment.

Sounds good, but it's a bad idea. First of all, it's always good to have a backup. If you work directly on the server, you won't have a local copy of your files in case of problems. If your remote server is down for whatever reason, you're locked out of your files. Plus, when you work directly on the Web, you need to be connected to the Internet the entire time you're editing your files—not a big issue if you have a cable modem or DSL, but a very big issue if you use a dial-up connection over your only phone line. But the biggest reason to work locally is because anything you do on the remote server—including pages with dummy text or links to bogus pages—is immediately live and visible to the world. That's not the best way to introduce the world to your vision.

Naming the Site

The folder name you choose in the Web Site Templates dialog box becomes the name of the new site. One of the most common mistakes when creating a site is forgetting to add a unique name for the folder, causing FrontPage to create a generic name such as mysite1 in the default folder. That's no big deal for your first site, but by the time you create a second or third site, you'll want to be able to distinguish them more readily. To change the name of the site, and thus the name of the folder in which it's stored, choose Tools, Site Settings. In the General tab (Figure 2.5), enter a new name in the Web Name field, and then click OK. You can see the name change automatically in the title bar of the FrontPage window and in the Folders view.

FIGURE 2.5

The Web name controls the folder name for the site. While it doesn't appear in the published site, using a meaningful name helps you organize your sites locally.

Importing Files and Folders

Creating a new site works well if you're starting from scratch, but you might have already designed a site using another program or inherited a site from someone else. In those cases, you need to import the site so that FrontPage recognizes it. To import a site, do the following:

1. Choose File, New to open the New task pane.

2. Choose More Web Site Templates from the task pane to open the Web Site Templates dialog box.

3. Specify the new location for your imported site. (FrontPage actually makes a copy of the files and folders in the existing site, so you need to specify a new location rather than the current location of the files.)

4. Double-click Import Web Site Wizard from the list of templates. FrontPage creates the new site and starts the Import Web Wizard to begin the transfer process.

5. On the Welcome screen of the Import Web Wizard (see Figure 2.6), choose how FrontPage should acquire the original files. There are a number of options:

   ■ **FrontPage Server Extensions or SharePoint Services**—If the site you're importing uses FrontPage extensions or SharePoint Services, this option will preserve those settings.

   ■ **WebDAV**—If the original site was uploaded using WebDAV (Distributed Authoring and Versioning) to provide version control (most commonly used in large development groups to protect files from being overwritten by other members of the team), this option will preserve the versioning controls.

- **FTP**—If you have access to the actual remote server where the files are currently stored, File Transfer Protocol (FTP) will transfer them directly from the server, including files that aren't accessible from the live site.

- **File System**—If the site was created by another program but is currently stored on your local computer or a CD, this option imports the files into a FrontPage folder structure. The original files remain in their original location, as well, so you need to remember to edit the correct version of the site after the import is complete.

- **HTTP**—This option downloads the pages and linked style sheets and graphics directly from the Internet. Unlike with the FTP option, additional pages, files, and folders on the server but not referenced on the site will not be downloaded.

FIGURE 2.6

The import option you choose depends on the location and contents of the original site.

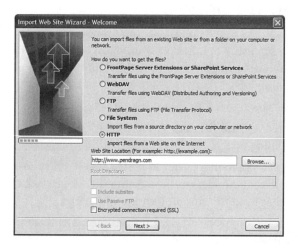

6. If the original site contains subfolders, such as an image folder, click the Include Subfolders check box to ensure you import everything.

7. Click Next.

8. In case you didn't get it right when you created the new site at the start of this process, FrontPage gives you one more chance to specify a new location for the imported site. Do so if necessary.

9. Click Next.

10. If you're importing a site from the Web, the next step is Set Import Limits, as shown in Figure 2.7. If you don't choose any of these options, the entire site

will be downloaded. Otherwise, you can limit the files that are transferred by choosing from the following:

- ■ **Import the home page plus linked pages**—Specifies how many pages of the original site you want to download from the Internet. The number you set in the Levels Deep field determines how far to dig down—the home page and all the pages linked from it (1 level), all the pages linked from those pages (2 levels), and so on.

- ■ **Import a maximum of**—Specifies the number of files to import based on kilobytes. If you want to download only 1,500KB of the site, FrontPage will start importing from the home page, then dig deeper until it reaches the maximum limit. Unless space on your local computer is really an issue, avoid this option. It's too easy to hit that maximum while essential elements of the site are still missing, thus defeating the purpose of the import.

- ■ **Import only HTML and image files**—Excludes non-HTML or image files, such as JavaScripts and external style sheets, from the import. As with the previous option, this is a good option to avoid. Many sites these days rely on external style sheets to control the design, and if you don't download it, the site's pages will be devoid of color, fonts, images, and even positioning.

FIGURE 2.7

If you only need the first level of pages from a live site, click Import the Home Page Plus Linked Pages, and set the number of levels to 1.

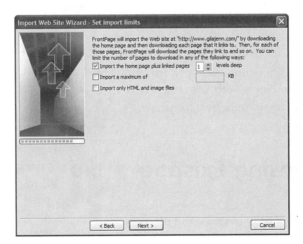

11. Click Next.
12. Click Finish.

After the import is complete, the new site will be listed in the Folders view.

Converting Existing Local Sites into FrontPage Sites

Using the Import Web Wizard on local sites makes a big deal out of something that's actually very simple. If you have a local site created in another program or inherited from another developer, there's a quicker way to convert it into a FrontPage site.

1. Choose File, New to open the New task pane.

2. Choose More Web Site Templates to open the Web Site Templates dialog box.

3. In the Specify the Location of the New Web field, use the Browse button to select the folder containing the existing site.

4. Click Open to return to the Web Site Templates dialog box.

5. Choose Empty Web Site.

6. Click OK.

You can use other site templates to perform this conversion, but the Empty Web Site template is the only one that doesn't modify existing pages or add new ones.

Opening and Closing Existing Sites

Once you've created or imported a site in FrontPage, it's easy to open and close it. To open a site, choose File, Open Site or File, Recent Sites. If you're going to be working extensively on one site for a while, choose Tools, Options and click Open Last Web Site Automatically when FrontPage Starts.

To close a site, choose File, Close Site.

note

It's time to get on my soapbox for a moment. The Import Web Wizard makes it technologically possible to import someone else's site onto your computer, images and all. Importing a site allows you to examine the table structure, images, and code that comprise the pages, which is a great way to learn advanced design techniques. If you use those pages and images as your own, however, you're stealing someone's intellectual property.

tip

You can open more than one site at a time in FrontPage. Each site opens in its own program window, but you can still copy and paste files between the two sites. This is particularly useful if you've created subsites related to a main site because you can ensure consistency of design and locate files easily in both sites to create links. For more information, see the sidebar "What Are Subsites?" later in this chapter.

Setting Page Options

Once you've planned your site and created the shell in FrontPage, you're almost ready to start developing it. Before you take off at a run, though, there are still a few things to consider. For one, it's difficult to anticipate what your visitors will have technologywise. Internet Explorer is the most popular browser, but there's still a core group of Netscape users, a handful of Opera aficionados, and a growing number of Mac users with Safari.

Most of the current versions of browsers can handle almost anything you can throw at them in FrontPage, but older browsers may not be able to interpret scripting languages or *cascading style sheets (CSS)*. Cascading style sheets enable you to control the design of your page from a master list of fonts, colors, positioning settings, and so on. To learn more about CSS, see Chapter 13, "Using Styles and Cascading Style Sheets."

Authoring Settings

When you first open FrontPage, a screen tip states that you're working in the default authoring settings. The authoring settings in the lower-right corner of the FrontPage window (shown in Figure 2.8) tell FrontPage the browser and server constraints under which you're working. In turn, FrontPage disables features that aren't supported by that browser or server.

FIGURE 2.8

The Default entry refers to the authoring settings for the server to which you'll be publishing your site. The Both entry refers to the browser expectations for your site's visitors.

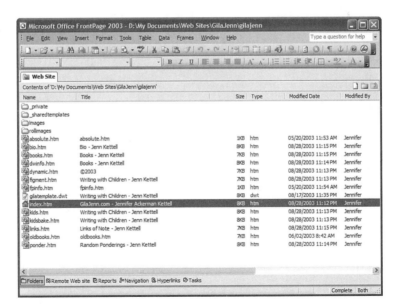

In most cases, the default settings are fine, and you may never have to change them. In the rare instance where you're designing a site that you don't plan to publish to a SharePoint-friendly server or for a limited audience with older browsers, you can modify them. Thus, if your remote server doesn't support Windows SharePoint Services, you can change the authoring settings to disable any features, such as Web components, that require it. If you need a site that can be viewed in Netscape 4, the positioning elements of cascading style sheets can be disabled.

To change the authoring settings, double-click either of the authoring settings in the FrontPage window or choose Tools, Page Options, and then click the Authoring tab. Either method opens the Authoring tab of the Page Options dialog box (see Figure 2.9). Unless you know exactly which features are available on your server or intended browsers, the only options you need to worry about are the FrontPage and SharePoint Technologies field and the Browsers field. As you change these options, you'll notice that the available features also change. You also can use the Custom settings to enable and disable the features of your choosing.

FIGURE 2.9

The default authoring settings are fine if you're publishing to a server with Windows SharePoint Services and intend for the site to be viewed using current browsers, but can easily be customized to meet specific needs.

Unfortunately, the results of changing the authoring options may not be what you intended. Even if you disable Web components, you can still add them; FrontPage won't do anything to stop you until you attempt to publish the site. Also, FrontPage can't change the past; while features may be disabled, if they were imported from another site or added before you changed the authoring settings, they will still appear on your pages.

Creating Pages

One assumes that after you've gone to all the trouble of creating a site, you'll want to actually add pages to it. The easiest way to create a new page is to click the New Page button at the top of the folder list. This adds a blank page to the file list and positions the insertion point to immediately rename the page.

Using Page Templates to Create a Page

You can also create a new page using page templates. Much like the Web site templates you used to create your site, this method lets you choose from a wide variety of page layouts and predesigned content. To create a page based on a template, do the following:

1. Choose File, New to open the New task pane.

2. In the New Page area of the task pane, choose More Page Templates to open the Page Templates dialog box (see Figure 2.10).

FIGURE 2.10

The tabs of the Page Templates dialog box let you organize your own templates as well as offering layouts for frame-based sites and style sheets.

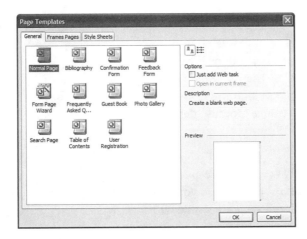

3. Choose a template. For a simple, empty page, choose Normal Page. You can examine other templates by clicking on them and looking at the Preview box.

4. Click OK.

Although the new page appears in the Design view, it doesn't really exist in the Web site until you save the file and give it a name. To do so, choose File, Save (Ctrl+S), or click the Save button on the toolbar. In the Save As dialog box, give the new page a name, and then click Save.

Creating from an Existing Page

If you already have a page that's designed the way you like, you can base a new page on that existing one. In the Folders view, right-click on the file on which you want to base the new page, then choose New from Existing Page from the context menu. Again, the new page isn't truly added to the site until you save it.

Page Formatting

Certain page-formatting options should be set early in the design process. These will prepare the page for the text and images that are to come, and will save time moving things around later.

Adjusting Page Size

You have no control over the screen size and resolution of your visitors' displays, so you want to size your design to suit the largest possible audience. To set the page size, click the page-size setting in the lower-right corner of the FrontPage window (see Figure 2.11), and then choose an option from the menu that appears. Notice that the actual screen dimensions are smaller than the full display sizes to account for the *chrome*—that is, the amount of space taken up by the menus and toolbars and such—of the average browser. The Modify Page Sizes option allows you to specify custom page dimensions.

note

Don't forget to save the file! Unlike other pages, newly created pages don't have an asterisk to note that they're unsaved. Also, if you choose File, Close, the page will disappear without any warning. Get in the habit of saving the file as soon as it's created, before you begin editing it.

note

Only the basic Web site and page templates are explained in this chapter, just to get you started. To learn about the other templates, see Chapter 3, "Using Wizards, Templates, and Themes."

FIGURE 2.11
Adjust the page
size to help you
design with min-
imal scrolling.
Customize these
settings using
the Modify Page
Sizes option.

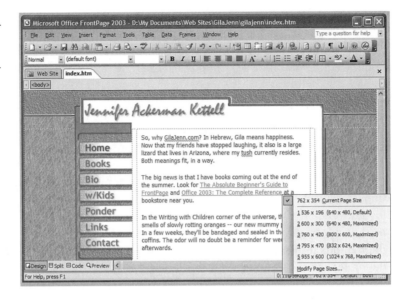

Setting Backgrounds and Text Colors

If the background of your site needs some color or a graphic, choose Format,
Background to change the default settings in the Page Properties dialog box, shown
in Figure 2.12. When choosing a background color, consider the color of the text
you'll be adding. If you're using a background image, choose one that won't over-
power the text with too much texture or stark lines and color.

FIGURE 2.12
The Formatting
tab of the Page
Properties dialog
box opens when
you choose
Format,
Background.

You can also set back-
grounds and text colors
using cascading style sheets. To
learn more about the full potential
of style sheets, see Chapter 13.

To set a background image, click the Browse button to locate an image file, then click OK. If the image file is smaller than the screen display, it will repeat itself horizontally and/or vertically to fill the space. This is known as *tiling*. To learn more about creating graphics, see Chapter 6, "Creating and Modifying Graphics."

Setting Page Margins

While you're in the Page Properties dialog box—which you can also access by choosing File, Properties—you can set the page margins in the Advanced tab (see Figure 2.13). Page margins determine how far from the edges of the screen the design appears. Internet Explorer and Netscape Navigator each use different margin settings to control page layout, so it's important to set all four margins to ensure the layout will be the same in both browsers. If you're planning to use tables to control the layout of your page, set each of the page margins to 0 because you can control the margins for your content within the table cells. To learn how to use tables for design layout, see Chapter 9, "Using Tables."

FIGURE 2.13

Netscape Navigator and Internet Explorer use different margin settings to control page layout, so you need to set four different options to cover both browsers.

Giving the Page a Title

You're not quite finished with the Page Properties dialog box just yet. Every page should have a title, which appears in the title bar of the browser window, and can be used to provide more information about your site than you can fit in a filename. To set the title of a page, click the General tab of the Page Properties dialog box, then enter the title in the Title field. Titles can use punctuation and spaces. Be brief, however, because titles are also used in Favorites lists, and lengthy ones cause grief to your visitors by widening the Favorites menu.

Saving Pages and Sites

You save Web pages in the same way you save documents in other Microsoft applications. That is, you click the Save button on the toolbar, use the File, Save menu command, or press Ctrl+S. The site itself is saved automatically.

If you're working on several pages at a time, you can save all of them by choosing File, Save All. If you created new pages that weren't previously saved, the Save As dialog box will prompt you to name and save each of those pages.

Deleting Web Sites

Suppose you were using a Web site as an experiment, or that you have a site that you're no longer maintaining. If so, you can delete the site within FrontPage. Here's how:

1. Open the site you want to delete.

2. In the folder list (View, Folder List, if it's not already visible), click the root folder of the site. The root folder is the top-most item in the folder list, containing the full path of the site.

3. Press the Delete key on your keyboard.

4. In the Confirm Delete dialog box, shown in Figure 2.14, choose which files you want to delete:

   ■ **Remote FrontPage information from this Web site only, preserving all other files and folders**—Removes the special files and folders used by FrontPage to manage the site, but leaves the site's pages and images on your local computer. This lets you save the site itself so that you can modify it later in another Web-design program or convert it back to a FrontPage site if you need it again.

   ■ **Delete this Web site entirely**—Deletes all the files and folders in the site, removing them entirely from your local computer.

FIGURE 2.14

The Confirm Delete dialog box offers two options for wiping out a Web site on the local computer.

5. Click OK.

Deleting the site from the local computer doesn't delete the published site on the remote server. Remember, however, that if you delete the local site, you won't be able to use FrontPage to maintain the remote site. If you want to completely wipe the site from the map, you need to delete the files on the remote server before you delete the local site. See the section "Creating and Deleting Folders" in Chapter 22, "Maintaining a Published Web," to learn how to delete pages and folders from a remote server.

Before you delete a site, be certain you also want to delete any subsites you may have contained within it. If you need to preserve a subsite, move it to another location before you delete the main site.

WHAT ARE SUBSITES?

Some sites start out small, but soon grow to mammoth proportions. Subfolders, created in the folder list, can help organize your pages. At some point, however, you may decide that a particular subfolder has grown so large that it's almost like a minisite in itself. At that point, you can convert the subfolder to a subsite. This enables you to maintain the pages within that subfolder independently of the main site.

To turn a subfolder into a subsite, right-click the folder in the folder list, then choose Convert to Web. The biggest advantage of using subsites is that you can publish all the files in the subsite without having to select them from the entire site. The downside is that the pages in a subsite aren't as readily accessible from the main site; any time you select that subfolder, it launches the subsite in a new FrontPage window rather than opening the folder within the main site.

THE ABSOLUTE MINIMUM

There's a lot to take in when it comes to site planning, and entire books have been written on the subject. At an absolute minimum, it's important that you think of your site as a set of interconnected pages, files, and folders rather than individual pieces. The more time you spend planning your site's design in advance, the less clean-up work you'll have to do later.

When it comes to creating sites and pages in FrontPage, just remember that the default options will work fine most of the time. Don't mess with the options unless you really need to. It's possible to design an entire site without ever opening the Page Options dialog box.

In this Chapter

- Choosing a good foundation for your site using templates
- Saving time with the magic of wizards
- Creating polished Web sites with dynamic Web templates
- Adding color, graphics, and fonts to an entire site using themes

3

Using Wizards, Templates, and Themes

The consistency of your site adds a level of professionalism and aesthetic value. It also makes your site easier to update. Consistency not only involves the navigation elements, but also the colors, fonts, layout, graphics, and writing style of your content.

One of the best ways to ensure consistency is to use themes and templates, whether they be those included in FrontPage, those downloaded from other sources, or those you create yourself. With these tools, colors can be set for your entire site, font styles are the same from page to page, and navigation tools are located at the same place on each page.

Using Templates

Templates are predesigned pages that contain page settings, formatting, graphics, and fonts. FrontPage has several default templates you can use, or you have the flexibility to create your own. Most templates incorporate a matching theme but also have predefined areas, where you can add your text and any additional images.

Page Templates

Page templates specify a unique page layout by determining where graphics and text are positioned on the page. Complex page templates also can incorporate forms, frames, Web components, or database elements to create discussion groups, guest books, and feedback forms.

To create a page using a template, do the following:

1. Choose File, New. The New task pane opens.

2. From the New page section, choose More Page Templates. The Page Templates dialog box opens.

note

Unfortunately, FrontPage is caught in a terminology sinkhole. Page templates, Web site templates, and dynamic page templates are all similar yet different features, confusing as that may seem. In a nutshell, *page templates* create individual pages, *Web site templates* configure entire sites, and *dynamic page templates* create pages with defined, editable regions. Each of these is covered in more detail in this chapter.

3. From the General tab, select the desired page template. Note that when you click one of the Web page template icons, a brief summary of the page template is displayed in the Description section, and a graphic representation is displayed in the Preview section of the tab.

4. Click OK.

Choosing the right page layout for the job can save you time and energy. The available page templates are as follows:

- **Normal**—Creates a blank page.

- **Bibliography**—Creates a simple page that allows you to create a bibliography containing a list of author names, book titles, and publication information.

- **Confirmation Form**—Creates a page that confirms information entered into a form on a separate page. This is most commonly used to confirm an order, to request information, or for site registration.

- **Feedback Form**—Creates a page with form elements to solicit feedback about a product or site. This template can be used in conjunction with the Confirmation Form template to reply to site visitors who submit the form.

- **Form Page Wizard**—Launches a wizard to lead you through the creation of a page containing a customized form with the fields you require. To learn more about forms, see Chapter 16, "Creating Forms."

- **Frequently Asked Questions**—Creates a page containing a table of contents at the top, with each entry linking to the answer listed below. After each entry is a link to return to the table of contents at the top of the page.

- **Guest Book**—Creates a form that's used to solicit comments from site visitors, as seen in Figure 3.1. The entries that are submitted through the form are appended to a separate HTML file, which is then included at the bottom of the Guest Book page using the Include Content Web component.

FIGURE 3.1

The Guest Book page template has a text field for visitors to submit comments about your site.

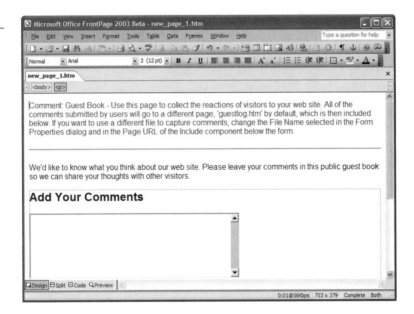

- **Photo Gallery**—Creates a photo-gallery page with placeholder images. This page can be customized using the Photo Gallery tools. To learn how to create and modify a photo gallery, see the section "Creating a Photo Gallery" in Chapter 6, "Creating and Modifying Graphics."

- **Search Page**—Creates a page that enables visitors to search for information in your site. The page also contains a quick guide to Boolean searches to aid visitors in narrowing down their search criteria.

- **Table of Contents**—Generates a table of contents page for your site. You can configure this page to update automatically as you add pages to your site, or you can adjust it manually to customize which pages are listed. For more information about the Include Content, Search, and Table of Contents Web components, see Chapter 18, "Adding Bells and Whistles with Web Components."

- **User Registration**—Creates a page with a form for visitors to register and access password-protected subsites within your Web site. This page won't work on all servers, and some Web-hosting companies won't allow you to use these types of registration forms, so it's best to ask your Web host before creating pages with this template.

Depending on the nature of your site, you might use several of these templates. For example, you might create a site with a photo gallery, a FAQ about how the images were captured and chosen, and a guest book for feedback about your site. As you can see, however, these templates are so specific that you might choose not to use anything other than the Normal template, adding form elements, Web components, and other features as you require. There isn't anything on a page template that you can't add to a page by yourself.

Web Site Templates

Whereas page templates form the foundation of a single page, site templates form the basis of an entire site. Additionally, they establish the site in FrontPage, enabling you to then work with the site's pages as a unit when publishing the site or creating link bars and site maps. For this reason alone, it's worth using the site template even if you only want to start with an empty Web site or a single blank page. For more about creating sites in FrontPage, refer to Chapter 2, "Creating Sites and Pages." To learn how to add link bars to your site, see the section "Adding Link Bars" in Chapter 12, "Creating a Navigation Structure." For help adding a table of contents, see the section "Adding a Table of Contents and Site Map to Your Web" in Chapter 18.

While the Empty Web Site and One Page Web Site templates are intentionally sparse, other Web site templates are incredibly full bodied, with preformatted pages to serve specific purposes, including navigation elements and Web components. These templates are still flexible, however, and can be modified to meet your needs. You can add your own content, and modify, add, and delete pages as you see fit, and the navigation elements will adjust themselves accordingly.

One of the drawbacks of using a template is that your site's layout has a canned look, meaning that it's similar to those of other FrontPage users. Luckily, the ability to apply customized themes and otherwise modify the appearance your site prevents this from becoming too much of a liability. You can use a template to form the basis of your site, but then modify the layout beyond all recognition to make it uniquely your own. As with page templates, however, you also can choose to start with an empty site and add all the same elements and components that appear in other Web site templates to new pages within your site.

To apply a Web site template, do the following:

1. Choose File, New. The New task pane opens.

2. From the New Web Site section, choose More Web Site Templates. The Web Site Templates dialog box opens (see Figure 3.2).

FIGURE 3.2

The Web site templates are as generic as the One Page and Empty Web Site options or as complex as the Personal Web Site or Customer Support templates.

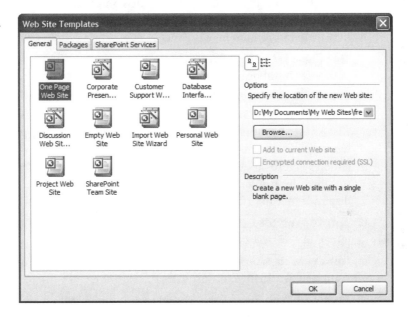

3. From the Options section, select the location for your new Web site using the down arrow and/or Browse button. To add the Web page template to the Web site that you are currently working in, select the Add to Current Web Site check box.

4. Choose the desired Web site template. Note that when you click one of the Web site template icons (the ones without the magic wands), a brief summary of the Web site template is displayed in the Description section of the tab.

5. Click OK.

The available Web site templates and wizards are as follows:

- **One Page Web Site**—Creates a site with a single page named index.htm. This template also creates an images folder to store any images you add to your pages.

- **Corporate Presence Wizard**—Creates a site to promote a business or corporation on the Web. The wizard can create pages to list products and services, solicit feedback from customers, and promote new features.

- **Customer Support Web Site**—Creates a site to interact with customers and provide additional information about a business and its products. The template creates all the elements of a discussion group, pages to download manuals and product updates, a frequently asked questions page, and a what's new page to promote new products.

- **Database Interface Wizard**—Creates a site that links to an Access or SQL database. Databases can be used as the backbone to an e-commerce solution or provide contact information for site members, among other uses.

- **Discussion Web Site Wizard**—Creates a site for a discussion group, otherwise known as a message board. If you want to limit your group to just members, the wizard will create an interface to register for access. The wizard also enables you to create a table of contents, to add a search feature, and to control the interface (frames, no-frames, or the ability to detect the browser and display either interface as appropriate).

- **Empty Web Site**—Creates a FrontPage Web site containing an images folder, but doesn't create any default pages.

- **Import Web Site Wizard**—Imports a site or pages from a site stored on the Web, a network drive, or locally.

- **Personal Web Site**—Creates a site to promote your personal interests and experiences. The template automatically creates pages to share your favorites, interests, and a photo gallery.

- **Project Web Site**—Creates a site to track or promote an ongoing project. The template creates pages for a discussion group, schedule, and archived information. This template is useful if you're working on a remote project team. You also can use it to describe a home remodel, a training program for an athlete, or other noncorporate projects.

- **SharePoint Team Site**—Creates a site using Windows SharePoint Services to utilize a calendar, library, task lists, discussion groups, and other features useful for a professional development team.

Wizards

If you look at the preceding list, you'll notice that many of the Web site templates are actually wizards. Wizards simplify the process of creating common types of pages and sites by walking you through a series of questions. The wizard then generates pages and content based on your answers. Simply fill in the requested information on each screen, then click Next to proceed to the next prompt.

FrontPage wizards can help you create forms and sites ranging from a single page to complex sites for discussions, database connections, or corporate promotion, as seen in Figure 3.3. You also can import an existing site into FrontPage using a wizard. To learn more about importing sites and pages, refer to the section "Importing Files and Folders" in Chapter 2.

FIGURE 3.3

With the double-click of an icon, the wizard launches and walks you through the automatic application process.

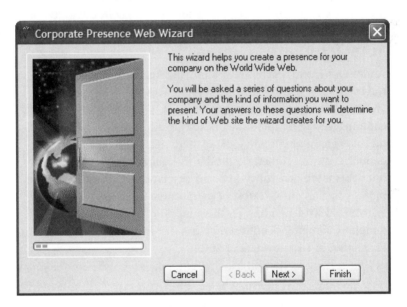

Modifying and Creating Templates

You don't have to be trapped using the standard page and Web site templates. Even a canned template can be dressed up and saved as something unique, to be used later on your own sites. If you're not of an artistic bent or want to include other advanced elements on your site without the hassle, you can find thousands of FrontPage templates on the Web.

To modify a page template, do the following:

1. Create a page using a page template.

2. Make the desired changes to the page.

3. Choose File, Save As. The Save As dialog box opens.

4. Click the Save As Type down arrow and choose FrontPage Template from the drop-down list that appears.

5. Give the template a new name.

6. Click Save. The Save As Template dialog box opens.

7. In the Title field, type a title for your template.

8. In the Description field, type a brief summary of your template.

9. Click OK.

The new template will appear in the My Templates tab of the Page Templates dialog box when you create a new page.

If you want to create an entirely new page template, simply create a page containing any elements you wish, then follow steps 3–9 in the preceding list.

Finding More Templates Online

Additional FrontPage templates may be found on the Internet. A good one-stop shopping site is FrontPage World (www.frontpageworld.com). This site contains tons of templates, with links to sites containing even more. If you look at these sites hard enough, you can sometimes find a free gem or two, but you should generally expect to pay for templates you find online. Most of them range in price from $15–$30, depending on the features of the template. Templates containing Flash or Swish elements can cost upwards of $50.

FrontPage also enables you to access additional page templates directly from Microsoft. To access more templates from Microsoft, do the following:

1. Choose File, New. The New task pane opens.

2. From the Templates section, choose Templates on Office Online. The Microsoft Office Online Web page opens.

3. In the blank search box, type **FrontPage** and press Enter.

4. The search is initiated; when it is complete, all the available FrontPage Web page templates are listed.

5. Select the hyperlink to the desired template, and then follow Microsoft's instructions to download it.

note

Flash is a multimedia graphics application developed by Macromedia. Flash files are saved with a .swf extension and can contain graphics, text, video, sound, and interactive elements. Swish is another application that can create .swf files, and is particularly popular with FrontPage developers. Chapter 8, "Adding Multimedia," has more details about this powerful addition to your site.

FrontPage Themes

A theme is a set of design elements and colors that you can apply to give your Web pages a professional look. Applying themes helps keep your pages visually consistent, as well as visually appealing.

When you apply a theme, all your headings, body text, colors, bullets, and so on will be automatically styled according to the theme. Themes also can include background images. You have the option of applying a theme to one page, to many pages, or to your entire Web site.

Themes do not define things like the location of navigation bars or the layout of your page. Instead, themes simply alter the appearance of color, fonts, and certain images on your pages, as shown in Figure 3.4.

FIGURE 3.4

When you select a new theme, the new colors, graphics, and fonts are applied to your Web page in an instant.

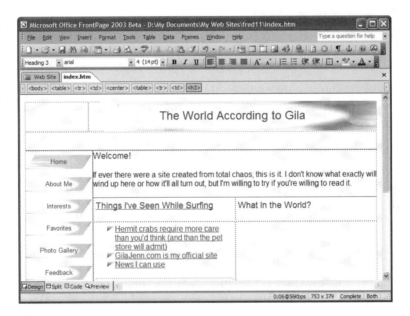

Applying Themes to Pages and Sites

To apply a theme to a page, choose Format, Theme. The Theme task pane opens, as shown in Figure 3.5. From the Select a Theme section, choose the desired theme. The theme you select will automatically be applied to the Web page on which you are currently working.

When you're applying a theme to only one page of a site at a time, remember to be consistent. If you use the Compass theme for one page and the Canyon theme for another, your site will lose its flow from page to page and could disorient your visitors.

FIGURE 3.5

The Theme task pane displays thumbnails of each available theme.

A better choice is generally to apply themes to an entire site. This ensures consistency throughout. Even better, you can change the theme on a sitewide basis when you're ready for a new look.

To apply a theme to an entire site:

1. Choose Format, Theme. The Theme task pane opens.

2. From the Select a Theme section, choose the desired theme. The theme you select will automatically be applied to the Web page on which you are currently working.

3. To apply this theme to your entire Web site, click the selected theme's down arrow. A file menu is displayed.

4. Choose Apply As Default Theme. A FrontPage message box opens, warning that applying the desired theme to the Web site will replace existing formatting.

5. To continue, choose Yes.

When you apply a theme to an entire site, any pages to which you'd previously applied a different theme will remain unchanged. Themes you apply locally—that is, to a page itself—take precedence over themes applied to the entire site. This same mindset applies when you start using cascading style sheets (CSS), so it's a good lesson to learn early. Cascading style sheets are the preferred method for controlling fonts, text and link colors, and even positioning on a page. To learn more about CSS, see Chapter 13, "Using Styles and Cascading Style Sheets."

Setting Theme Options

At the bottom of the Theme task pane are options to enhance or modify a theme. Although these changes are generally subtle, they can make your site stand out at least a bit from others using the same theme. Another good use of these options is if you want to give a slightly different look to one section of your site while still having it appear related to the whole. These options are as follows:

- **Vivid Colors**—Choosing this option makes some of the text and graphic elements on your Web page appear even brighter. This varies by theme, so examine the differences in the thumbnails before applying this option.

- **Active Graphics**—Choosing this option animates certain theme components, such as rollovers on navigational elements.

- **Textured Background**—Choosing this option applies a textured background to the page.

Modifying a Theme

You can modify a theme to meet your needs. Modifications can be made to a theme's colors, graphics, and/or text. In doing so, you can create a unique theme based upon elements of other themes.

Changing Colors

You can choose to use a different color palette, change the color scheme, or modify a color using FrontPage's color wheel. To modify the colors of a theme, do the following:

1. Choose Format, Theme. The Theme task pane opens.

2. From the Select a Theme section, choose the desired theme.

3. To modify the theme, click the selected theme's down arrow, then choose Customize. The Customize Theme dialog box opens, as shown in Figure 3.6.

4. Click the Colors button in the What Would You Like to Modify? section. A new dialog box opens to enable you to adjust the theme's colors, as shown in Figure 3.7.

5. Make the desired changes in the Color Schemes, Color Wheel, and/or Custom tabs.

6. Click OK twice.

FIGURE 3.6

The Customize Theme dialog box enables you to modify a theme's colors, graphics, and text.

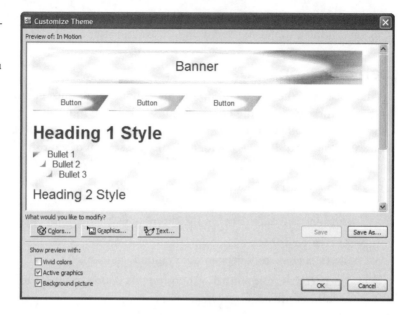

FIGURE 3.7

FrontPage offers several methods for adjusting colors in a theme, either using the predetermined color schemes, generating a scheme based on a selection on a color wheel, or by customizing individual elements.

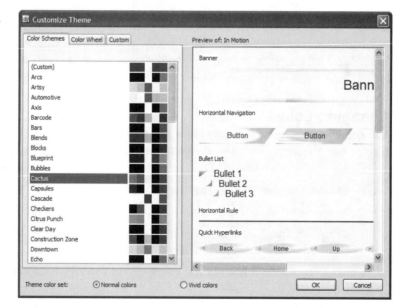

Changing Graphics

With FrontPage, you have the option of changing a theme's background picture, bullet icons, navigation buttons and bars, and banners. To modify the graphics of a theme, do the following:

1. Choose Format, Theme. The Theme task pane opens.

2. From the Select a Theme section, choose the desired theme.

3. Click the selected theme's down arrow and choose Customize. The Customize Theme dialog box opens.

4. Click the Graphics button in the What Would You Like to Modify? section. A new dialog box opens to enable you to change graphics, as shown in Figure 3.8

FIGURE 3.8

If the Active Graphics option button is selected, you can change the normal, selected, and hovered states of navigational elements.

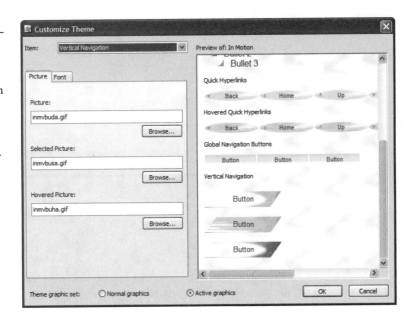

5. Make the desired changes to the graphic items. In the case of navigation elements and banners, you also can customize the font used for the element's text.

6. Click OK twice.

Changing Text Styles

Changing the font in a theme can give it a new look with very little effort. You can change the font for the body and headings of your pages. To modify the font used by a theme, do the following:

1. Choose Format, Theme. The Theme task pane opens.

2. From the Select a Theme section, choose the desired theme.

3. To modify the theme, click the selected theme's down arrow, then choose Customize. The Customize Theme dialog box opens.

4. Click the Text button in the What Would You Like to Modify? section. A new dialog box opens to enable you to change the fonts used by the theme, as shown in Figure 3.9.

FIGURE 3.9

You can change
the font for the
theme's major
text elements in
the Customize
Theme
dialog box.

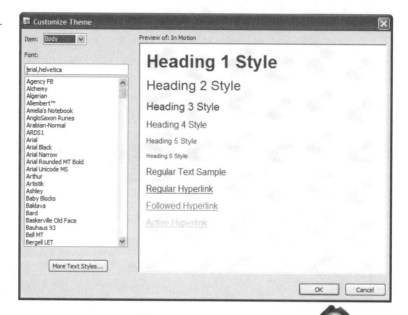

5. Make the desired changes to the text settings.
   When you select a font name, the font will
   be displayed in the preview window.

6. Click OK twice.

If you want to dig deeper into this feature, you can
edit the CSS styles for other page elements and
change the size, color, and decoration of the text,
as well as the font. To do this, click the More Text
Styles button, then edit the style as you would in
any other style sheet. To learn more about editing
cascading style sheets, see the section "Modifying
Styles" in Chapter 13.

Dynamic Web Templates

The page templates found in previous versions of
FrontPage are simply a starting point for the page
layout; once a page is created, the layout can be
easily changed to the point that the template is no
longer recognizable. Dynamic Web templates,
which are new to FrontPage 2003, are different in
that they enable you to create editable regions on

note

The font list displayed
in the Customize Theme
dialog box lists all the fonts
installed on your computer. This
doesn't guarantee that those fonts
are installed on the computers of
your site's visitors, however. If
you're changing fonts for text elements, stick with the most common fonts, such as Arial, Times
New Roman, Verdana, Helvetica,
and Courier. You can list multiple
fonts separated by commas. You
also can add a generic font type,
such as sans-serif or serif.

the page, thus blocking access to areas such as the navigational elements while still enabling you to add and modify the content of, say, your main content area and your sidebars. Dynamic Web templates can also apply graphics, themes, and style sheets that aren't included in standard page templates.

Dynamic Web templates can save you from being your own worst enemy in that if you protect consistent content such as navigation bars and page banners, you can't add menu items that don't appear elsewhere on your site or insert the wrong site logo. As your site grows, this is likely to become a bigger issue than when you're first starting out. You'll be adding pages that might branch into directions you didn't anticipate when you first designed your navigation menu, and it's easy to forget that these additions need to be made consistently to old pages as well as future ones.

If you're a Web designer creating pages that might be edited by others, you can set the page banner, a copyright notice, and the site-navigation components in areas that can't be edited, leaving only the main content area free for changes. A practical example of this would be a commercial site where you design the layout and navigation, while another person adds the marketing content. The marketing staffer can go wild with the fancy prose while the navigation and other page elements are untouchable.

The other benefit of using this kind of template is that it remains attached to a page even after you've added content. Thus, you can update all the pages using that template at once simply by modifying the template, without disturbing the content on any pages that are using it.

Creating a Dynamic Web Template

A dynamic Web template starts as a basic page. If you create this page and immediately save it as a dynamic Web template, you won't have to worry about remembering to change the file format later.

To create a dynamic Web template, do the following:

1. Create a new page, using whichever page template suits your needs.
2. Select File, Save As. The Save As dialog box opens.
3. Click the Save As Type down arrow and choose Dynamic Web Template from the drop-down list that appears.
4. Type a name for the file in the File Name field. The correct file extension will automatically be added by FrontPage.
5. Click Save.

Once you've created the template page, design it just as you would any other page, adding elements or content that you wish to appear on all the pages to which the template will be attached. The best way to lay out your page is using tables. This will enable you to create your consistent content in certain cells and define others as editable regions.

Defining Editable Regions

A dynamic Web template is divided into editable and noneditable regions. You must define at least one editable region on a template before you can attach it to a page. To do this, perform the following steps:

1. Select an area on the page that should have unique content—usually a table cell or cells.

2. Choose Format, Dynamic Web Template, Manage Editable Regions.

3. In the Editable Regions dialog box, shown in Figure 3.10, give the new region a name.

FIGURE 3.10

The Editable Regions dialog box automatically contains a defined region for the page title.

4. Click Add.

5. Click Close to return to the document window.

Once you've created an editable region, it will be labeled and outlined in Design view, as shown in Figure 3.11. Be sure to save the template to preserve the editable region.

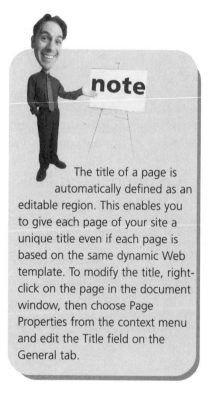

note

The title of a page is automatically defined as an editable region. This enables you to give each page of your site a unique title even if each page is based on the same dynamic Web template. To modify the title, right-click on the page in the document window, then choose Page Properties from the context menu and edit the Title field on the General tab.

FIGURE 3.11

The label around the defined editable region won't show up when you publish the final page based on the template, but it serves as a guide when designing the template and attached pages.

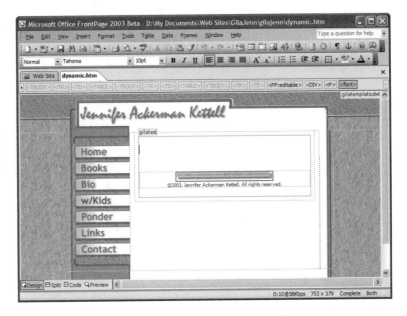

Attaching a Dynamic Web Template to a Page

Once you've created a dynamic template and defined one or more editable regions, it's ready for use. To attach a dynamic Web template to a page, do the following:

1. Create a new page.
2. Choose Format, Dynamic Web Template, Attach Dynamic Web Template. The Attach Dynamic Web Template dialog box opens.
3. Select the desired dynamic Web template.
4. Click OK.

FrontPage will automatically place all the elements from the dynamic Web template on the new page. If the page already has content on it, you'll be prompted to determine which editable region should contain it, as shown in Figure 3.12.

Modifying Dynamic Web Templates

Aside from consistency and not having to reinvent the wheel on every page in your site, one of the biggest advantages of using dynamic Web templates is having the ability to change the entire site simply by modifying the template. To do this, open the template itself in FrontPage by selecting the .dwt file in the Folders view. Then, you can change themes, update a copyright year, or radically change the colors and graphics on a site to give it a whole new look. When you save the file, you'll be prompted to update all the pages to which the template is attached.

FIGURE 3.12

FrontPage will
prompt you to
put preexisting
content into an
editable region
when you
attach the
dynamic Web
template.

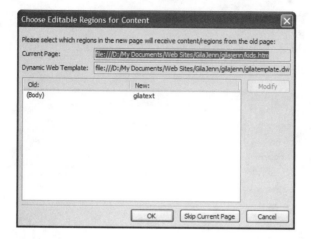

You can even modify the editable regions on your template. To add a new editable
region, select the area and then choose Format, Dynamic Web Template, Manage
Editable Regions, and then name and add the new region just as you did when creating the initial regions. To delete an editable region, again use the Manage Editable
Regions dialog box, select the name of the region, then press Remove.

EDITING EDITABLE REGIONS WITH CARE

When editing dynamic templates, you need to be careful with the editable regions. If you
delete an editable region, you'll be prompted to find a new location for any content that's
contained in those regions on pages created from the template. This includes any graphic
or other elements in that region.

For example, say you have an editable region for a sidebar on your pages that contains a
nested table with cells for the sidebar heading and the text below. If you delete the sidebar
editable region in the template, you'll be prompted to move everything that was in the
sidebar of each page into another region. If you elect to move this content into, say, the
main body text of the page, the graphic heading and the table will appear along with the
text itself. This can really mess up the formatting of your pages.

THE ABSOLUTE MINIMUM

You don't have to become overwhelmed by such complex elements as discussion groups, guest books, and link bars. There's no shame in using the tools FrontPage provides—relying on Web site and page templates to create these elements for you. Similarly, not everyone has an eye for design and color. Themes take the guesswork out of the design process. If the idea of using one of the canned themes bothers you, use them as the foundation for your own themes or download themes from the Web that might not be as familiar to Web surfers. Just know that at an absolute minimum, you can create a full-featured site using templates and themes that will get the job done more than adequately.

Dynamic Web templates are an exciting addition to FrontPage because they offer the consistency of templates and themes with the flexibility to design an entire page layout and protect it. If you're the do-it-yourself type, you'll want to master using this feature.

PART

Designing Webs and Pages

4

ADDING TEXT

FrontPage allows you to work with text as if you are using Microsoft Word instead of a state-of-the-art Web-design tool. Thanks to this application's user-friendly format, you don't have to worry about cracking the HTML code. Instead, you are free to point and click your way to cool-looking text. It's like driving an automatic instead of a stick shift. So sit back and enjoy the ride.

Working with Text

Text is one of the most important elements you can add to a site. It gives your site a voice that can be used to enlighten, antagonize, humor, or provoke deep thought. At a minimum, text directs—even a photo gallery site can benefit from text describing the images or telling users how to get to the top or bottom of the page. Because text is so crucial, FrontPage offers several methods of formatting and controlling text. Figure 4.1 highlights where these methods are found in FrontPage, which can serve as a roadmap while you read this chapter.

FIGURE 4.1

The road map for adding text. FrontPage has a large number of text-enhancement tools that make text formatting a snap.

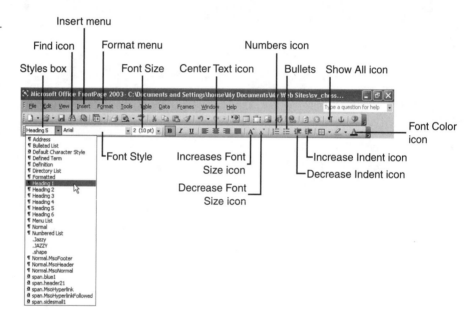

With FrontPage, you can brighten up drab text in a matter of moments. With just a few quick clicks of the mouse, you can change font: type, style, point size, color, and special effects. In addition, you can add symbols (✍) in a flash, eliminating the dull task of memorizing character code numbers.

Most of FrontPage's text enhancements are contained on the Font dialog box, shown in Figure 4.2. The Font dialog box is accessed from the Format menu.

Formatting Text

FrontPage gives you the flexibility of working with a variety of existing documents ranging from HTML files (formatted text) to word-processing documents (unformatted text). This versatility allows you to update documents on the fly. No more having to retype additional text. Instead, you get to insert text using cut and paste, a simple process we've all come to love in Word.

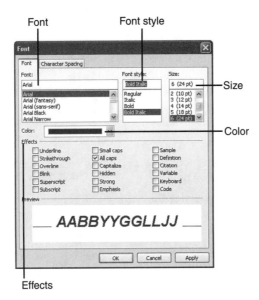

FIGURE 4.2

You'll be like a kid in a candy store with all the easy-to-use text tools found in the Font dialog box.

To cut and paste text in FrontPage, do the following:

1. Copy the existing text that you want to insert.

2. Place the insertion point where you want to paste the new text.

3. Choose Edit, Paste (or right-click to bring up the context menu, then choose Paste). The new text is inserted.

Adjusting Font Size

FrontPage has different ways of allowing you to adjust the font size of your text, based upon your needs.

When you're not really sure which point size you want, do the following:

1. Select the text you want to change.

2. Choose Format, Font (or right-click, then choose Font). The Font dialog box opens.

note

What's the point? Point size refers to the measured height of fonts. (One point = 1/72 of an inch.)

3. Adjust your text by selecting the desired size. Use the up and down arrows to access the available point-size options. By default, FrontPage uses seven standard font sizes, ranging from 1 (8 pt) to 7 (36 pts). The fonts move up and down in two-point increments.

4. View the results of your selection in the Preview box at the bottom of the Font dialog box.

When you know exactly which point size you want to use, do the following:

1. Select the text you want to change.

2. On the Formatting toolbar, click the Font Size down arrow to display a drop-down list of point sizes.

3. Select the desired point size.

To resize your text on the fly in two-point increments, click the Increase or Decrease Font buttons (refer to Figure 4.1) located on the Formatting toolbar.

Changing Text Colors

There are so many choices for working with color, you'll feel like you're back in Kindergarten art class. In FrontPage, you can select from a variety of color options:

- **Automatic**—Your basic black text.
- **Document**—Lists all the colors that are currently being used on your page. This feature comes in handy when you want to ensure that you use the exact same hue of blue text throughout your entire document.
- **Standard**—The basic color palette compatible with most Web browsers. This is usually the safest set of colors to use on your Web site.

tip

If the font size you want isn't on the list, don't panic. Selecting the Normal option in the Font Size field of the Formatting toolbar or Font dialog box will change the font size options to allow you to type in point sizes not on FrontPage's default list.

tip

If you're not using one of FrontPage's seven standard font sizes, the Increase and Decrease Font buttons won't be accessible on the Formatting toolbar.

■ **More Colors**—The most powerful color feature. It allows you to specify an exact color by
its hex value. If you are so into colors that
you've got their number, then you're really
going to love this feature. Here is where you
can combine colors until you get just that
right shade you're looking for. Last, but certainly not least, you can also "pick up" a
color, using the eyedropper tool, from a
graphic and match it to your text. Talk
about the perfect accessory.

It's a good idea to use
colored text sparingly. On
the Web, colored text is usually
reserved for hypertext links.
Remember, your goal is to delight
your viewers, not confuse them.

To change text colors, do the following:

1. Select the text you want to change.

2. Choose Format, Font (or right-click, then
   choose Font). The Font dialog box opens.

3. Choose Color. As soon as you open the Color box, the current text color is
   denoted by a small indentation.

4. Select the desired color. Your selection is displayed in the Preview box at the
   bottom of the dialog box.

To change font color on the fly, select the text you want to change, then click the
arrow to the right of the Font Color button on the Formatting toolbar (refer to
Figure 4.1) .

CRAFTING YOUR MESSAGE

When you are designing a Web page, remember that more is not always better. Try to aim
for cutting your text back to at least half of what you would normally present in hard-copy
format. Shoot for having text that is tight, crisp, and clean. Get right to the point, and then
move on.

Also, don't forget to proofread your text for spelling and grammar. Although you may not
get Brownie points for picture-perfect text, people aren't too forgiving when it comes to
glaring typos or stomping on the English language.

Inserting Symbols

Every Web page seems to contain at least one symbol ($\frac{1}{2}$) or special character (©) that doesn't normally appear on a standard keyboard. Just as in Word, you can insert these characters directly into your document. Here's how:

1. Position the cursor where you want to insert the symbol or special character.

2. Choose Insert, Symbol.

3. In the Symbol dialog box, browse through the various fonts to find the symbol or special character you want to insert. When you click on a symbol, you'll see its name displayed in the bottom corner of the dialog box.

4. When you've found the character you want to insert, click it, and then click Insert.

note

Be careful when inserting symbols into your pages. If you use a symbol from a font that's not installed on your visitors' computers, they may see a different character or symbol entirely. Play it safe by only choosing symbols from the font you're using for your content, usually Times New Roman, Arial, or one of the other standard fonts.

Changing Fonts

Changing fonts in FrontPage is as easy as changing fonts in Word. When you're not really sure which font you want, do the following:

1. Select the text you want to change.

2. Choose Format, Font (or right-click, then choose Font). The Font dialog box opens.

3. Choose the desired font in the Font box. Use the up and down arrows to access the available font options. As you make your selection, you'll see an example of the font displayed in the Preview box, contained at the bottom of the Font dialog box.

4. When you've found the font you want, click OK.

tip

As an added feature, FrontPage stores the last 16 symbols or special characters that you've inserted into documents or Web pages in the Recently Used Symbols box.

When you know exactly which font you want to use, do the following:

1. Select the text you want to change.

2. On the Formatting toolbar, click the Font down arrow to display a drop-down list of fonts, and select the one you want to use.

Changing Your Default Fonts

In FrontPage, you can designate the font that you would like FrontPage to use by default when no other font has been specified. FrontPage sets this default as Times New Roman, but you can change this to Arial if you prefer a sans-serif font.

1. Choose Tools, Page Options. The Page Options dialog box opens.

2. Click the Default Fonts tab.

3. In the Design View and Code View section of the tab, choose the font you want to use as the default.

4. Click OK.

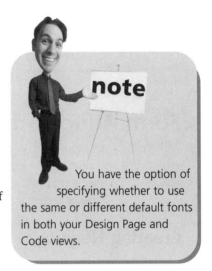

note

You have the option of specifying whether to use the same or different default fonts in both your Design Page and Code views.

Your Defaults Aren't Necessarily Your Visitor's Defaults

When it comes to Web-page design, it's tempting to jazz up your text using cool fonts like Algerian, Cow-Spots, and ChowMein (see Figure 4.3). Unfortunately, if your viewers don't have the same specialty fonts on their computer, their Web browser will substitute another font in its place. Sometimes a substitute font can really mess up the look of your Web page.

If you want to maintain control over how your Web page looks, it's a good idea to stick with the common fonts found on most computer systems, such as Arial, Courier, and Times New Roman (again, see Figure 4.3). Save the ChowMein for headings, which you can create as graphics and insert where needed. For more information about graphics, see Chapter 6, "Creating and Modifying Graphics."

FIGURE 4.3

Battle of the fonts: specialty versus tried and true.

> Specialty Fonts
> ALGERIAN, COW-SPOTS, CHOW MEIN
>
> Common Fonts
> Arial, Courier, Times New Roman

TOO MANY FONTS (LIMITING FONTS ON A PAGE)

When your eyes are bigger than your tummy and you overdo it at the buffet, you usually end up with a big stomachache. Well, that's how most of us feel when Web pages binge on too many fonts, as shown in Figure 4.4.

The intention of text on a Web page is to convey information, not to make viewers feel nauseous. A well-designed Web page needs only two or three fonts, at the maximum, to get the point across.

Using **too** many fonts looks weird.

Formatting Paragraphs

In FrontPage, you can control the appearance of your paragraphs in terms of indentation, alignment, and line spacing. To make your life easier, FrontPage enables you to select paragraphs and apply multiple formatting enhancements all at once. This feature comes in handy for making the paragraphs on your Web site look consistent.

Creating Headings

A paragraph heading is a style that displays text that is large, bold, italic, and so on. FrontPage features both built-in and user-defined paragraph headings.

To apply a built-in paragraph heading, do the following:

1. Select the text you want to include in the heading.
2. Choose Format, Style. The Style dialog box opens.
3. From the Styles list, select the desired paragraph heading (Heading 1, Heading 2, Heading 3, and so on).

To apply built-in paragraph headings on the fly, select the text you want to include in the paragraph heading and choose the desired paragraph heading style from the Styles box (refer to Figure 4.1). Click the down arrow to display a list of the available paragraph heading styles.

To create a user-defined paragraph heading, do the following:

1. Choose Format, Style (or right-click, then choose Style). The Style dialog box opens.
2. Click the New button. The New Style dialog box opens.
3. Type a name for your new paragraph heading in the Name (Selector) box.
4. Click the Format button. A drop-down menu opens.
5. Choose Paragraph. The Paragraph dialog box opens.
6. Format the paragraph heading's alignment, indentation, and spacing. Watch the Preview box to see your paragraph heading under construction.
7. When complete, click OK on all the open dialog boxes.

Centering Text

To center text on a page, do the following:

1. Select the text you want to center.
2. Choose Format, Paragraph. The Paragraph dialog box opens.
3. In the Alignment box, click the down arrow to display the drop-down list.
4. Click Center.
5. Click OK.

To center your text on the fly, select the text and click the Center Text button (refer to Figure 4.1) on the Formatting toolbar.

Indenting Text Using Block Quotes

Block quotes are used if you are inserting quotations from another work (like a passage from a book, a poem, or your favorite recipe), or when you just want to offset text by having it be further in from the margins of the page.

1. Select the text you want to indent using block quotes.
2. Choose Format, Paragraph. The Paragraph dialog box opens (see Figure 4.5).
3. Change the Indentation options by clicking the arrows in the Before Text and After Text boxes.
4. Click OK.

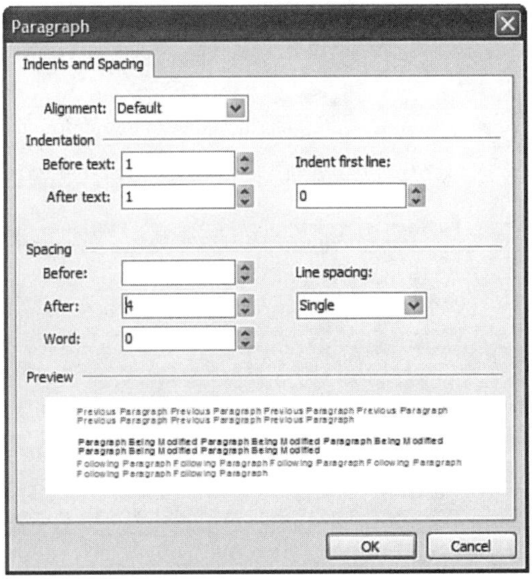

FIGURE 4.5

Offsetting your paragraphs with the click of a mouse: indenting block quote text.

To indent text using block quotes on the fly, select the text and click the Increase Indent button (refer to Figure 4.1) located on the Formatting toolbar. If you find that you have increased the text too much, use the Decrease Indent button (again, refer to Figure 4.1) on the Formatting toolbar to make adjustments.

Breaking a Line Within a Paragraph

When you break a line within a paragraph, you create a new line without adding any space between the new line and the line above it. To break a line within a paragraph, do the following:

1. Insert the mouse at the place you want the break to occur.
2. Choose Insert, Break (or right-click, then choose Break). The Break dialog box opens.
3. Choose Normal Line Break.
4. Click OK.

You can accomplish the same result faster by simply pressing the Shift+Enter key combination to insert the break.

If you want to know where you have inserted line breaks, click the Show All button on the Formatting toolbar (refer to Figure 4.1). Line breaks are marked with left pointing arrows, as shown in Figure 4.6.

FIGURE 4.6

Clicking the Show All button on the Formatting toolbar reveals paragraph line breaks instantaneously.

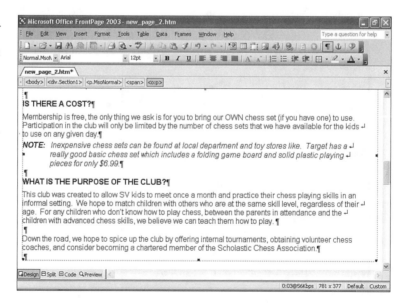

Making Lists

When FrontPage sees a list, it sees the text as a series of paragraphs. There are several types of lists used on the Web:

- **Bulleted**—In a bulleted list, each list item appears with a symbol or bullet before the entry. This is also referred to as an unordered list because it doesn't matter what order the items appear in.

- **Numbered**—In a numbered list, each list item appears with a number before the entry. This is also referred to as an ordered list because the numbering of each item implies that they follow sequentially.

- **Nested**—A nested list is a list that's a mix of bulleted and numbered items, such as a list of sequential steps with various options available at each step.

- **Definition**—A definition list includes a list of terms and definitions, such as entries found in a glossary or dictionary

---

BREAKING TEXT INTO READABLE BLOCKS

Although I love to read, I can't remember ever wanting to stay home and curl up with a good computer. The way people read print versus the way they read online is as different as night and day. When I sit down at the computer to read text, I usually want the Web author to cut to the chase. For some reason, the whole online experience can make us a little crabby and impatient.

When you design your Web pages, keep in mind that your visitors will probably scan the text, paying attention to only those sentences and paragraphs that really interest them. Even though you probably don't want to hear this, your visitors won't read everything you write. With that in mind, they'll like you more if you break your text into readable chunks. Aim for plenty of white space, structure text into multiple paragraph headings, and use meaningful headlines to convey what each section is really about.

Making Bulleted Lists

To make a bulleted list, do the following:

1. Select the text you want to make into a bulleted list.

2. Choose Format, Bullets and Numbering. The Bullets and Numbering dialog box opens.

3. Choose the Plain Bullet tab.

4. Select the bullet style you want to use.

5. Click OK.

To bullet a list on the fly, select the text and click the Bullet button on the Formatting toolbar.

Setting the Bullet Style

When you create a bulleted list in FrontPage, the default bullet is a black circle. As you just saw, you can change the bullet to a black square or other symbol. If your design calls for something with even more punch to it, such as a bullet you create yourself to match the graphics of your site, you can create your own bullet style. To create a bullet style, do the following:

1. Choose Format, Bullets and Numbering. The Bullets and Numbering dialog box opens.
2. Choose the Picture Bullet tab.
3. Select Specify Picture.
4. Click Browse, and locate the graphic file that contains the bullet style you want to add.
5. Select the file and click Open.
6. Click OK.

Of course, this method assumes that you've created a graphic for your bullet. This graphic can be created in any graphics application, such as Photoshop, and saved as either a GIF or JPG. To learn more about creating graphic bullets, see Chapter 7, "Adding Shapes, Word Art, and other Special Graphics."

Making Numbered Lists

To create a numbered list, do the following:

1. Select the text you want to make into a numbered list.
2. Choose Format, Bullets and Numbering. The Bullets and Numbering dialog box opens.
3. Choose the Numbers tab (see Figure 4.7).
4. Select the desired number style.
5. Click OK.

To number a list on the fly, select the list to be numbered and click the Numbering button on the Formatting toolbar (refer to Figure 4.1) .

Changing the Numbering of a List

If you decide that you want to change the numbering of a list in FrontPage, making that change is a snap. You have the flexibility of starting your numbered list at any number.

To change a numbered list, do the following:

1. Select the numbered list text to be changed.
2. Choose Format, Bullets and Numbering (or right-click, then choose List Properties). The List Properties dialog box opens.

3. Choose the Numbers tab.

4. In the Number Start At box, type the number you want the numbered list to begin with. Or, use the up and down arrows to scroll through the list of available numbers.

5. Click OK.

FIGURE 4.7

With FrontPage you can quickly number a list.

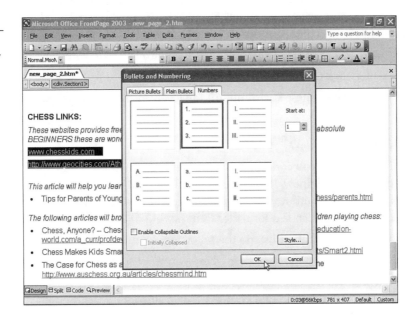

Nesting Lists

In FrontPage, you can build outline lists and assign different styles to the various levels. You have the option of formatting your text to include bullets and numbers.

To create a nested list with numbered entries containing bulleted subentries, do the following:

1. Place the cursor where you want to create a nested list.

2. Choose Format, Bullets and Numbering (or right-click, then choose List Properties). The Bullets and Numbering dialog box opens.

3. Choose the Numbers tab.

4. Choose the box with the style of numbers or letters that you want to start with.

5. Click OK.

6. Type the text for each item that you want included in the nested list, pressing Enter after each entry.

7. When you have typed the last item, press Enter twice. This ends the list.

8. To place each item on the correct level, select the items, then click the Increase Indent button (refer to Figure 4.1) on the Formatting toolbar twice. You need to click that button twice to format each and every level you want in your nested list.

9. To apply numbering, lettering, or bulleted styles to the different levels, insert the cursor on the level or sublevel, and choose Format, Bullets and Numbering (or right-click, then choose the Bullets and Numbering box). The Bullets and Numbering dialog box opens.

10. In the Numbers list, click the box with the style you want to use.

11. Click OK.

12. Repeat these steps until all the levels in the list are formatted.

Creating a Glossary of Terms

In FrontPage, you can build a definition list, which is a fancy way of saying a glossary—you know, like the ones usually found at the back of a textbook. Definition lists allow your viewers to click on specially highlighted words to see what they mean, which is a lot easier than having to leaf back through a big, bulky book.

To make a definition list, do the following:

1. Place the mouse cursor where you want to type the word to be added.

2. Click the down arrow next to the Style field on the Formatting toolbar (refer to Figure 4.1), and choose Defined Term from the drop-down list that appears.

3. Type the word you want to define on the page and press Enter.

4. Type the definition on the page. If you look at the Style field in the Formatting toolbar, you'll see that this line is automatically formatted in the Definition style.

5. When you are finished, press Enter twice.

If you find that FrontPage doesn't work as stated here—this happens sometimes—you can manually format your definition lists. Simply type the definition term on one line, then the definition on the next. Select the definition term, then use the Style field on the Formatting toolbar to choose the Definition Term style. Do the same for the definition, selecting the Definition style.

Adding Comments to a Page

Remember when you were a kid how fun it was to write with invisible ink? You'd write your secret message in lemon juice and nobody could see it until you held it up to a light bulb. Well, FrontPage has a great feature that's kind of like that.

In FrontPage you can leave yourself notes, called comments, on a Web page that appear when the page is being edited, but are invisible when the page is being viewed online. This is a good feature for Web-page designers who want to pass along notes to other members on a team, for people who like to use Post-It notes, or for those of us who are just nostalgic for our secret decoder ring.

To include comments on a Web page, do the following:

1. Place the mouse cursor where you want to add the comment.
2. Choose Insert, Comment. The Comment dialog box opens, as shown in Figure 4.8.
3. Type your text in the Comment box.
4. When you are finished, click OK. Your comments will appear in colored text on the page. The comments will be added to the HTML code for your page, but will only be visible if a visitor chooses to view your source code. Otherwise, the comments are invisible and won't detract from your design.

To edit an existing comment, do the following:

1. Select the comment you want to edit.
2. Choose Format, Properties to open the Comments dialog box. You can also double-click on the comment to open the Comments dialog box.
3. Make your changes to the text.
4. Click OK.

FIGURE 4.8

Adding comments in FrontPage is like having electronic Post-It notes.

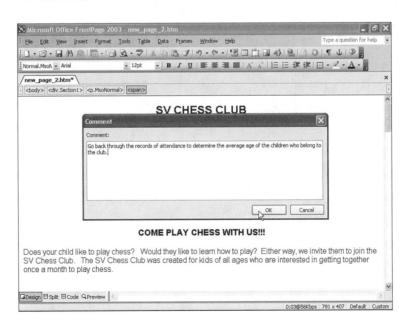

Using Borders and Shading Around Text

To really make your text stand out, FrontPage enables you to surround it with a border or to apply a shading effect to it.

Adding a Border

To add a border, do the following:

1. Select the text around which you want to place a border.

2. Choose Format, Borders and Shading. The Borders and Shading dialog box opens, as shown in Figure 4.9.

3. Click the Borders tab.

4. Choose the desired border setting from the Settings list (options include Box, Shadow, and Custom).

5. Change the border style by making a selection from the Style list.

6. When you are finished, click OK.

To specify that only particular sides of the text should get borders, click the diagram's sides in the Preview section of the Borders tab or use the buttons to apply/remove borders.

FIGURE 4.9

Make text leap right off the page by adding a nifty border.

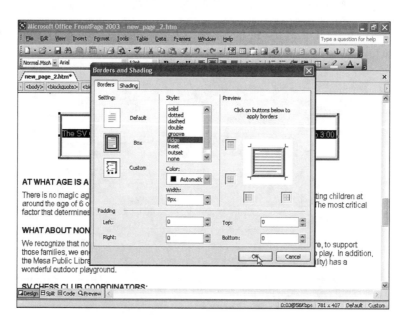

Adding Shading

To shade text, do the following:

1. Select the text you want to shade.

2. Choose Format, Borders and Shading. The Borders and Shading dialog box opens.

3. Click the Shading tab.

4. Choose the desired background color and foreground color from the fill options listed.

5. When you are finished, click OK.

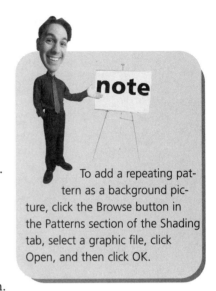

note

To add a repeating pattern as a background picture, click the Browse button in the Patterns section of the Shading tab, select a graphic file, click Open, and then click OK.

Using Find and Replace

FrontPage really acts like Word when it comes to using the Find and Replace feature of the program. Although FrontPage may not have all the bells and whistles that Word has, it's pretty darn close. You can search for and replace almost any kind of typed phrase, including whole words and matching case. An extra benefit is that you have the option of searching through all the pages on your site (great when you need to make a global change to your entire Web site) or just the current page.

Running a Basic Find and Replace Search

To run a basic Find and Replace operation, do the following:

1. Choose Edit, Find. The Find and Replace dialog box opens.

2. Type the text you're looking for in the Find What box.

3. Click the Replace tab.

4. Type the replacement text in the Replace With box.

5. Click Replace All to find and replace text all at once, or click Replace to find and replace text one word/phrase at a time.

6. If you choose Replace All, FrontPage will display a message box after performing the operation indicating how many replacements were made. If you choose Replace, you must click Replace, Find Next, or Close until the search is complete. At the end of the search, FrontPage will display a message box indicating that your search is complete.

Building Advanced Searches

FrontPage allows you to perform Find and Replace operations as simple as the one listed previously or as complex as limiting the operation to specific pages or even content within specific HTML tags. To perform an advanced Find and Replace operation:

1. Choose Edit, Find. The Find and Replace dialog box opens.

2. Type the text you're looking for in the Find What box.

3. In the Find Where field of the Search Options section, select the search options regarding which pages you want FrontPage to include in its search.

4. In the Direction field, select the direction in which you want the search to be performed.

5. Select the Advanced options, like Match Case, you want included in the search.

6. When you are finished, click the Replace tab, as shown in Figure 4.10.

7. Type the replacement text in the Replace With box.

8. In the Find Where field of the Search Options section, select the replace options regarding which pages you want FrontPage to include in its replace operation.

9. In the Direction field, select the direction in which you want the replace to be performed.

10. Select the Advanced options you would like included in the replace, such as matching a whole word exactly rather than a portion of a word.

11. Click Replace All to find and replace text all at once, or click Replace to find and replace text one word/phrase at a time.

12. If you choose Replace All, FrontPage will display a message box after performing the operation indicating how many replacements were made. If you choose Replace, you must click Replace, Find Next, or Close until the search is complete. At the end of the search, FrontPage will display a message box indicating that your search is complete.

note

One of the Advanced replace options in FrontPage is Regular Expressions. A regular expression is merely a pattern that describes character combinations in text. If you want to run a Find and Replace operation using Regular Expressions, all you need to do is select the applicable box on the Replace tab. How easy is that? If you tend to use the same regular expressions on multiple searches, use the Query field's Save button to save an expression, and use the Open button to open it in a later search.

FIGURE 4.10

FrontPage's powerful Find and Replace feature can save you hours of editing time.

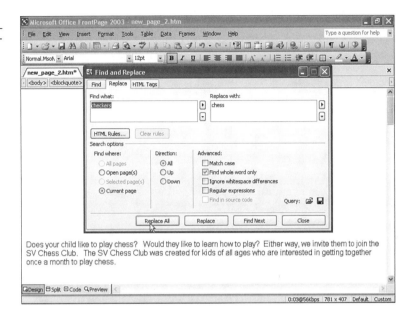

THE ABSOLUTE MINIMUM

With the text-formatting skills you have mastered in this chapter, you are ready to collect the trophy for winning the information highway race. Your text should now set your Web page out from the crowd. As opposed to looking dull and boring, or cluttered and busy, your Web pages should now look clean and polished.

At the bare minimum, you should have learned that it doesn't take a lot of work to make your Web site look professional. Just making a few formatting enhancements like colored text, a few simple fonts, bulleted and numbered lists, indentations, and consistent paragraph headings are really all it takes to create a Web site that is pleasing to the eye.

You should have also learned that one of FrontPage's most powerful features is that changes to your text can be done in a snap. With a quick Find and Replace, you can change a Web site for a chess club into a checkers club in seconds. Now that's awesome Web authoring.

CREATING LINKS

I once heard someone refer to the Internet as the largest library in the world, with all the books dumped on the floor. If that's an accurate description, then a tool that can help you sort through that big mess would be worth its weight in gold. Hyperlinks are that tool. By adding hyperlinks to carefully selected sites on the Web, you can direct your visitors to additional information or entertainment.

Links don't only control access to the World Wide Web at large, however. They also can make the world a bit smaller by allowing your visitors to find specific information within your sites and pages. Links can even personalize the user experience by providing direct e-mail contact to you, the Webmaster.

Links: The Key to Getting Around the Internet

The Internet is made up of billions of Web sites that reside on millions of different computers. Each site has its own unique address, as does each page within a site—much as an apartment building has a street address, and each apartment in that building has a unique number. When you create a link, your page is considered the *source* of the link, while the page to which you're linking is called the *target*.

Linking to Existing Pages

To link to an existing page, do the following:

1. Select the text to be hyperlinked.

2. Choose Insert, Hyperlink (or click on the Hyperlink button, located on the Standard toolbar). The Insert Hyperlink dialog box opens, as shown in Figure 5.1.

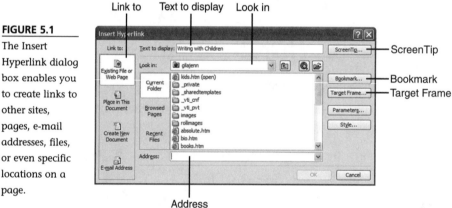

FIGURE 5.1

The Insert Hyperlink dialog box enables you to create links to other sites, pages, e-mail addresses, files, or even specific locations on a page.

3. In the Address field, type the URL (for example, www.gilajenn.com) of the external Web site. If the URL is lengthy or fraught with slashes and underscores, you can cut and paste it from your Web browser into the dialog box.

4. Click OK.

The Hyperlinks dialog box offers many options to help you create and format your link:

- **Link To**—The various choices (an existing file, a Web page, a bookmark, a new document, or an e-mail address) to which you can target your links.

- **Text to Display**—Highlighted text on the Web page you are currently designing that will become the link.

- **ScreenTip**—Used to create a text message that is displayed when a mouse cursor passes over it.

- **Look In**—The various locations (your computer, an intranet, or the Internet) where a target link can be located.

- **Bookmark**—Used to create a flagged location on a Web page (for example, the top of a page).

- **Target Frame**—Used to direct the link to open the target page in a different frame or new window.

- **Remove Link**—Used to delete a link. This option appears in the Edit Hyperlink dialog box, which you access by right-clicking on the link and then choosing Edit Hyperlink from the context menu. Other than this option, the rest of the dialog box is identical to the Insert Hyperlink dialog box.

- **Address**—The target location of the link.

- **Parameters**—This is an advanced feature that allows you to create a hyperlink that queries a database and links to the page containing the results of the query.

- **Style**—Used to format the appearance of hyperlink text.

You also can create links on the fly directly in the Design view. Simply type the URL directly onto your Web page and press Enter. FrontPage automatically converts the URL into a link. If you want the link to be more descriptive than the boring URL, select the hyperlink and then type in a new name. This over-typing will change the text but maintain the link.

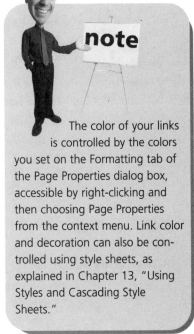

note

The color of your links is controlled by the colors you set on the Formatting tab of the Page Properties dialog box, accessible by right-clicking and then choosing Page Properties from the context menu. Link color and decoration can also be controlled using style sheets, as explained in Chapter 13, "Using Styles and Cascading Style Sheets."

LINKED SITES, LIKE PEOPLE, DO CHANGE

One of the dangers of adding external links to your Web site is the rapid rate of attrition on the Internet. The great site of today may well be gone tomorrow. Therefore, it's a good idea to check your links on a periodic basis. One method is to test each link one at a time, but that's a very time-consuming process. Luckily, FrontPage has a report feature that will do this all for you. With just a few clicks of the mouse, FrontPage will happily scour through all the files of your Web site and test all your links. The Hyperlink report is explained in Chapter 19, "Testing Your Web."

Even if you run the hyperlink report religiously and maintain broken and missing links, you should still make time to manually visit every link target at least once a month. The content of a site is subject to change with little or no advance notice, and domains are bought and sold in seconds. The site that offered in-depth book reviews one day could easily become another owner's porn site the next—not exactly the content to which you want to be linking if your site is about new book releases.

Linking to New Pages

When you're designing the first few pages in your site, you can kill two birds with one stone by linking to a new (blank) page, which has the added bonus of creating the page at the same time the link is established. To link to a new page, do the following:

1. Select the text to be hyperlinked.
2. Choose Insert, Hyperlink (or click on the Hyperlink button, located on the Standard toolbar). The Insert Hyperlink dialog box opens.
3. From the Link To options, choose Create Document.
4. In the Name of New Document field, type the name of the new file you want to link to.
5. In the When to Edit option, choose either Edit the New Document Later or Edit the New Document Now.
6. Click OK.

Be sure to save the new page before closing it. If you close a new page without first adding content to it, FrontPage doesn't prompt you to save, and you lose the file.

Linking Within a Page

If you need to direct visitors to a specific portion of the page that's currently displayed, as is often the case with Frequently Asked Questions (FAQ) pages or when referencing a particular paragraph in your text, you can set anchors within your page that can then serve as link targets. In FrontPage, these anchors are called *bookmarks*.

To create a bookmark, do the following:

1. Position the cursor where you want to insert the bookmark. You don't have to select text or a graphic to set a bookmark, but you want the anchor to be close to the content you're referencing.
2. Choose Insert, Bookmark. The Bookmark dialog box opens, as shown in Figure 5.2.

3. In the Bookmark Name field, type the name you want to assign to your bookmark. The name should be meaningful, particularly if you're going to set more than one bookmark on a page or will be linking to it from another page later.

4. Click OK. A blue flag will appear where your cursor was originally located, representing the new bookmark. This flag will appear only within FrontPage to remind you of the bookmark; it won't appear on the actual page when you publish it to the Web.

The next step is to create a link to that bookmark. You can link to a bookmark on the same page or on a different page. To link to a bookmark on the same page, do the following:

1. Select the text to be hyperlinked.

2. Choose Insert, Hyperlink (or click on the Hyperlink button, located on the Standard toolbar). The Insert Hyperlink dialog box opens.

3. Choose Place in This Document from the Link In options. The dialog box changes to show all the bookmarks for the page, as shown in Figure 5.3.

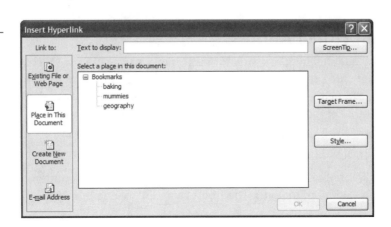

4. Click a bookmark to select it.

5. Click OK twice.

If you want to link to a bookmark on a different page, select the page just as you would when creating any other link, then click the Bookmark button. The book-marks for the selected page will appear. After you've made your selection, you can close the Insert Hyperlinks dialog box as normal.

CREATING A FAQ USING LINKS

Many Web developers like to include a FAQ list on their Web site. A FAQ is nothing more than a series of frequently asked questions that people might have. When the visitor clicks on a question, he or she is magically transported to the answer, which is ordinarily located farther down the page.

When you create a FAQ, it's a good idea to do the following:

- Provide your user with a way to return to the questions (for example, a Return to Top link) after they've read each answer. Visitors hate having to use the scroll bar too much. You can create a Return to Top link by setting a bookmark at the top of the FAQ, then using it as the target of these hyperlinks.

- Reiterate the question when you give the answer. Visitors may have short memories, so give them a break. At the same time, be sure the question is identical in both locations. If the question is worded differently, it can disorient visitors.

- Make sure your links all go to the right place. Visitors will get annoyed if a question goes to the wrong answer.

- Add white space to the bottom of your page. Bookmarks near the bottom of the page won't be able to be displayed properly at the top of the browser window if there's not enough text below it to fill the screen. You can add white space simply by adding empty paragraphs to the bottom of the page. A classier way of adding white space, however, is to add a graphic or other filler to that area.

Linking to an E-mail Address

Every site should offer a way for visitors to contact either the Webmaster or the owner of the site. This enables visitors to get personal answers to their questions. It also can help you because visitors will often inform you if a link is broken or if there are other problems with your site. Think of it as free site testing.

To create a link to an e-mail address, do the following:

1. Select the text to be hyperlinked.

2. Choose Insert, Hyperlink (or click on the Hyperlink button, located on the Standard toolbar). The Insert Hyperlink dialog box opens.

3. In the Link To options, choose E-mail Address. Fields specific to e-mail links will appear, as shown in Figure 5.4.

FIGURE 5.4

E-mail links require different options than other link types.

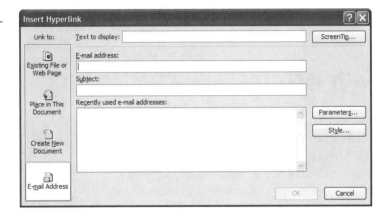

4. In the Address field, type the e-mail address. As soon as you begin typing, you'll notice that FrontPage automatically inserts Mailto: before the address.

5. You can provide a Subject line for the e-mail if you like. This will appear as the subject of any messages sent from this link.

6. Click OK.

The Mailto: designation specifies that the link should open a new e-mail message window rather than connect to a page or site. When a visitor uses an e-mail link to send you a message, the message may not get to you until the visitor opens his or her e-mail application and manually sends the message.

The subject line is optional, but can be used to good advantage. If you have multiple e-mail links within your site, you can customize the subject line depending on the page. This will enable you to track which pages visitors are accessing and where they're encountering issues.

Linking to Download a File

Another use for links is to give your visitors access to files that they can download. A customer-support site might use this to disseminate software updates to their users. The method for creating these links is identical to linking to a page, except that your target is a file rather than a Web page.

The user experience in dealing with certain files can vary. If your file is a Word or PDF file, and the visitor has Microsoft Word or Adobe Acrobat Reader installed, the file will appear in the browser window. If the visitor doesn't have the correct application installed or chooses to save the target file rather than following the link directly, the file will be downloaded to his or her computer.

Linking with Pictures

Linking with pictures—navigation buttons, photograph thumbnails, clip art, and so on—is done in the same manner as linking with text. Select the image, then create the hyperlink. Whereas text links are underlined by default, pictures acquire a colored border when used as a link. These can be unsightly and generally aren't necessary.

To modify picture link borders, do the following:

1. Click on the picture.

2. Choose Format, Properties (or right-click the picture, then choose Picture Properties). The Picture Properties dialog box opens.

3. On the Appearance tab, shown in Figure 5.5, change the Border Thickness setting. If you set this to zero (0), the border will be removed, but the link will remain.

4. Click OK.

If you're going to make files available from your site, be absolutely certain that they're virus free. Nothing can kill a site faster than exposing your visitors' computers to a virus. Not only will they warn others to stay away, but they also can file a complaint with your Web host to have you shut down.

FIGURE 5.5
In most situations, you'll want to completely remove the border around a picture link by setting the Border Thickness to zero.

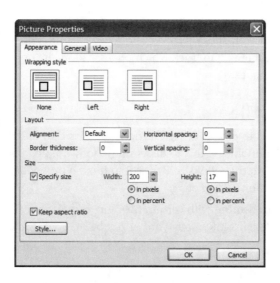

Targeting Links

By default, when a user clicks on a link, the new page opens in the same browser window as the source page. In most cases, this is fine because Web surfers want to be able to navigate from site to site without opening new windows all over their screens. There are times, however, when you'll want to keep a page available while opening a link target in another window. This is known as *targeting your link*.

A good time to take advantage of the open-a-new-window technique is when you want to send your users to an external link, but not lose them. An example of this would be if you've created a FAQ with the questions on one page and the answers on another. By launching the answers in a new window, the site visitor can toggle between windows to return to the question list at any time.

To set a link to open in a new window, do the following:

1. Select the hyperlinked text.

2. Choose Insert, Hyperlink (or click on the Hyperlink button, located on the Standard toolbar). The Edit Hyperlink dialog box opens.

3. Click the Target Frame button. The Target Frame dialog box opens, as shown in Figure 5.6.

FIGURE 5.6

The Target Frame dialog box enables you to specify where to open the link target—in the same window as the source, in a specific frame of a frame-based site, or in a new window.

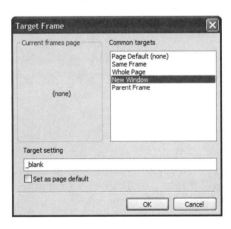

4. Select New Window. If you want every page to open in a new window, click the Set As Page Default box.

5. Click OK twice.

Consider carefully before setting the default to always open a hyperlink in a new window. Every open window uses computer resources, which in turn can slow your visitor's computer down. Web surfers generally like to control how many windows they have open at once, and if every link on your site opens yet another window, those surfers will be turned off (and tune your site out). You should only open a new window when absolutely necessary, such as when you're sending a visitor to another site for related information, but reason that they'll probably still want to view your site.

Dressing Up Your Links

In FrontPage, you can configure your pages to change how hyperlinks look when the user rolls his or her mouse over them. This is a good way to alert your visitors to the fact that a link is active.

To change the appearance of links, do the following:

1. Choose File, Properties (or right-click, then choose Page Properties). The Page Properties dialog box opens.

2. Click the Advanced tab.

3. In the Styles section, click the Enable Hyperlink Rollover Effects box.

4. Click the Rollover Style button. The Font dialog box opens.

5. Make the desired changes to the Font, Color, and/or Effects settings. Your changes will be displayed in the Preview box.

6. Click OK twice.

An even better method for controlling the appearance of links and creating rollovers is to use cascading style sheets (CSS). To learn more about them, see Chapter 13.

ScreenTips

Another neat feature of FrontPage is that it enables you to create a ScreenTip hyperlink. When your Web site visitor moves his or her mouse over the hyperlink, text in a little message box is displayed. ScreenTips only work in Internet Explorer and the most recent versions of Netscape, Mozilla, and Opera, so not all your visitors may see them.

To create a ScreenTip link, do the following:

1. Select the text or image to be linked to a ScreenTip.

2. Choose Insert, Hyperlink (or click on the Hyperlink button, located on the Standard toolbar). The Edit Hyperlink dialog box opens.

3. Click the ScreenTip button. The Set Hyperlink ScreenTip dialog box opens.

4. Type the text you want displayed.

5. Click OK twice.

Removing a Link

The quickest and easiest method for removing a link is to just delete the applicable text or picture. However, because you may want to hang on to the related text or picture, FrontPage gives you a method for only removing the link.

To remove a link, do the following:

1. Select the text or picture whose hyperlink you want to remove.

2. Choose Insert, Hyperlink (or click the Hyperlink button, located on the Standard toolbar). The Edit Hyperlink dialog box opens.

3. Click the Remove Link button.

Maintaining Links with the Hyperlinks View

FrontPage has a nifty tool to give you a birds-eye view of all your links: Hyperlinks view. This graphic map enables you to trace the path of your links. You will find that this comes in really handy when you're trying to determine just where all your links go.

To access the Hyperlinks view, do the following:

1. Choose View, Hyperlinks.

2. All the hyperlink target locations for that page are displayed, as shown in Figure 5.7. Click the plus sign on a page to expand the list of sublinks. Or, click the minus sign to contract the list of sublinks for a page.

FIGURE 5.7
Hyperlinks view shows how the pages in your site and on other sites are connected with hyperlinks.

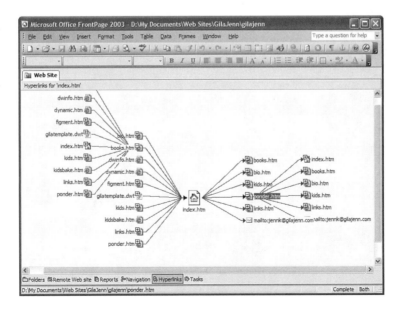

THE ABSOLUTE MINIMUM

Links are a simple tool with tremendous potential. At an absolute minimum, you should become comfortable with creating links to other pages within your site and to related sites elsewhere on the Web. Anything else you want to try, from bookmark links to file downloads, is just gravy.

Cascading style sheets are the preferred method for controlling the appearance and rollover states of links, but there's no shame in using the simpler methods available in FrontPage, such as using the Page Properties dialog box. The bottom line is that you want to help your users get around your site and the Internet. How you accomplish that is up to you.

The absolute minimum requirement for creating links, however, is maintaining them. Broken links don't help your users get around and don't help you build a good reputation for your site. Keeping links under control is one of the most critical jobs of a Webmaster. Fortunately, FrontPage recognizes the importance of this, providing not only the Hyperlinks view but also several reports to help you maintain your links. To learn more about the hyperlink reports, see Chapter 22, "Maintaining a Published Web."

6

CREATING AND MODIFYING GRAPHICS

They say a picture is worth a thousand words, and that certainly can be true when you add graphics to your Web site. In the case of a graphical medium such as a Web site, graphics can serve many purposes, including providing pictorial support for your text or to illustrate a point, showcasing products you may have for sale or examples of your work, and breaking up large blocks of text that may be tiring or monotonous to visitors' eyes.

That said, when it comes to using graphics on your Web site, it's not just a matter of picking a graphic (or many graphics) and inserting them on your pages; there is much more to consider.

The more graphics you use on a page, the longer it can take for that page to load on your visitors' browsers; that's why you need to choose your images wisely. Use only as many as you absolutely need, and modify them to fit the unique conditions you may have set up on a page. For example, you may want to crop or resize a graphic so that it's not as large on your page and won't take as long to download.

Understanding Graphics Formats

The term *graphics format* refers to the type of file—and its properties, such as the number of colors it can display—created when you store an image on your computer. There are numerous graphics file formats, but the two used most often on a Web site are

- **GIFs (Graphics Interchange Format)**—A type of graphic that can use as many as 256 colors. GIFs are typically used for small images and illustrations as well as for very short animations.

- **JPGs or JPEGs (Joint Photographic Experts Group)**—This type supports as many as 16 million colors and is typically used for digital photography, simple screenshots, and larger images.

Certain types of graphics files—and for Web sites, this is especially true for JPG images—use something called a *compression algorithm* to shrink an image's file size to as little as 5% of its original size. This sounds great from your standpoint as a Web designer because the smaller an image's file is, the faster it should load when visitors open a page containing it on your site. With such compression, however, comes some loss in detail, which may or may not be obvious to the eye. For example, a JPG

note

There are two other types of graphics files that are sometimes used on Web sites: Windows bitmaps or BMP files, and PNG files. In general, the use of BMP files is discouraged because they are often very large and can take your site visitors a long time to download. The other, PNG, is new and supported by FrontPage, but still not in as wide a use as GIF and JPG files. It was created to get around copyright issues surrounding the use of GIF files, which use a special compression scheme first distributed on CompuServe. You may find digital camera software, as well as graphics software, that support this format, which can also be used for images on your FrontPage site.

image won't always display lettering, line drawings, or very small images with the same detail and clarity because of its high compression rate.

You can create images such as GIFs and JPGs using a number of different programs and/or hardware. For example:

- If you have a scanner attached to your PC, you can scan images into your PC and, using the scanner's software—or using the Scanner or Camera wizard in FrontPage—save the acquired image file in either the GIF or JPG image format.

- If you have a digital camera that you can attach to your PC, you can download images from the camera into your PC using either the camera's software or the Scanner or Camera Wizard and save them in GIF or JPG format (depending on the type of camera and the types of image formats it supports).

- You can create drawings using programs such as Jasc Software's PaintShop Pro, Adobe PhotoShop, and even Microsoft Paint and save them in either GIF or JPG format.

The Rules of Adding Images

Although the purpose of this chapter is to show you how to insert images and fit them to your needs, there is some additional information you should know.

First, graphics should be used carefully because the inclusion of many different graphics on one page or even the use of one or two very large graphics can appreciably slow the loading of that page in a visitor's Web browser. This is especially true if that user is connected to the Internet via a dial-up (phone and modem) rather than a high-speed (satellite, cable, or DSL modem) connection. If you're using dial-up, you'll hit the same problem when you visit your own site.

Second, there tends to be a temptation, especially among new site designers, to use any and all graphics they think are particularly cool or beautiful or funny. Too often, these graphics are used even when they have nothing to do with the subject matter at hand. Instead of enlivening or enriching a page or pages on a site, they end up distracting from it.

For these reasons, among others, you may want to follow these rules of the road when working with Web graphics:

- Think about your images before you add them. Select a small number of images you think will work best. You can always save the rest to use later with new pages you add.

■ Reduce the size of large image files so that they don't take too long to download over the Internet (but don't make the images themselves so small that they are difficult to make out).

■ Try to match your images to your page content.

■ When you want to create a collection of images, consider using a photo gallery to do so. You will learn how to put one together in this chapter.

Sources of Images

When you first start your Web site, it's important to have an idea about where you can find images you can use on your Web pages. Microsoft FrontPage can help you there, both in providing access to some clip art you can download and in helping you acquire and organize other images from additional sources, such as your scanner, your digital camera, various graphics programs, and the Internet. For example, you can organize images already contained on your computer using the Microsoft Clip Organizer tool in FrontPage.

Using the Microsoft Clip Organizer

The Microsoft Clip Organizer is available within FrontPage (as well as within other Microsoft Office programs you may have, such as Microsoft Word) to enable you to organize your artwork into one main collection, which is then divided by specific categories (such as symbols and technology) for easy reference and copying.

To open Clip Organizer and organize your media files, also called *clips*, into collections, do the following:

1. Open the Insert menu, choose Picture, and select Clip Art.

2. The Clip Art task pane opens at the right side of the FrontPage window. Click Organize Clips (see Figure 6.1).

3. As shown in Figure 6.2, a dialog box opens, inviting you to allow the organizer to search for clips on your PC. Click Now.

In step 3 you can click the Options buttons to specify which drives and folders you want the organizer to search (letting you exclude other areas).

Clip Organizer searches your drive(s) for image and media files—including multimedia files, such as videos and sound clips, discussed in Chapter 8—to include in the master collection, and then divides them up by keywords that the Organizer adds.

Media files are separated into individual collections to better categorize them so that you can find them quickly. Depending on the size and number of drives you have, and the number of media files that are on those drives, this process may take from under a minute to several minutes.

When the operation is complete, Clip Organizer opens in the Collection List view, as shown in Figure 6.3.

FIGURE 6.1

The Clip Art task pane— choose Organize Clips.

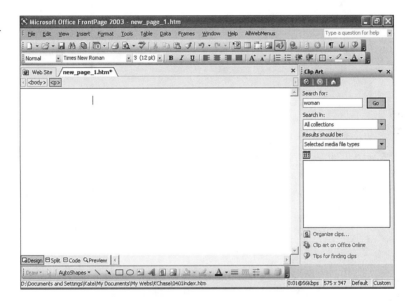

FIGURE 6.2

Microsoft Clip Organizer enables you to assemble and categorize any or all images on your PC into one convenient, easy-to-reference location.

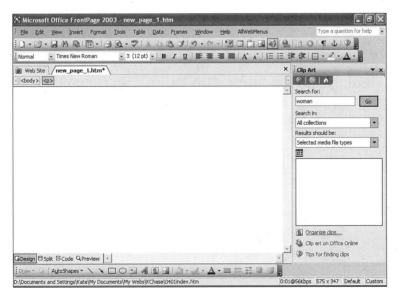

FIGURE 6.3

By default, Clip Organizer creates collections for you, but you can always add more.

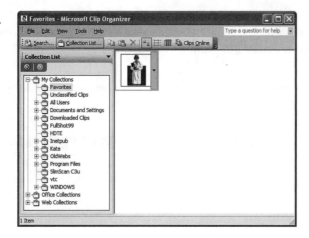

About Other Images and Media

You may notice that when you use Clip Organizer to collect all your scanned documents, digital photos, sound clips, and such into collections, they won't have keywords to help you search for them as the FrontPage included clip art does. Fortunately, you can add them. Here's how:

1. Right-click on a clip to which you want to add keywords.

2. Select Edit Keywords.

3. In the Keyword text box, type the first search word you want to associate with this clip. When you're finished, click Add.

4. Repeat step 3 until you've added all the keywords desired. Then click OK to exit, or click the Previous or Next buttons to move backward or forward in your collection to select another clip.

Finding and Adding a Clip Using Clip Organizer

After Clip Organizer searches your drive(s) to compile your collections of clips, you can then use it to locate those clips quickly in order to add them to your site. To locate and add a clip, do the following:

1. With FrontPage open to the page where you want to add the clip, click the location on the page where you want to insert it.

2. Open the Insert menu, choose Picture, and select Clip Art. The Clip Art task pane opens.

3. In the Search for box, type a keyword that corresponds to the type of clip you want to find, such as **building** or **person** or **dog**. Then click Go.

4. Clip Organizer conducts its search. Assuming it locates any clips that relate to the keyword you typed, Clip Organizer lists the clips found, as shown in Figure 6.4.

5. To use a clip located there, right-click on the clip, and choose Copy.

6. Right-click the spot in the page where you want to insert the clip and select Paste.

FIGURE 6.4

Keywords enable you to search your collections of clips much more quickly than looking through the various folders on your drive(s).

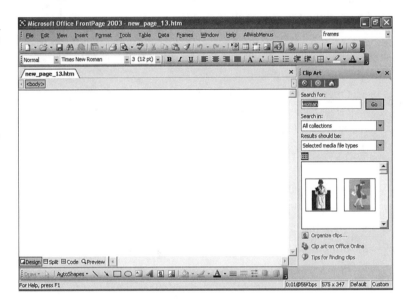

HANDLING ANIMATED GIFS

You've no doubt visited Web sites that contain animated GIF files. If not, Microsoft includes some examples in its clip-art collection for use with FrontPage, such as a seedling that grows from a freshly planted seed into a large, healthy plant. These are often attention getters for a site, especially when used judiciously (meaning not too often and when added to the right types of pages).

That said, animated GIFs are still just GIFs. The only difference is that an animated GIF uses three or more individual GIFs to create the motion effect. Programs such as Jasc Software's PaintShop Pro and others enable you to create your own animated GIFs. These programs then assemble and compress your animated GIF into a single GIF file, which you can insert on your Web pages just like any other GIF.

Downloading Clip Art

One of the truly neat things about FrontPage is that Microsoft makes available to you a special large online collection of clip art, photographs, and various media files, including sounds, which you can download to Clip Organizer and easily insert into your pages. There is no charge for this service; it's one of the benefits of being a FrontPage user.

You can either open your FrontPage Web site to the page where you want to insert the downloaded clip art or just download the clip art to Clip Organizer and then copy it to the page or pages you want later.

To access the Microsoft Office Clip Art and Media Web site, do the following:

note

To use the Microsoft Office Clip Art and Media site to download clip art, you need to be connected to the Internet.

1. Open the Insert menu, choose Picture, and select Clip Art. The Clip Art task pane opens.

2. Click the Clip Art on Office Online link to open your Web browser and connect to the Microsoft Office Clip Art and Media Web site.

3. Scroll down to Browse Clip Art and Media and click a category to open that category and display the first group of available clip art.

4. Click the check box below any graphic to select it.

5. Click Next to move to the next page in the collection, and make additional selections.

6. When you've selected all the images you want, double-click the Download (number) Items link on the left side of your browser window, as shown in Figure 6.5.

7. In the Terms of Use Policy dialog box, click the Accept button.

8. Click Download Now, click Save, and then click Save again.

This process downloads the files from the Microsoft Web site into Microsoft Clip Organizer, where they will be available for your use. When you're notified that the download is complete, click Open to launch Microsoft Clip Organizer.

To use a clip-art graphic you've just downloaded, do the following:

1. From Microsoft Clip Organizer, point to the graphic you want to insert, right-click, and choose Copy.

2. Return to your Web site page, position your cursor where you want to insert the graphic, right-click, and choose Paste.

FIGURE 6.5

The Microsoft Office Clip Art and Media site enables you to choose from thousands of clips (sounds and photos as well as icons and standard clip art) and download them into Microsoft Clip Organizer for use in your Web site.

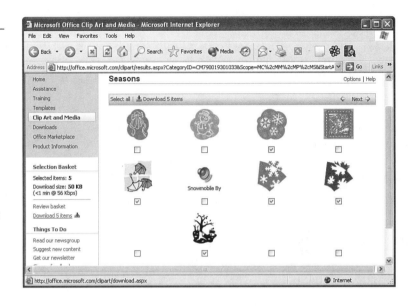

Adding Digital Photography

If you have a digital camera that you can attach to your PC, you can use FrontPage to download images from the camera into your PC. After the images have been downloaded from the camera, you can easily place them on your Web pages.

To use FrontPage to download images from your camera, do the following:

1. Connect your camera to the PC (if it's not already) and make certain the camera is turned on.

2. In FrontPage, open the page on which you want to insert the photo.

3. Open the Insert menu, choose Picture, and select From Scanner or Camera. The Insert Picture from Scanner or Camera dialog box opens.

4. If your camera isn't already shown in this dialog box, click the Device down arrow and select the camera from the drop-down list that appears.

5. Next to Resolution, select Web Quality.

6. If you want the photos added to Microsoft Clip Organizer, click the Add pictures to Clip Organizer check box to check it.

7. Click the Insert button, which launches the Scanner and Camera Wizard.

tip

You can also launch the Scanner and Camera Wizard by simply attaching your digital camera to your PC (often, this is done by a cable attached to your COM or serial port or USB port on the back—or front—of your PC) and turning your camera on. Alternatively, click the Start button, choose My Pictures, and click the Get Pictures from a Scanner or Camera link.

8. Click Next.

9. The wizard displays a preview of the pictures on your camera, as shown in Figure 6.6. By default, all photos are selected. Click the green check mark next to any image you *don't* want to download to uncheck it, and then click Next.

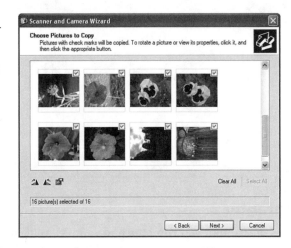

10. Select the location where you want your photos downloaded (usually, the My Pictures folder or a folder within it).

11. If you like, click the Delete Pictures from My Device After Copying Them check box to select it. Then click Next.

12. The pictures are copied from your camera to your PC; use the screen that appears to monitor the progress of the operation. When the copy is complete, click Next.

13. Under Other Options, click Nothing. Then click Next.

14. From the Completing Scanner and Camera Wizard screen, double-click the link to the folder where you just copied your photos to open that folder.

15. Click the image you want to add to your Web page, right-click, and choose Copy.

16. Return to FrontPage, right-click the spot where you want to insert the photo, and choose Copy. As shown in Figure 6.7, the photo appears on your page.

FIGURE 6.7

An example of an inserted photo on a FrontPage Web page, downloaded from a digital camera and copied from the My Pictures folder.

If the digital photo you want to add to your page has already been downloaded to your PC, it most likely was placed in your My Pictures folder. To add it to your page, do the following:

1. Click the Start button and choose My Pictures.

2. Locate the photo you want to use, right-click it, and choose Copy. (If the photo is in a subfolder under My Pictures, double-click the subfolder to open it.)

3. In FrontPage, open the page in your site to which you want to add the photo.

4. Right-click the spot where you want to place the photo and choose Paste.

Additionally, you may have regular photographs taken from a nondigital camera you want to add to your site. For this, you need an optical scanner. Here's how to add these types of photos to your page:

1. Place the photo you want to scan in the scanner.

2. Open FrontPage to the page where you want to insert the photo, and click the position on the page where it should be inserted.

3. Open the Insert menu, choose Picture, and select From Scanner or Camera.

4. When the Scanner or Camera Wizard opens, select your scanner and click OK.

5. When the Scanner window appears, select Web Quality and then click either Insert (for an automatic insertion) or Custom Insert (which lets you make additional choices, such as whether to scan in color or greyscale).

The photograph is then scanned into your PC through FrontPage, and the digitized image appears where you intended to place it.

Inserting Other Images

After you decide you want to add an image or images to a page or pages on your site, it's wise to identify the image and decide where it (or they) best fits.

To insert an image on a page, do the following:

1. In FrontPage, open the page to which you want to add the image. Be sure you are in Design view.

2. Click the location on the page where you want to insert the image.

3. Open the Insert menu, choose Picture, and choose one of the options listed for the source of your image, as shown in Figure 6.8. (For normal images, you will usually choose Clip Art or File.)

FIGURE 6.8

FrontPage enables you to add graphics from a number of different sources.

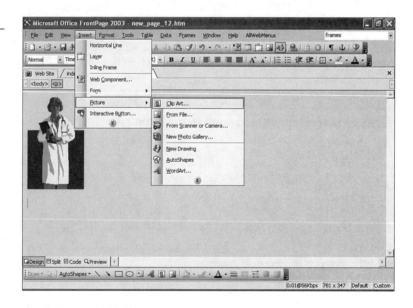

When you perform step 3 to add an image, as shown in Figure 6.8, you'll have a number of different source options available to you. These include the following:

- **Clip Art**—Use this option when you want to use an image from the collections of clips stored on your PC or downloaded from the Internet.

- **File**—Select this if you want to insert a graphic that is stored on your PC.

- **Scanner or Camera**—Choose this when you want to scan an image from a print source (like a print photograph or document) or acquire an image directly from your digital camera.

- **New Photo Gallery**—You can choose this if you want to create a full gallery of images.

- **Flash**—This is the choice to make when you want to insert a Flash animation (you need to obtain the animation before you use it) rather than a still image into your page.

- **New Drawing**—Select this option to open a drawing window on your page that enables you to create an original piece of artwork using selections from the Drawing toolbar.

- **AutoShapes**—Choosing this option opens the AutoShape toolbar, letting you select the type of shape you want to include. (Learn more about this in Chapter 7, "Adding Shapes, WordArt, and Other Special Graphics.")

- **WordArt**—Select this option to create WordArt, allowing you to create very stylized graphics for words. (This is also discussed in Chapter 7.)

- **Video**—This option enables you to add a supported video file, such as one you've obtained or created using your Web cam or other digital camera. (This is covered in more detail in Chapter 8, "Adding Multimedia."

Moving an Image

If, after you've inserted an image, you decide that it should be placed elsewhere on the same page or on another page altogether, it's easy to rearrange. If you simply need to move a graphic to elsewhere on the same page, you can click on the graphic and simply drag it to its new location.

Otherwise, use these steps to move an image:

1. Right-click the image you want to move and choose Cut. Alternatively, click the image to select it, open the Edit menu, and choose Cut.

2. Right-click the preferred destination for the image (this may require you to open another page) and choose Paste. Alternatively, click the preferred location, and then open the Edit menu and choose Paste.

note

To remove a graphic after you've inserted it, simply click the graphic to select it and press the Delete key on your keyboard. Alternatively, after selecting the graphic, open the Edit menu and choose Delete.

Modifying a Graphic in FrontPage

Chances are that after you add a graphic to your Web page, you'll need to modify it in some way—for example, resize it, rotate it, crop it, and so on. You can easily do so using FrontPage's Pictures toolbar, as well as by using the Picture Properties dialog box.

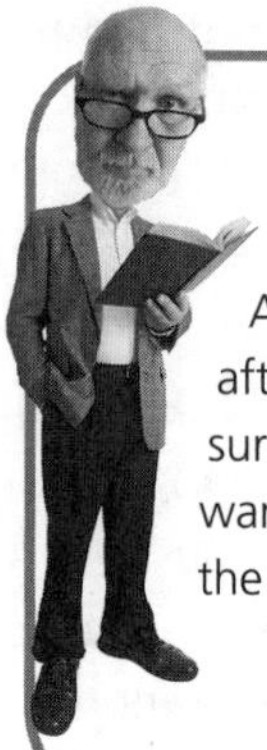

tip

Always check your image after modifying it to make sure the results are what you wanted. If they aren't, repeat the operation or undo it.

Using the Pictures Toolbar

Perhaps the fastest way to make changes to the images you'll include on your Web site is through the use of the Pictures toolbar. By default, this toolbar is normally hidden from your view. To make it visible for your use, do the following:

1. Open the View menu, choose Toolbars, and select Picture.
2. After the toolbar appears, as shown in Figure 6.9, click one of the buttons to use a tool available there.

FIGURE 6.9
To see what each button on the Pictures toolbar does, simply run your mouse across it. A ScreenTip will appear, reporting the button's function.

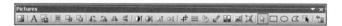

Among the tools available to you on this toolbar are the following:

- Insert Picture from File
- Text
- Auto Thumbnail
- Position Absolutely
- Rotate
- Adjust Brightness/Contrast
- Crop

■ Set Transparent Color

■ Adjust Color Level

You will learn about using several of these tools when working with images in the remainder of this chapter.

Resizing Graphics

The simplest way to resize a graphic is to do so after you've inserted it into a Web page. You might do this to make the image smaller so that it fits in the area of the page to which it's been added. Note that you also can make a graphic larger than it normally is, but you might have poor results because the image may become fuzzy and distorted.

To undo any changes you make to your graphics using the Pictures toolbar, simply click on the toolbar's Restore button.

Follow these steps to resize a graphic:

1. Right-click the graphic you want to resize and select Picture Properties.

2. The Picture Properties dialog box opens. If it is not already displayed, click the Appearance tab (see Figure 6.10).

FIGURE 6.10

The Picture Properties dialog box's Appearance tab lets you adjust your graphic's width and height and specify whether those values should be expressed in pixels or as a percent.

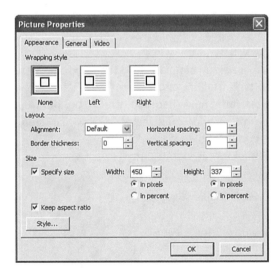

3. Type a new value in the Width and Height boxes or use the down and up arrows next to them to increase or decrease the value.

4. If you want to express the value in pixels rather than as a percent or vice versa, click the In Pixels or In Percent option button underneath the Width and Height boxes. For example, specifying a width of 60% resizes the graphic to 60% of its original size.

5. Click to check or uncheck the Keep Aspect Ratio check box. (Checking this box instructs FrontPage to maintain the image's original proportions when it is resized.)

6. Click OK.

Rotating Graphics

Sometimes, especially when using a digital photo, you may find the orientation of the graphic is just wrong: It's upside down or sideways, or points to the right when you want it to point to the left.

When this happens, you can simply rotate the graphic until it displays correctly on your page. Here's how to accomplish this:

1. Click the graphic you want to rotate.

2. On the Pictures toolbar, click the Rotate Left, Rotate Right, Flip Horizontal, or Flip Vertical button.

Adjusting Color, Brightness, and Contrast

Another modification you can make to your graphics is to adjust their color level, brightness, and contrast to make them look as good as possible on your page.

Adjusting Color Level

Color level refers to the degree of color saturation applied to an image. For example, suppose you've taken a digital photo of a little girl in a bright orange dress, and you want to use the image on your site. When you acquire the photo from your camera, however, you notice that the orange color seems to glow like neon, almost hurting your eyes. In this case, you might want to adjust t
he color level to desaturate it a bit, dulling the neon to a nice orange.

To adjust an image's color level, do the following:

1. Click the image whose color level you want to adjust.

2. On the Pictures toolbar, click the Color button and choose Automatic from the list that appears.

The result should be that the image becomes slightly less vibrant.

tip

If you want to wash out the color to reduce it further, or even change it to grayscale, you can select either of those options in step 2 instead of choosing Automatic.

WHAT'S A WEB-SAFE COLOR PALETTE?

Not all colors are supported by all Web browsers, especially when the browser in question is older or is built into a hand-held device.

So what happens when a Web browser is told, in the process of displaying a Web page, to reproduce a color it doesn't support? Usually, the browser will do one of two things: substitute a color it does support or try to combine two supported colors to match it as closely as possible (this is referred to as *dithering*). The results may not seem very satisfactory to you as a Web designer. For example, the perfect apple red you use might come out as pink or even orange when viewed through a browser.

In the course of learning the art of Web design, you may hear the term *Web-safe color palette* (also called a *browser-safe palette*) and wonder what it is. Put simply, this is a group of colors that should display properly in all browser types. Beyond that, they are designed to work with Web access devices that may be capable of showing far less color range than the millions of different shades many of today's PCs—and their video cards—can. Some devices can only display 256 or fewer colors. Also, PCs and Macs have 40 colors in a 256-color palette that they won't render quite the same. For this reason, a Web-safe color palette typically offers 216 colors.

Adjusting Brightness

As you probably know, brightness, with respect to images, describes the level of light available in an image's display. Increasing the brightness of an image can reveal some of the detail contained in darker regions of that image. If the brightness is increased too much, however, detail can be lost in areas of the image that were already light.

To adjust a graphic's brightness, do the following:

1. Click the image whose brightness you want to adjust.

2. On the Pictures toolbar, click the More Brightness button to increase the brightness or the Less Brightness button to decrease it.

Adjusting Contrast

Contrast refers to the overall difference in brightness levels of both light and dark regions of an image. Adjusting contrast also can be used to help increase image detail.

Follow these steps to adjust a graphic's contrast:

1. Click the image whose contrast you want to adjust.

2. On the Pictures toolbar, click the More Contrast button to increase the contrast or the Less Contrast button to decrease it.

Cropping Graphics

To crop a graphic is to select a specific part of a full image and cut the rest of the image away. This is useful when you only want to use part of a picture (for example, the part containing a face or a person) and remove superfluous areas (such as sky or white space). You can also use cropping to reduce the size of a full-size image.

To crop an image, do the following:

1. Click the image you want to crop.

2. On the Pictures toolbar, click the Crop button. FrontPage outlines the entire image with a dotted line.

3. Move your cursor to one of the corners of the dotted outline, and drag it until the outline contains roughly the part of the image you want to keep, as shown in Figure 6.11.

FIGURE 6.11

With cropping, you can specify how much of an image you want to keep for use on your Web page.

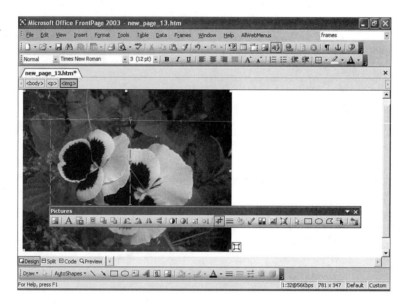

4. To adjust the outline, repeat step 3 as needed on the other corners until only the area of the image that you want to keep is framed in the dotted outline.

5. Click the Crop button again.

Making Images Transparent

Think of a transparent image as one that blends into the background of your Web page, even if the background of the image and the background color of the page don't originally match.

Let's consider an example of such an image, using one of FrontPage's clip-art samples, as shown in Figure 6.12. As you can see, it's a female medical professional drawn against a white background. If you copy and paste this piece of clip art to a Web page with a white background, the image will appear transparent—that is, you'll see the woman and the blue area behind her, but the white parts of the image will blend into the white of the page.

FIGURE 6.12

The FrontPage clip-art image and its white background.

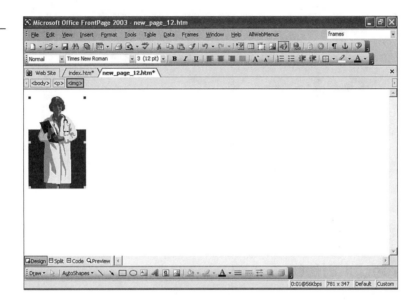

But what happens if you have a pale green background for your page? Unless you set this image to be transparent, the white in the image will be displayed when you paste it into your page.

To make the white on the image blend in with the pale green background of the Web page, take these steps:

1. With the page that contains the image open in FrontPage, click the Set Transparent Color button on the Pictures toolbar.

2. Click on the white part of the image.

The image's white background becomes transparent, changing to match the page's background—in this case, pale green, as shown in Figure 6.13.

Here is another way to make an image transparent:

1. Right-click on the image and select Picture Properties.

2. Click the General tab.

3. Click the Picture File Type button.

4. In the Picture File Type dialog box, under Settings, click the Transparent check box to check it.

5. Click OK twice to return to the page.

FIGURE 6.13

By clicking the Set Transparent Color button on the Pictures toolbar, you can modify the background color of the image to match that of your page.

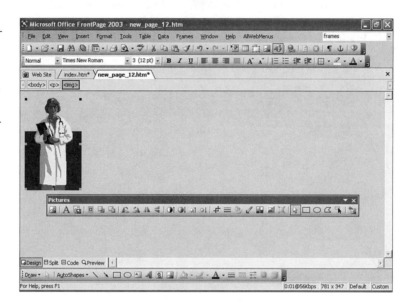

Adding Special Effects

There are certain special effects you can apply to your graphics to further customize how they appear on your page. For example, you can add bevels and drop shadows to your images.

Bevels

Beveling an image gives it a bit of a 3D appearance with crisp sides that appear to drop down into the page itself. To create this effect, do the following:

1. Click the image you want to bevel.

2. On the Pictures toolbar, click the Bevel button.

Look at the image again and you'll see that all four sides appear to bevel or drop down into the page. Click the Bevel button again, and you'll see the effect change somewhat.

Drop Shadows

Do you want to create a shadowing effect? FrontPage lets you add this for WordArt and AutoShapes through the use of the Drawing toolbar, located at the bottom of the FrontPage window.

Here's how to create drop shadows:

1. Click the image to which you want to apply a drop shadow.
2. On the Drawing toolbar, click the Shadow Style button.
3. Click to select the shadow type you want to use for the image.

For this option, you may want to experiment a bit. It's possible that shadows may not work well for all images.

Setting Picture Properties

There are a number of different ways you can change the size and alignment of an image. In FrontPage, one of the most common ways is to use the Picture Properties dialog box's Appearance tab, shown in Figure 6.14. To open this dialog box, right-click the graphic you want to modify, and choose Picture Properties from the short-cut menu that appears.

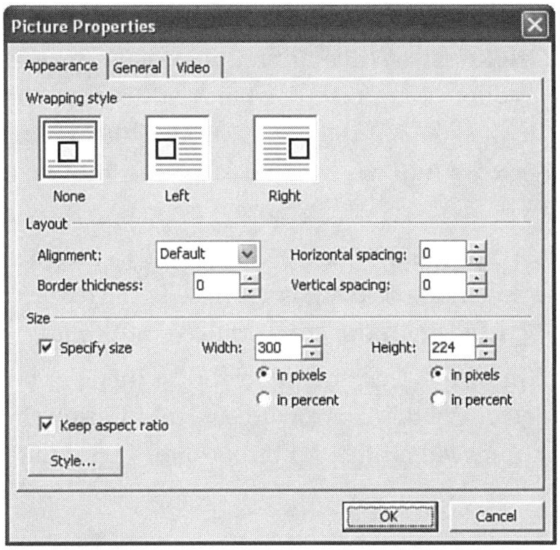

FIGURE 6.14

The Picture Properties dialog box's Appearance tab enables you to modify many aspects of an image.

Aligning Graphics

Alignment refers to the position of an object, usually relative to another object or to an entire entity, such as a Web page. FrontPage makes it relatively simple to adjust the alignment of your graphics—as well as your text—to get the best fit for your page design.

To change the alignment of a graphic on your Web page, as well as how text on that page wraps around the graphic, do the following:

1. Right-click the graphic you want to modify and select Picture Properties. The Picture Properties dialog box opens.

2. If the Appearance tab is not displayed, click it to display it.

3. Under Wrapping Style, select one of the following:

   ■ **None**—Choose this option if you don't want any text near the graphic to wrap around the image.

   ■ **Left**—Choose this option if you want the image to appear at the left of page with the text wrapped to the right of it.

   ■ **Right**—Select this option if you want the image to appear at the right of the page with the text wrapped to its left.

4. In the Layout section, make the following adjustments:

   ■ **Alignment**—Click the Alignment down arrow to select the image's orientation on the page (center, left, right, and so on).

   ■ **Border Thickness**—While not an alignment issue, this option is available to allow you to change border thickness; click the up arrow to increase the thickness of the border around the image, or click the down arrow to decrease it (0, set by default, means that no border will be added).

   ■ **Horizontal Spacing**—Click the up arrow to increase the horizontal spacing of the image or the down arrow to decrease it; this lets you set any spacing needed on the left or right of an image.

   ■ **Vertical Spacing**—Click the up arrow to increase the vertical spacing of the image or the down arrow to decrease it; this allows you to specify any spacing needed on the top or bottom of an image.

Adding Text Descriptions to a Graphic

There are two different ways you can, and perhaps should, add text to a graphic you insert on a page. Such text can offer unique information that can help identify the graphic and place it in context.

The ways to add text are as follows:

■ In the form of a caption

■ In the form of a text description that can be read by those who may not be able to see the image itself (for example, people with visual disabilities who access your page using a special reader tool to tell them the contents of your page)

To add a caption, you first insert a text box, in which you can then type the information you want to appear with the image. To add a text box to an image, do the following:

1. Click the image to which you want to add a text box caption.

2. On the Pictures toolbar, click the Text button.

3. Point to the area on the picture or page where you want the upper-left corner of the text box to appear. Then, while holding your left mouse button down, drag your mouse down and to the right to expand the text box to the size you want, as shown in Figure 6.15. When the text box is the correct size, release the mouse button.

4. Click within the text box and type the caption as you want it to appear. To change the font, right-click, choose Font, and then choose the font you wish to use.

Image captions often appear in a smaller font size than the main text on the page; sometimes italics are used.

FIGURE 6.15

The text box for the caption can appear imposed on the image itself or to the top, bottom, or side of the image.

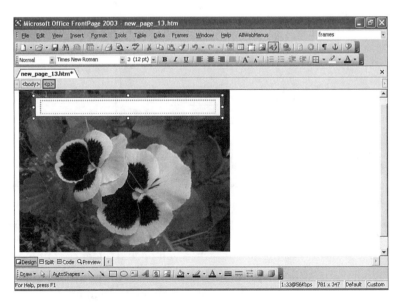

Beyond adding a caption, it's also wise to add a text description to an image. This description will appear when a visitor's mouse moves across the image, or will provide information for those with visual difficulties—or even Web-browser problems—that prevent them from properly viewing your image. These descriptions tend to be short and to the point.

Here's how to add a text description:

1. Right-click the image to which you want to add a text description, and choose Picture Properties from the shortcut menu that appears.

2. Click the General tab.

3. Under Alternative representations, type a short description of the image in the Text box, as shown in Figure 6.16.

4. Click OK.

FIGURE 6.16

Use this option to provide a description of the image in case a visitor is prevented from viewing the image itself.

Organizing Pictures with Thumbnails

Thumbnails are reduced-size versions of images (or documents or pages) and are useful because they enable visitors to preview an image before opening the larger version, which is apt to take longer to download. Depending on the version of Windows you have and how it's configured, images stored on your hard drive may already display as thumbnails when you open a folder containing them.

What occurs with a Web thumbnail image is a little different from with regular (nonthumbnail) images. Like a regular image, a thumbnail is also included in a page when it opens in a browser. However, unlike a regular image, the thumbnail can be clicked to open a separate page containing the full-size image.

In this way, you can include more images on a page without making the page take too long to open. You also can easily organize thumbnails into a single row or even multiple rows organized by category.

To convert a full image on a Web page into a thumbnail image, do the following:

1. With the page containing the image open in FrontPage in Design Page view, click on the image to select it.

2. On the Pictures toolbar, click the Auto Thumbnail button.

To view or modify the properties of your site's thumbnail images, do the following:

1. With your site open in FrontPage in Design view, click the Tools menu and choose Page Options.

2. In the Page Options dialog box, click the Auto Thumbnail tab (see Figure 6.17).

FIGURE 6.17

The Page Options dialog box contains a number of tabs to adjust various options, including Auto Thumbnail.

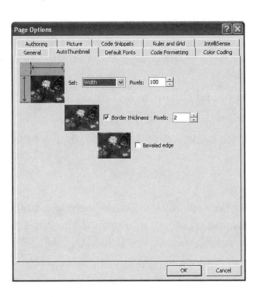

3. Make changes as desired to the width and height, the border thickness (if left unchecked, no border is applied), and the bevel settings.

4. Click OK.

Working with Photo Galleries

A photo gallery on a Web site is a great way to offer your visitors a collection—or even multiple collections—of images organized into specific categories or themes. For example, if you're selling artisan crafts on your site, you could place all your kitchen-related products in one gallery, all your baby-related products in another, and so on. Such galleries can reside as separate collections or be linked together into a Web album through the addition of a link bar (see Chapter 12, "Creating a Navigation Structure," for more information).

A gallery is a smart way to create a photo collection and avoid placing too many oversized images on your individual pages. By organizing the images into galleries, those who want to view your images can do so, while those who don't—or who suffer from much slower connections—can opt out of opening lots of images while still being able to view your regular pages.

FrontPage's Photo Gallery feature enables you to select from a number of professional-looking layouts, as you will see.

Creating a Photo Gallery

To create a photo gallery, do the following:

1. After you create or open the page to which you want to add a photo gallery, click the spot on the page where you want the gallery inserted. (Be sure you're in Design view.)

2. Open the Insert menu and choose Web Component.

3. In the Component Type list, click Photo Gallery.

4. In the Choose a Photo Gallery Option list, click to select the layout style that you want to use.

5. Click Finish.

FrontPage opens the Photo Gallery Properties dialog box, which enables you to add images to your gallery. This dialog box should open to the Pictures tab by default; if not, click that tab to select it, and then do the following:

1. Click the Add button, and choose either Pictures from Files or Pictures from Scanner or Camera from the list that appears. (In this example, choose Pictures from Files in order to add files already stored on your PC to your gallery.)

2. In the dialog box that appears, locate the first picture you want to add to the gallery, click it to select it, and click the Open button.

3. To adjust the thumbnail size for the image, click the down or up arrow next to both the Width and the Height boxes.

4. If you want to include a caption with the first image in your gallery, type the caption you want to use in the Caption field.

5. To add a description for the first image, type the description you want to use in the Description box.

6. Repeat steps 1–5 to insert each photo or other image you want to include in your gallery. The results should look similar to what's shown in Figure 6.18.

7. When finished, click OK.

FIGURE 6.18

The properties for each image in the gallery are set by you in the Photo Gallery Properties' Pictures tab.

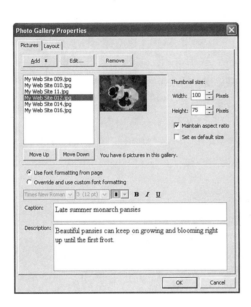

Editing Pictures in the Gallery

At any point, you can adjust or edit the pictures in your gallery, as well as the gallery itself. For instance, you can change the picture order, modify the thumbnail size, or rotate or crop the picture.

To edit a picture in your gallery, do the following:

1. In the page containing your gallery, right-click the image you want to edit and choose Photo Gallery Properties from the shortcut menu that appears. The Photo Gallery Properties dialog box opens (refer to Figure 6.18).

2. Click the Edit button.

3. The Edit Picture dialog box opens. From here, you can do the following:

   ■ Under Picture Size, change the width and/or height of your picture by clicking the appropriate up or down arrows.

   ■ Under Rotate Picture, click a button to modify the orientation of the image.

- Under Crop Picture, click the Crop button, then point to the preview of the picture and drag to draw an outline around the part of the image you want to keep. Adjust the outline until only the part of the image you want is displayed, and then click the Crop button again.
- To cancel your changes, click the Reset button.

4. Click OK.

To change the order of the pictures in your photo gallery, do the following:

1. In the page containing your photo gallery, right-click any image on the page and choose Photo Gallery Properties from the shortcut menu that appears. The Photo Gallery Properties dialog box opens (refer to Figure 6.18).

2. In the list of images, click an image you want to move.

3. Click either the Move Up button or the Move Down button.

4. Repeat as needed until the images appear in the desired order.

THE ABSOLUTE MINIMUM

In this chapter, you learned what you need to know in order to create graphics and add them to your Web site. For example, you learned how to create basic art work for your site and how to make it transparent in order to blend in with the page background. In addition, you discovered resources available to you in obtaining additional clips for your site.

You learned how to use Clip Organizer to find all media clips on your system and to automatically add them to the collections available when you create new pages. You also learned how to modify your picture properties and set options for features such as thumbnails. In addition, you learned that Using FrontPage, you can easily modify the graphics you use to customize them to your specific needs and desired effect.

With your new-found knowledge from this chapter, you are equipped to bring your pages to life by adding photographs, stunning or humorous artwork, and graphics that you can modify to meet your needs.

IN THIS CHAPTER

- Creating and modifying drawings
- Adding text to drawings
- Making and working with shapes
- Understanding and converting vector images
- Designing and utilizing image maps

7

ADDING SHAPES, WORDART, AND OTHER SPECIAL GRAPHICS

The past two chapters taught you a good deal about working with so-called regular images—clip art, photographs, and other graphics you may be ready to include in your site. But FrontPage enables you to add even more types of graphics, such as your own drawings, shapes, WordArt (a special art collection originally available only to Microsoft Word users), and even image maps. You can customize these images to make them unique to your site and your needs.

Creating a Drawing

Care to create something all your own for one of your pages? Perhaps you want to draw a simple flag, make a sign, or let your child add a freehand expression. For this, you can use FrontPage's drawing tools, including the Drawing toolbar, as shown in Figure 7.1.

FIGURE 7.1

The paintbrush, line, fill, and color options on the Drawing toolbar.

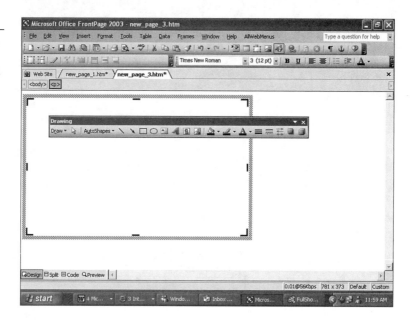

To get the lay of the land, move your mouse over any of the toolbar options to display a ScreenTip with the option's name.

So you can get the hang of using these tools, I'll walk you through the process of creating a simple drawing right on your Web page. To start, click the Line Style down arrow on the Drawing toolbar and choose the thickness you want to use for the first line you want to draw. Then click, the Line Color down arrow to pick a color for your line. Finally, to start a drawing right on a page, do the following:

1. Open the page on which you want to create the drawing, and point to the location on the page where you want it to appear.

2. Open the Insert menu, choose Picture, and choose New Drawing.

3. When the drawing outline appears on the page, move your mouse pointer to the Drawing toolbar and select the option that you want to use.

4. Bring your mouse pointer back to the drawing outline, point to a location within it, and click and drag your mouse to draw (see Figure 7.2).

FIGURE 7.2

Your drawing is contained within the drawing outline, which normally gives you plenty of room to add regular content.

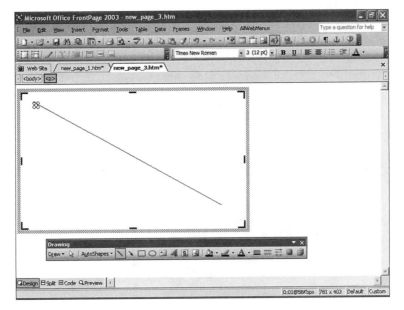

Be prepared to experiment here, and don't be frustrated if your first result isn't perfect. If you need to start over again, simply click the drawing outline (which you'll see momentarily) and click Delete, then try again.

Adding Text to Drawings

Chances are you'll want to include text as part of your drawing—perhaps to label it, to offer a message, or even to sign your name or provide a copyright mark.

The easiest way to accomplish this is through the addition of a text box to your drawing. Any text you add then appears within the dimensions of the box.

Here's how to add a text box:

1. From the Drawing toolbar, click on the Text Box button.

2. Click the spot in the drawing outline where you want to place the text box.

note

Do you have a drawing that you've already created on paper? If so, and if you have a scanner, you can simply insert the scanned drawing into your page. To do so, first place the drawing in your scanner. Then, in FrontPage, open the Insert menu, choose Picture, and select Scanner.

3. Drag the mouse pointer (usually down and to the right) until you've created the size text box you want to use (make sure it's big enough to hold the text you want to add), and release the mouse button.

4. Click inside the text box, and then type your text, as shown in Figure 7.3.

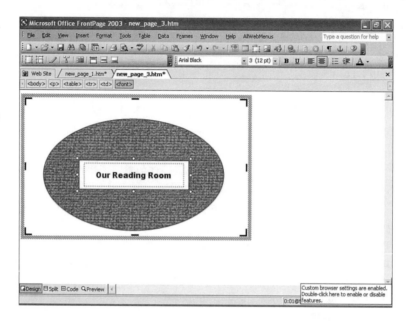

Don't like the default font or its color? You can tailor it to fit your needs.

To change the font of text in your text box, do the following:

1. Right-click within the text box.

2. Choose Font from the shortcut menu that appears.

3. From the Font dialog box, select the desired font, font style, and size. The selected font is displayed at the bottom of the window.

4. Click OK.

note

If you've already typed the text and then want to change it, highlight the text before you perform the preceding steps. This will automatically adjust your existing text.

Creating Shapes

You probably noticed that the Drawing toolbar includes some basic shapes that you can use when creating your own page graphics. You may not know, however, that

FrontPage also includes AutoShapes to give you a helping hand when adding common shapes such as rectangles (good for banners), stars, hearts, and even flowchart components to your page. These AutoShapes are a nice bonus for those of us who have less advanced art skills and would like to spend more of our time creating good content for our pages.

Using the Drawing Toolbar

To add an AutoShape directly from the Drawing toolbar to the page, do the following:

1. Click the spot on the page where you want to insert the AutoShape.
2. Click the AutoShapes option on the Drawing toolbar.
3. From the AutoShapes menu, select the desired AutoShape category, then click on the AutoShape you wish to use.
4. A cursor appears on the page. Click and drag down and to the right to create the size shape you want to use.

Using AutoShapes

To give you an idea of how you can use AutoShapes in your work, let's add a banner shape to a new page. (After you add the banner, refer to the instructions in the section "Adding Text to Drawings" earlier in this chapter to add text to the banner.

To create a new banner, follow these steps:

1. Open the File menu, choose New, and select New Page to open a new page for this exercise.
2. Click a spot at the top of the page where you want to insert the banner shape.
3. On the Drawing toolbar, click the AutoShapes down arrow and choose Stars and Banners from the menu that appears.
4. Choose the vertical scroll shape in the bottom-left corner of the Stars and Banners submenu.
5. Point to the top of your page and drag to the right and down to draw the banner shape, as shown in Figure 7.4.
6. To add text to the banner, follow the instructions found in the section "Adding Text to Drawings" earlier in this chapter.

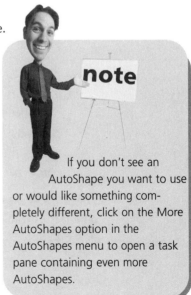

note

If you don't see an AutoShape you want to use or would like something completely different, click on the More AutoShapes option in the AutoShapes menu to open a task pane containing even more AutoShapes.

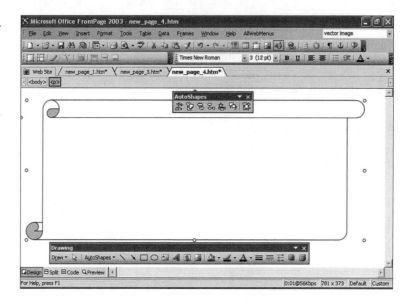

Creating WordArt

The WordArt feature is available within FrontPage to add very stylized, colorful, specialty text to your page—which, in essence, becomes some of the artwork for that
page. WordArt can make for a suitable banner to identify the page's content, as
introductory text for an article that then reverts to normal text, and so on.

To select and create WordArt text for your page, do the following:

1. Open the page on which you want the WordArt to appear, and click the spot
   on the page where it should be displayed.

2. Click the WordArt button on the Drawing toolbar (or open the Insert menu,
   choose Picture, and select WordArt) to open the WordArt Gallery dialog box.

3. Double-click the gallery option you want to use. The Edit WordArt Text dialog
   box opens.

4. Select the font and size you want to use, and then type the text as you want
   it to appear.

5. Click OK.

The result may look something like that shown in Figure 7.5, where a side-leaning
option is used to create a heading for a New Features section. Notice, too, that the
result produces a WordArt toolbar, which you can use to edit text and the finished
image.

FIGURE 7.5
WordArt can be a great addition to a page as a label, title, or banner for a feature because it gets attention.

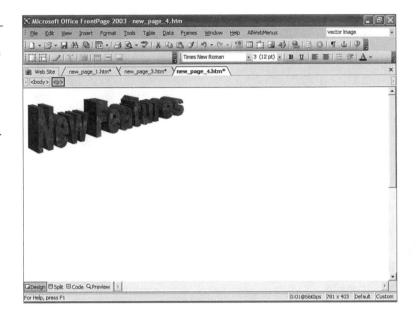

If you open the View menu, choose Toolbars, and select WordArt, you will see that WordArt has its own toolbar, from which you can insert (additional) WordArt, edit text, view the WordArt gallery, format AutoShapes, and make other changes, such as character spacing, to your WordArt design as you like.

WHY YOU DON'T WANT TO USE WORDART FOR BODY TEXT
WordArt is intended for short text. Because its stylized appearance can make it more difficult to read than a straightforward font, you want to use it sparingly, and not for normal body text.

note

Text boxes for WordArt, as with other shapes and image maps you'll work with in this chapter, generally give you a very limited area in which to include text. For this reason, avoid creating situations in which you need to place a great deal of main or body text within a WordArt image. It's also usually not so easy to customize the look of the text within such a text box.

Moving and Resizing Drawings, Text, Shapes, and WordArt

What if you decide that the drawing, shape, text box, or WordArt you've added to your page is not positioned exactly where you want it to be? The answer, of course, is to move it to the desired location. To do this, you can usually simply cut and paste. Follow these steps:

1. Point to the graphic or text box you want to move, right-click, and choose Cut from the shortcut menu that appears.

2. Point to the location where you want the object to appear, right-click, and select Paste.

tip

If you want to copy, rather than move, an existing graphic to a new location or to multiple locations, follow the preceding instructions given, but select Copy rather than Cut in step 1.

Alternatively, you can sometimes simply click on a shape or graphic and drag it to the new position.

You can cut or copy and paste any number of times, as needed, to either copy or move additional images or to repeat the same image.

FrontPage also enables you to resize your graphics and text boxes to better fit your needs and the layout of your Web page. You may want to do this to make a graphic or text box smaller because a page area is crowded or to expand the graphic if you want it to stretch across the width of a page when it currently does not.

To resize a graphic object, do the following:

1. Click on the image or text box you want to resize.

2. At the edges of the image or text box, you'll see a series of circles, or selection handles. Move your mouse pointer to one of the selection handles; when the pointer changes to a crosshair, drag the handle inward (to reduce the size of the text or graphic) or outward (to increase the size of the text or graphic), as shown in Figure 7.6.

3. Release the mouse button. You might need to repeat these steps for additional selection handles to get the size right.

note

You can resize your image proportionally by dragging one of the corner handles up, down, to the left, or to the right.

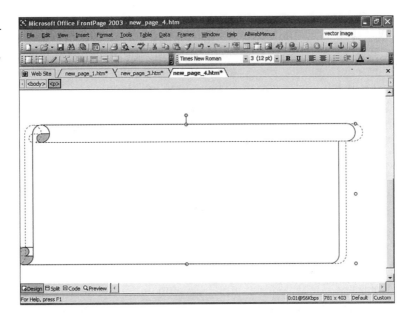

Converting Vector Images to GIF or JPG

Two primary graphic file formats—GIF and JPG—are used with Web pages.
FrontPage, however, can work with far more file formats, including at least one vector image format.

UNDERSTANDING VECTOR GRAPHICS

A vector image, often called a *vector graphic*, refers to a specific type of image created by
using a series of lines. Vector images offer more flexibility (for selecting, resizing, moving,
and so on) and operate using less memory than another type of images called bitmap
images, which are created through the use of dot patterns. However, the types of images
you're apt to use most frequently are neither vector not bitmap, but JPG and GIF.

For the best range of file conversion, however, it's best to use software specifically
designed to convert graphics from one file format to another. Jasc Software's
PaintShop Pro (www.jasc.com) and Alchemy Mindworks Graphic Workshop
(www.alchemymindworks.com) are two good examples of software that can do this for you.
However, one issue you should be aware of is that whenever you insert an image into
a Web page, FrontPage will check the file format and, in the process of saving the
Web page, automatically convert the file into JPG or GIF format for you (with certain
limitations—for example, if FrontPage doesn't recognize the file type it can't do this).

Image Maps

When is a picture or image more than just something pretty or colorful on your Web page? In truth, there are a number of different situations in which an image is actually put into service to do more than just sit on a page. In this section, you'll learn about a special type of image called an *image map*, which enables you to transform a graphic into a navigational tool.

When you create an image map, you separate different areas of an image into regions (called hotspots) that link to individual pages. For example, suppose your Web site features reviews of various types of computer equipment. In that case, you could use an image of a computer to create an image map. Users could click the PC monitor in the image to get data about monitors, click the keyboard to read up on keyboards, and so on.

Choosing a Map-worthy Graphic

Not every graphic lends itself to becoming an image map. You need to evaluate a graphic's map-worthiness on a case-by-case basis, taking into account certain basic rules:

- The image must be of sufficient size, clarity, and overall quality to work well as an image map so that you can easily distinguish the different elements within.

- The general topic of the image should fit the theme of the site, page, or whatever it is supposed to represent. For example, if you want to create an image map to cover astrology signs, you probably don't want to use a picture of a kitchen.

- There should be enough distinct regions or elements within the image to serve as individual hotspots or regions in the map.

- The image should be well positioned on a page so that it can be easily located and used by your visitors.

Creating Hotspots

A *hotspot* is part of a larger image file or image map that, when clicked (or when rested on by the mouse pointer), acts as a hyperlink to another file or document.

By definition, an image map contains two or more hotspots; fewer than that, and there is no reason to create an image map or an individual hotspot (you can just make the entire image one big link).

To add a hotspot to an image you want to use as an image map, do the following:

1. In FrontPage, open the page containing the image you want to use.

2. Switch to Design view.

3. Click the image to which you want to add the hotspot.

4. On the Pictures toolbar, click to choose the hotspot shape you want to use: rectangular, circular, or polygonal.

5. Back on the image, drag your mouse pointer to create the shape you want to use for the hotspot.

6. Release the mouse button. The Insert Hyperlink dialog box opens.

7. Locate the file or page you want to use as the link from this hotspot, and click OK.

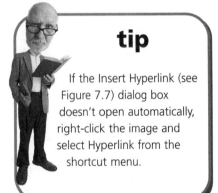

tip

If the Pictures toolbar isn't currently available (meaning that it's grayed out or hidden), right-click the image and select Show Pictures Toolbar.

Adding Text to a Hotspot

Besides adding a hyperlink to a hotspot, you can also add text. This is useful when you want to use the hotspot to provide information in addition to or instead of a hyperlink to another page. (Be aware that a text box will generally be visible all the time, not just when a visitor's mouse moves over or clicks the hotspot.)

tip

If the Insert Hyperlink (see Figure 7.7) dialog box doesn't open automatically, right-click the image and select Hyperlink from the shortcut menu.

FIGURE 7.7

Choose the link the hotspot should use from the Insert Hyperlink window.

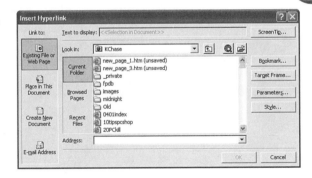

To add a text box and text to a hotspot, do the following:

1. In FrontPage, open the page containing the image with the designated hotspots.

2. Switch to Design view.

3. Click the image that contains the hotspot to which you want to add text.

4. Click the Text button (the one with a blue *A* on it) on the Pictures toolbar.

5. A text box appears. Type the text you want to add. Then press Enter or click on another spot on the page.

tip

If the Pictures toolbar isn't currently available to you (meaning that it's grayed out or hidden), right-click the image and select Show Pictures Toolbar.

THE ABSOLUTE MINIMUM

The ability to add images of various types and then customize them to fit your very special needs is a big step in turning you from an amateur Web designer into one who can turn out a highly polished, very snazzy site. Fortunately, you've now mastered some of the critical operations, including creating a drawing and customizing it, inserting a text box in or around an image to label it or express your thoughts, and using AutoShapes and WordArt to further enhance the graphical appeal of your site. You also have learned how to move and resize your images for best results and produce an image map with hotspots that link to other pages or sites.

8

ADDING MULTIMEDIA

Now that you've learned the basics of adding essential text and images to your site, it's time to look at a richer media environment—one that enables you to include both sound and video or other moving images. Used correctly, such inclusions can add tremendous pizzazz to an otherwise ordinary Web site.

Although FrontPage makes it quite simple to add such content to your site, there are some important things you need to know about using multimedia content—starting with what's available for use, as well as legal and usability issues. After all, you want to get the right results from your audience, not annoy or incense anyone.

Defining Multimedia

Published text, recorded voices and music, pictures, and moving images are all different forms of media. Multimedia, by contrast, combines different forms of these media into one overall presentation.

For example, professionally recorded CD-ROMs often combine moving images and still shots with music and voice narration to take advantage of both sight and sound to capture the viewer's attention and imagination. Chances are you can probably recall some fancy Web sites where you were treated to such presentations as well. Some Web-based news sites or special information sites, like those focused on space travel, put multimedia possibilities to good use.

A WORD ABOUT COPYRIGHTS

Copyright refers to the right of the creator, producer, or owner of a particular work to publish or distribute that work exclusively. Music and other sound files (including recordings of broadcast productions), artwork, stories and articles, movies and animations, and many other types of work are often copyrighted, and appear with the © symbol.

All too frequently, new Web designers—and, unfortunately, some established ones—pay scant attention to copyright laws, often using the copyrighted work of others. At best, this generates threatening letters from the work's creators or their duly-appointed legal representatives; at worst, it is a formula for disaster, leading to lawsuits, financial losses, and damaged reputations. Copyright law is recognized and enforced on a federal level, and those who misuse copyrighted material can be charged with a federal felony.

For this reason, you should avoid using anyone else's copyrighted material without express permission to do so. In such cases, written permission is better than a simple oral agreement because the latter may offer you no legal protection if you have no proof of contract.

To learn about copyrighting your own multimedia creations and other such work you produce and publish to your Web site, as well as the fair use of the copyrighted works of others, visit http://lcweb.loc.gov/copyright/title17/, http://fairuse.stanford.edu, and http://www.whatiscopyright.org.

Working with Sound Files

Many Web designers are tempted to add music and other sound files to their sites, and there are many legitimate reasons to do so. For example, a Web site specializing in music sales might want to share samples of its collection. Likewise, a company that has written theme music for radio or TV ads might want to play that theme for visitors arriving at the site. Other sites might choose to add music to commemorate holidays, such as Christmas or Halloween.

Of course, not all sound files contain music. For example, a sound file might include a short recorded script or skit, a voiceover offering a company slogan, or even a full-length audio presentation such as a speech.

Sound (and video) files available through a Web site can normally be played in one of three ways:

- Via support enabled through the Web browser and/or operating system
- Through a multimedia application such as Windows Media Player or RealPlayer
- Via the use of plug-ins, which are application modules designed to play a specific type of file format through a Web page

Types of Sound Files

You've already learned that there are two basic genres of sound files: music and nonmusic. Now let's talk about different sound file formats, particularly those supported by FrontPage.

STREAMING AND DOWNLOADABLE AUDIO

There are two major types of audio files that you can add to your site (and to some degree, the same is true for video, discussed later in this chapter). These are

- The types your visitors can download fully and then play later on their computers, often referred to as a standard sound file
- Those that play automatically when the visitor views a page that contains a sound file; this can be a standard sound file used as background sound for a page, or a streaming audio file used to deliver an Internet-encoded talk show, radio program, news, or other sound recording

Because Web visitors (especially those using less–than-high-speed Internet connections) don't always like the delayed gratification of waiting to download a large sound (or video) file before they can play it, streaming audio was developed. The chief difference between a standard sound file and a streaming audio file is that the latter doesn't require the visitor to download the entire file before the file begins to play; the same is true with streaming video. Instead, the streaming audio is sent in chunks that quickly begin to play either through the Web browser or a plug-in, even before the rest of the file is received.

Neither method works perfectly for those on slow connections. They'll either have to wait for a long download in the case of a standard sound file or risk pauses and breaks in a streaming audio (or video) file.

MIDI and WAV Files

Two of the oldest—and still quite popular—sound file formats are MIDI (Musical Instrument Digital Interface) and WAV (Wavetable) files, both considered standard sound files. Both formats are universally supported by most of today's Web browsers.

MIDI files are created either by hardware musical devices attached to a computer (such as a MIDI keyboard) or through software alone and use the .mid file extension.

WAV files are usually short sound files that can be recorded (and played) through a number of software programs (including Windows Sound Recorder) and use the .wav file extension.

RealAudio Files

RealNetworks' RealAudio sound format—played through its RealPlayer application or plug-in—is considered by most to be the standard for Web-based streaming-audio file presentations. Visit www.real.com for more information. The file extensions most often used for RealAudio format files are .ra and .ram (older).

MP3 Files

MP3 files, which can be played on most software audio players and are considered standard rather than streaming audio, were developed to allow for longer, crisper-sounding audio files while using a special compression algorithm to reduce file size. In fact, files that might have been 50MB or more using other file formats were reduced to 3–4MB with MP3. MP3 files make this reduction in size possible by removing extraneous audio data that the human ear cannot hear. MP3 files typically end with the file extension .mp3.

Before MP3 files, most Web-based sounds were fairly short in size, offering only a few seconds of audio play so that they wouldn't take a prohibitively long time to download from the Internet. After MP3 was adopted, however, entire songs and presentations could be recorded and made available on the Web for download and collection (and are often burned to CDs for storage and later play in CD sound systems). This has resulted in some legal problems because music artists and sound distributors don't always want their music released in this way because it can affect music sales.

Adding Sound

To add a sound file to one of your Web pages that will play automatically when someone opens the page, follow these instructions:

1. In Design view, right-click anywhere on the page to which you want to add a sound and choose Page Properties from the shortcut menu that appears.

2. The Page Properties dialog box opens. Click the General tab (see Figure 8.1).

FIGURE 8.1

In the Page Properties dialog box's General tab, you can specify the sound file you want to use and how many times (if any) the sound should replay for visitors.

Page Properties   ? ☒

General | Formatting | Advanced | Custom | Language |

Location: unsaved:///new_page_15.htm
Title: New Page 15
Page description:
Keywords:

Base location:
Default target frame: ...✎

Background sound
Location: file:///D:/WINDOWS/Media/ringin.wav   Browse...
Loop: 2 ⬍ ☐ Forever

OK   Cancel

3. Click the Browse button in the Background Sound area.

4. Locate and select the sound file you want to use, and then click the OK button.

5. If you want the sound file to loop, specify the number of times it should do so in the Loop box (type 0 if you don't want the sound file to loop). To loop the sound forever, click the Forever check box to select it.

6. Click OK.

What if you simply want to make a sound file on your site available for download by interested visitors, rather than automatically playing the file for them? First, select the page to which you want to add the link to download the sound file. Then, before you create the link, move the sound file to your site in FrontPage:

note

Avoid checking the Forever check box to replay a sound continuously; your visitors probably won't like it. Typically, you want to replay the sound no more than once or twice.

1. Click Start, My Computer and locate the sound file you want to copy to your Web.

2. Right-click the file and choose Copy.

3. Locate your FrontPage Web, open it, right click within it, and choose Paste.

After you've done this, do the following:

1. Open the page where you want to add the link.

2. Type an identifying title for that link, such as **Link to download and play Our_Welcome.wav (59Kb)**.

3. Select the title, and click the Hyperlink toolbar button.

4. From the Insert a Hyperlink dialog box, choose Existing File or Web Page, and then select the sound file to which you want to connect the link. Click OK to finish.

note

If your sound file is the only thing contained on a page, you may instead want to delete the entire page from your Web.

Removing Sound

If you later decide you want to remove a background sound file that you added to a page, do the following:

1. In Design view, right-click the page that contains the sound file you want to delete and choose Page Properties from the shortcut menu that appears.

2. Delete the text that appears in the Location box in the Background Sound area.

3. Click OK.

SOUNDING THE WRONG NOTE (ADDING UNNECESSARY MUSIC)

As wonderful as adding sound to a site can seem, there are drawbacks. Even if you love a particular song or sound byte, it's not safe to assume that everyone else will. And even if your visitors share your audio tastes, imagine how those people who regularly return to your site feel when they get hit with the same sound each and every time?

Even people who enjoy listening to sound over the Web won't like everything they hear, and some users, particularly new ones with less experience, may jump away from your site rather than try to stop the sound (which can usually be done by clicking the Stop button on the browser toolbar). This is especially true when you're adding background sound, such as you did earlier, because the user isn't being presented with media controls to start and stop the sound from playing.

It's smart to include sound sparingly. If you add a sound file to every Web page, you lessen the impact you create when you add it to just a select page or two. Remember, too, that you may slow a visitor's transit through your site while the file is being downloaded to his or her computer.

Working with Video

The addition of video to a Web site can transform it. Video changes your site from a provider of text and still images to one that offers a rounder multimedia experience to your visitors.

You can employ video to do the following:

- Offer a product or how-to demonstration.
- Treat your visitors to an amusing video clip.
- Display a recorded speech or other presentation or performance.
- Provide a tour of your home (for example, if you're offering it by Web for sale) or company.
- Show newsworthy video footage.

Naturally, however, you want the inclusion of video to fit. You wouldn't, for instance, do well to include a movie of your dog learning a new trick on a page where you're trying to sell people your mortuary's services. And because video often takes longer to download and open for your visitors than audio files, it's that much more important that you use it to enhance or enrich your visitor's experience rather than simply to up the cool factor. For this reason, you should plan the inclusion of video and its placement carefully before you actually add the file.

Types of Video Files

Several different video file formats exist. This section outlines the most common formats and discusses which types of software are most often used to play them for your visitors.

MPEG Files

MPEG (pronounced em-peg, and short for Moving Pictures Experts Group) provides one of the best available video formats, offering better quality video than most and three different standards that work at different screen resolutions. Such video files usually end in the file extension .mpg. Most video players today support the play of MPEG videos.

QuickTime Files

QuickTime video and animation files, developed by Apple Computer, also can be played on computers that have the QuickTime player installed. Such files usually end in the .mov or .qt file extensions. To find out more, visit www.quicktime.apple.com.

AVI Files

AVI (Audio Video Interleave) files are another type of video format specifically tied to Microsoft Windows, where AVI still serves as a (now, lower-end) video standard. The file extension for this type of video is .avi. It is playable through Windows Media Player.

Adding Video

The process of inserting a video file into one of your Web pages is virtually identical to the process you followed earlier for adding an audio file. To add video, follow these steps:

1. With the page in which you want to insert a video open in Design view, Click the location on the page where you want the video (actually, an icon representing it) to appear.

2. Open the Insert menu, choose Picture, and select Video.

3. Locate and select the video file you want to insert, and click the Open button.

Removing Video

Should you later wish to remove a video file from a Web page, you can either delete the entire page (if the video file is the only real content on that page) or simply remove the video file along with any references to it. To delete the video file, do the following:

1. Click the video file on the page.

2. Press the Delete key on your keyboard or open the Edit menu and choose Delete.

note

What happens if you accidentally remove a video file you didn't intend to delete? If you haven't performed any other actions in the meantime, you can open the Edit menu and choose Undo Clear to restore the file. Otherwise, just re-add the video that was removed in error.

Setting Properties for Video

After you choose to insert a video onto a page or pages on your site, you might want to specify how that video will behave when played. For instance, you can change the video file itself (if you want to add a new one or if you accidentally selected the wrong video file), specify whether the video file loops automatically for replay, and whether the file begins to play the moment a mouse is passed over it or when the file is opened with the page itself.

To modify your video play properties, do the following:

1. Right-click the video on your page whose properties you want to modify and choose Picture Properties from the shortcut menu that appears.

2. The Picture Properties dialog box opens. Click the Video tab to display it, as shown in Figure 8.2.

FIGURE 8.2

The Picture Properties dialog box's Video tab enables you to specify the video to be played, whether the video should be looped, and how the video initiates play.

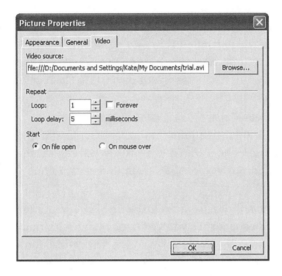

3. To change the video file to be played, click the Browse button in the Video Source area.

4. In the dialog box that appears, locate and select the video you want to play, and click Open.

5. To specify how many times (if any) the video should be looped, type the desired number in the Loop field in the Repeat area. (If you don't want the video to loop at all, type 0.) Click the Forever check box if you want the video to loop endlessly.

6. If you specified that the movie should be looped, type the number of milliseconds that should pass before the video repeats.

note

Avoid checking the Forever check box to replay your video continuously. This is apt to annoy your visitors, especially if there is other content on the same page that they want to view.

7. In the Start area, click the On File Open option to play the file automatically for visitors when they open the page that contains the video file, or click the On Mouse Over option to delay the file's play until the visitor moves his or her mouse pointer over the file.

Working with Flash

Macromedia Flash is a multimedia platform that works well for site visitors regardless of the browser being used. It's also supported for use with FrontPage, which means you can include Flash content in your site. Such content can take the form of animation, Flash movies, or professional presentations.

To use Flash, you need a Flash file to insert on a page on your site; FrontPage enables you to add such files ending in these file extensions: .spl, .swf, and .swt. The way most people obtain Flash content is to find a site online that freely distributes a file or files recorded in that format (search using the Google search engine, for example), although you can also record your own using Flash-creation software like that available from Macromedia (www.macromedia.com).

For your site visitors to view such Flash files, their computer must have the Flash plug-in installed so that the file can automatically download to their browser and play. You can point those visitors who don't already have the plug-in installed to a page on the Macromedia site that enables them to download and install the plug-in free of charge.

It's also important to note that Flash files take one of two major forms: one that is added to a regular Web page just as you've already done with audio and video, and another that takes up an entire page in your Web. The second form is where the Flash animation itself becomes the Web page—usually the opening page—rather than an animation simply played within a page.

Because this topic could easily take a chapter—indeed, a book—all its own, let's look at how you can add a Flash animation or movie to an existing page on your site. Before you do this, you need to have a Flash file to use for this purpose.

Adding a Flash Animation

To add Flash animation, do the following:

1. With the page to which you want to add a Flash file open in Design view, click on the spot on the page where the link to the Flash file should go.

2. Open the Insert menu and choose Web Component.

3. The Insert Web Component dialog box opens (see Figure 8.3). Click the Advanced Controls option in the Component Type list on the left.

4. In the Choose a Control list, click Flash.

5. Click Finish.

6. Locate and select the Flash file you want to use, and click Open, which puts a placeholder to the desired file onto your page.

FIGURE 8.3

Add Flash ani-
mation to your
site by choosing
the Advanced
Controls option
in the Insert Web
Component dia-
log box.

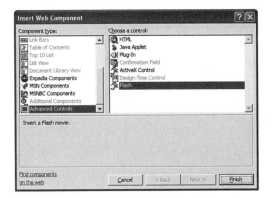

Setting Playback and Looping Options

After you've inserted your Flash movie or animation into a page, you can customize how this
media will be played for your site's visitors, much
as you did when adding other types of video files.
The process for doing so, however, varies slightly
because you won't be working with the Picture
Properties dialog box.

To customize your Flash movie, do the following:

1. Right-click the Flash file placeholder on your
   page and choose Flash Properties from the
   shortcut menu that appears.

2. The Flash Properties dialog box opens. Click
   the General tab (see Figure 8.4).

3. In the Playback area, as shown in Figure
   8.4, click any of the following check boxes to
   check (or uncheck) them:

   ■ **Auto Play**—Plays automatically without any prompt from the visitor.

   ■ **Loop**—Plays again when the animation is finished.

   ■ **Show Menu (a special menu just for Flash)**—Displays special
   options available for Flash users.

   ■ **SWLiveConnect**—Tries to establish communication between a plug-in
   (such as would play a Flash animation) and the JavaScript used in a
   Netscape browser so that an animation can play in Netscape.

4. Click OK.

> **note**
>
> Notice in Figure 8.4
> that the Flash Properties
> dialog box contains a Web
> address for the Internet Explorer
> Code Base page, as well as a
> Web address for the Netscape
> Plugins page. These enable peo-
> ple who visit your site to access
> the appropriate Macromedia
> Web page to download the Flash
> plug-in required for viewing Flash
> movies regardless of what type of
> browser they use.

FIGURE 8.4

When you select an option such as Auto Play, you're specifying that the Flash file play automatically for the visitor.

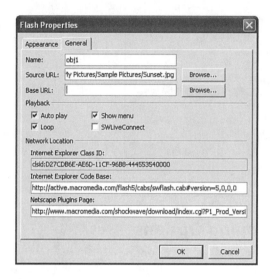

TOO MUCH MOTION CAUSES SEASICKNESS

Ask 10 different people how much they like animation or other moving pictures on a Web site, and you'll probably get at least three distinctly different opinions. Some are wowed by it and think it truly adds something to their experience, while others are either indifferent to it or truly loathe it.

The smartest way to fend off a bad reaction, short of avoiding such content altogether, is to limit the amount of motion you use. This means you should create or pick your animated/movie files carefully, use them judiciously, and avoid options such as Auto Play so that you give your visitors the choice of not viewing what they don't want to see.

THE ABSOLUTE MINIMUM

When you are ready to add multimedia options like sound and video files to the pages in your site, come back here for a refresher course. In this chapter, you learned to appreciate the use and reproduction of copyrighted work, identify and briefly understand the various audio and video file formats you can work with in FrontPage, insert a sound file onto your page and then set the properties for its playback through the page, link to a sound file so that others can download it, add a video file to a page and specify playback options, and show a Flash animation on a page on your site—or on its own.

With your new knowledge, you can greatly enhance your site by using sound and video to educate, entertain, and tempt your visitors. Consider strategic ways you can implement multimedia to get your site's message to your visitors.

9

USING TABLES

Now that you've learned about the different kinds of content you can add to a Web page—from text to images to multimedia—you may be thinking that you need a way to organize it all on your pages. Good thinking! The whole point of putting a Web site on the Internet is because you hope it will be something that someone wants to see. And the best way to make your site inviting and easy to use is to lay out your content in a cohesive and organized manner.

When tables were first incorporated into HTML, they were intended only for use in presenting tabular data. It quickly became apparent, however, that tables were useful for far more than just that; these days, tables are the most widely used tool in the HTML bag of tricks for creating page layouts. In fact, virtually every major Web site uses tables as the basis of its page layout. Even FrontPage's templates use tables extensively.

If you were writing your site from scratch without the use of a tool like FrontPage, learning how to code tables properly would be a time-consuming and aggravating task. Tables have lots of little quirks that are hard to understand unless you design your page in a visual environment. Even seasoned Web designers sometimes get headaches from trying to make table-based page layouts work correctly when coding by hand. However, FrontPage makes it easy even for beginners to dive right in and start creating complex tables from scratch.

Table Anatomy

Tables may seem complicated, but in actuality the basic concept is pretty simple. Tables occupy a rectangular area of a page, or even the entire page, and divide it into sections. These sections can be arranged vertically from top to bottom, where they are called *rows*. Inside the rows, you can have sections arranged horizontally across the page to form *columns*. A table may have any number of rows and columns, but every table has at least one row and one column in each row. The individual sections created by the intersection of rows and columns are referred to as *cells*. Content (images and text) inside a cell always stays inside that cell, allowing you to decide how everything on your page should go. The basic structure of a table is shown in Figure 9.1.

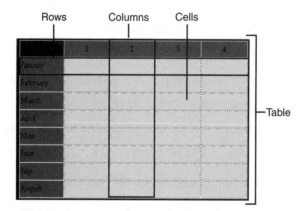

FIGURE 9.1
A table divides a page into sections so that you can organize your page content.

For even more complex layouts, cells can span across multiple columns or multiple rows. The only requirements are that every cell remains a rectangular region and that the number of rows and columns remains consistent over the entire table when you take into account the spanned cells. (See the section "Merging and Splitting Cells and Tables" later in this chapter for information about cells that span multiple rows and columns.)

Creating Tables

To use a table, the first step, of course, is to create one. FrontPage gives you several different ways of creating tables, and what you ultimately use is going to mainly depend on which method you feel the most comfortable with. Once a table is on the page, you can work with it in the same way no matter how you created it.

Inserting Tables from the Toolbar

The absolute quickest way to get a new table on a page is to use the Insert Table button on the Standard toolbar, shown in Figure 9.2.

FIGURE 9.2

Use the Insert Table button on the Standard toolbar to add a table quickly.

To insert a table using the Insert Table button, do the following:

1. In Design view, click in the page to set the cursor where you where you want the table to appear.

2. Click the Insert Table button on the Standard toolbar.

3. In the grid that pops up, drag the mouse to select the number of rows (up to four) and columns (up to five) to include in your table. Don't worry if your final table needs more columns and rows than this; you can insert them later.

4. Click the mouse button again to select the rows and columns you want to create the table.

Inserting Tables from the Menu

Although it may not be as quick as inserting tables using the Standard toolbar's Insert Table button, the simplest way to add a more complex table to your page is to insert it using the Insert Table dialog box, which you open using the Table, Insert, Table menu command. This is especially useful when you're new to tables because the Insert Table dialog box shows you all the table properties from the outset and lets you customize your table and specify the initial number of rows and columns.

To insert a table into a page using the Insert Table dialog box, do the following:

1. In Design view, position the cursor where you want the table to be inserted.

2. Choose Table, Insert, Table from the menu.

3. In the Insert Table dialog box, shown in Figure 9.3, choose the initial options

for the table. For now, limit your actions to using the Size area to specifying the initial number of rows and columns in the table.

FIGURE 9.3

When you
insert a table
using the menu,
you get a
chance to set
the table's ini-
tial properties
in the Insert
Table
dialog box.

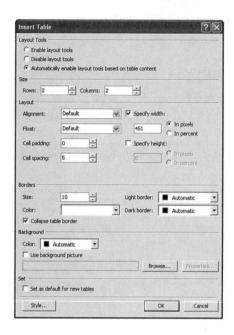

Inserting a table in this manner is the fastest way to get a table if you know the number of rows and columns you will want, if you want to specify initial table dimensions, or if you want your table and cell properties to differ from the defaults.

Drawing Tables

Another useful (and fun) way to insert tables is to use FrontPage's Draw Table feature. Use this method if you want to be able to create a free-form table on the page using the mouse pointer. Although it's not as easy to get pixel-perfect column and row dimensions using this method, it is very useful for getting started creating a page layout or some other irregularly sized template.

To draw a table, do the following:

1. Choose Table, Draw Table from the menu. Your mouse pointer will turn into a pencil icon, indicating that you are in Draw mode, and the Table toolbar will automatically open. If the toolbar is already open—you can access it manually by right-clicking in the toolbar area of the application window, and then selecting Table—you can simply click the Draw Table button on the Table toolbar.

2. Click where you want the table to start on the page, and drag to form the outer dimensions of the table.

3. Wherever you want rows and columns in the table, click on one side of the table and drag a line across to the other side, or from the top to the bottom. A dotted line appears where the column or row border will go, as shown in Figure 9.4.

4. Release the mouse button to create the column or row.

5. Repeat steps 3 and 4 to add all the rows and columns to your table.

FIGURE 9.4

FrontPage's Draw Table tool offers an easy way to quickly create free-form tables.

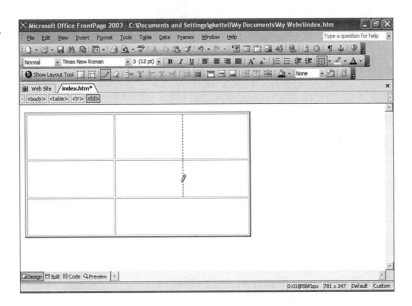

Creating Tables from an Excel Spreadsheet (or Access Database)

The purpose of a Web site is to present information. It's not surprising, then, that it is often necessary to take information from other applications—such as, say, data from an Excel spreadsheet—and show it on the Web.

Because of the grid-like nature of a spreadsheet, it's a natural fit to display the data in a table in FrontPage. FrontPage provides the ability to automatically convert Excel spreadsheet data into a table when it is pasted into the Design view. The table is automatically created during the paste operation, based on the contents of the spreadsheet.

To paste Excel spreadsheet data into a table, do the following:

1. Open the spreadsheet in Excel.

2. Using your mouse, select the cells that you want to include on the page.

3. Choose Edit, Copy from the menu.

4. In FrontPage Design view, click the cursor in the place where you want the table to be inserted.

5. Choose Edit, Paste from the menu. The data is automatically inserted as a table, as shown in Figure 9.5.

FIGURE 9.5

An Excel spreadsheet pasted into FrontPage is automatically inserted as a table.

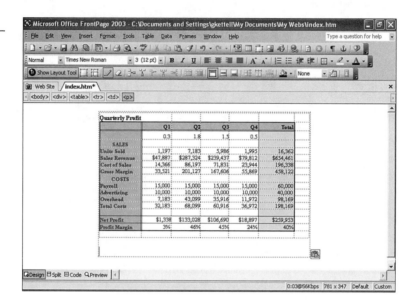

By default, FrontPage preserves the formatting of the pasted-in spreadsheet. If you want to change the formatting to use the table and text formatting already in use on the Web page, click the Paste Options icon in the lower-right corner of the new table and choose Use Destination Styles. You could also choose Keep Text Only, but that will only paste the text from the spreadsheet; you will lose any table formatting.

This copy-and-paste technique also works for Access database tables.

Converting Text to Tables

In addition to converting formatted data from Excel or Access, you can paste just about any

tip

Although copying and pasting is a handy way to insert data from Excel or Access in a page, it's only a snapshot of your data. If you want the data in the table to automatically update when the spreadsheet or database changes, you'll need to use data connections. See Chapter 17, "Databases," for more information about database connections.

type of formatted text into FrontPage and format it as a table. A common use for this is to paste data from a comma- or tab-separated text file.

To insert formatted text as a table, do the following:

1. Open the text file in a text editor such as Notepad.

2. Select the portion of the text you want to include, and copy it to the clipboard using Edit, Copy.

3. In FrontPage, select Design view and position the cursor where you want the table to be inserted.

4. Choose Edit, Paste from the menu.

5. Select the text in FrontPage, and choose Table, Convert, Text to Table.

6. In the Convert Text to Table dialog box, shown in Figure 9.6, choose a character or paragraph mark, such as a tab or comma, to use for separating the columns of text. These separators in the text will be used to determine which column the text goes in.

Converting text to tables is a useful feature. Sometimes it is also useful to remove a table while leaving only the text behind. To do this, select the table itself by clicking in it and choosing the **<table>** button in the tag list at the top of the page. Then use the Table, Convert, Table to Text to automatically remove the table.

FIGURE 9.6

Use the Convert Text to Table dialog box to create a table from formatted text.

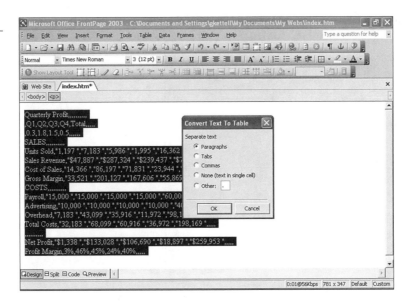

Table and Cell Properties

You now know several different ways to create tables in FrontPage. But that is just the beginning! Now you can customize the look of your tables with everything from text properties and spacing to cell colors and background images.

Some properties apply to individual cells of a table, while others affect the entire table at once. Let's start out by discussing the table properties.

Table Properties

You set table properties by clicking anywhere in a table and choosing Table, Table Properties, Table from the menu (or, if you prefer, by right-clicking anywhere in the table and choosing Table Properties). This opens the Table Properties dialog box, shown in Figure 9.7. This dialog box, you may have noticed, bears a striking resemblance to the Insert Table dialog box. In fact, it is the same dialog box with only a few minor differences:

- You can't set the number of rows and columns any lower than the number of rows and columns already in the table. You can, however, add more.

- There's now an Apply button. This is useful to apply the changes you have made without closing the dialog box. If you use this, note that the Cancel button will only cancel changes made since the last Apply. (You can always use Edit, Undo from the menu to undo any undesired changes.)

FIGURE 9.7

Use the Table Properties dialog box to change a table you've already created.

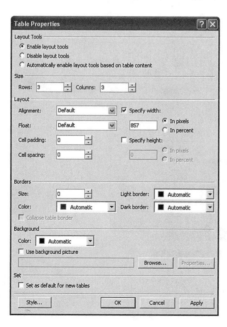

Table Properties

The first options on the Table Properties dialog box enable you to set general options for the table. They are as follows:

- **Layout Tools**—These options allow you to enable or disable layout tools. Layout tools give you extra controls to use in Design view for creating layout tables. (Layout tables are described later in this chapter.)

- **Size**—Use these options to add additional rows and/or columns to your table.

Table Layout Properties

The Layout section of the Table Properties dialog box enables you to choose options that describe how the table will be displayed in the browser. These options are as follows:

- **Alignment**—Choose whether the table will align to the left, the right, or the center of the page. The default alignment is left.

- **Float**—Choose whether text should flow around the table on the left or the right. This is discussed later in this chapter in the section titled "Floating Tables."

- **Cell Padding**—Sets the amount of space between the cell boundaries and the content in the cell.

- **Cell Spacing**—Sets the amount of space between cells.

- **Specify Width**—Checking this option allows you to set the overall width of the table. This can be in fixed pixel or percentage widths. A table with a percentage width will grow or shrink as the object containing it (or the page itself) grows or shrinks.

- **Specify Height**—Checking this option allows you to specify a height in either pixels or a percentage. Some older browsers, particularly Netscape 4.7 and earlier, don't handle table heights correctly. If you want your pages to be viewable in these older browsers, you may just leave this unchecked (or set to 100%).

Border Properties

The Borders section of the Table Properties dialog box is where you can set the look of the border lines surrounding the table and between the rows and columns. The settings in this area are as follows:

- **Size**—Set the width to use for the table borders. Set this to zero (0) if you want no borders—the usual setting for layout tables.

- **Color**—Select a color to use for the table border. This only applies if the table border is set to something other than 0.
- **Light Border, Dark Border**—These options allow you to add a border that has a two-color 3D effect.
- **Collapse Table Border**—If you specify that you want a border shown, a border is drawn by default around each cell in the table as well. Checking this option makes the border a single pixel wide at the cell boundaries. Unchecking this option makes it two pixels wide (one pixel for each cell).

Table Background Properties

The Background section of the Table Properties dialog box lets you set a color or an image to serve as the background for the entire table.

- **Color**—Choose a color to use for the background color of the table.
- **Use Background Picture**—Choose an image to use as the background. Click the Browse button to find an image either in your Web directory or elsewhere on your computer.

Other Table Properties

There are a few remaining settings in the Table Properties dialog box:

- **Set As Default for New Tables**—If you want to reuse your table properties throughout your site, check this check box; as a result, table properties you set here will be used whenever you insert a new table, with the notable exception of background settings and table size.
- **Style**—Clicking this button allows you to set cascading style sheet properties for the text you display in the table. (See Chapter 13, "Using Styles and Cascading Style Sheets," for more information about using styles and cascading style sheets.)

Cell Formatting

In addition to setting properties for the entire table, FrontPage allows you to set properties for individual cells or a selection of several cells.

You set cell properties by clicking in a cell, or by making a selection over multiple cells and choosing Table, Table Properties, Cell from the menu. (Alternatively, right-click the selection and choose Cell Properties.) This opens the Cell Properties dialog box, shown in Figure 9.8.

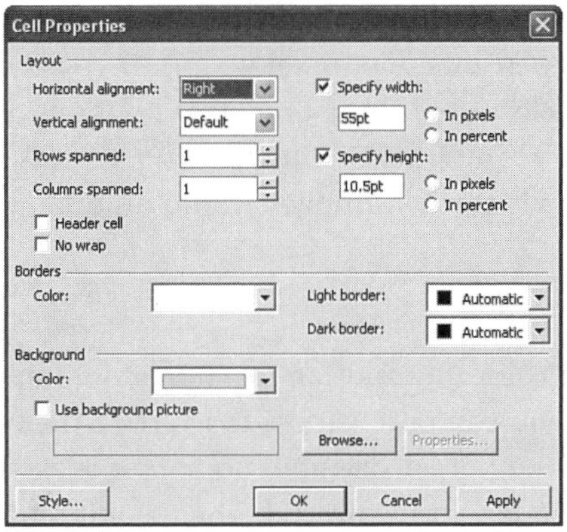

FIGURE 9.8

Use the Cell
Properties dialog
box to change
settings for indi-
vidual table
cells.

The settings in this dialog box are described in the following sections.

Cell Layout Properties

Table cells are almost like mini Web pages unto themselves. The cell layout properties reflect this by giving you control over text alignment inside the cell. In addition,
these properties enable you to control other aspects of the cell, including the
following:

- **Horizontal Alignment**—This option lets you set the alignment for text in
  the cell. Options are Default, Left, Right, Center, and Justify, and these have
  the same effect on text in the cell that the similar settings for the page or a
  paragraph have. The Default setting varies depending on the browser viewing the page, but is usually left alignment.

- **Vertical Alignment**—This lets you set vertical alignment for text in the cell.
  Options are Top, Middle, Baseline, and Bottom. Baseline and Bottom are similar, but differ slightly in that the Baseline setting aligns text according to the
  bottom of the font, not counting descenders in lowercase letters, while the
  Bottom setting includes those descenders.

- **Rows Spanned, Columns Spanned**—Specifies the number of rows and
  columns this cell occupies. In general, it's better to leave this set automatically by using the Merge and Split Cells feature, or the Draw Table mode to
  create a table.

- **Header Cell**—Sets this cell as a header cell, giving it some unique properties.
  Header cells usually appear in the top row of the table and are used for column titles.

- **No Wrap**—This option is supposed to tell table cells not to wrap text.
  However, it frequently does not work. If you have content that you don't want
  to wrap, you can use a spacer image to force the cell wider.

■ **Specify Width, Specify Height**—Enables you to set a height or width for the table cells in either percentage or pixel widths. If you are setting the cell properties of multiple cells at the same time, these options are initially grayed out to prevent you from accidentally setting all cells the same. However, you can override this by simply clicking an option.

Adding Cell Borders

You can set border and border color information for individual table cells as well as for the entire table. However, you can only choose to override the color specified for the table. If the table is set with a border size of 0, no border is displayed for the cell. If there is a border, however, these settings override the default settings chosen in the Table Properties dialog box:

■ **Color**—Select a color to use for the cell border.

■ **Light Border, Dark Border**—These options enable you to add a border that has a two-color 3D effect.

Adding a Background Color or Graphic

Table cells can have their own background color or image. These settings override the settings for the table itself.

■ **Color**—Choose a color to use for the background color of the cell.

■ **Use Background Picture**—Choose an image to use as the background. Click the Browse button to find an image either in your Web directory or elsewhere on your computer.

Automatically Formatting a Table

Even people who are not design impaired sometimes like a little help setting up initial table layouts. The Table AutoFormat option in FrontPage allows you to choose from almost 40 predefined table layouts designed to give you nice-looking tables. Click somewhere in a table and choose Table AutoFormat from the Table menu to open this dialog box, shown in Figure 9.9.

The AutoFormat layouts are for formatting tables for use in displaying tabular data and provide a wide variety of styles that can be applied to tables to set borders, shading, font, and color information. Each format allows special settings to be made for the heading, first and last column, and last row of the table.

FIGURE 9.9

FIGURE 9.9

The Table
AutoFormat dia-
log box lets you
choose from
dozens of prede-
fined table lay-
outs.

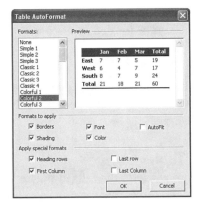

note

Due to limitations of
HTML, it is not possible to
position a table directly in the center of the page and have text flow
around both sides. As with
images, left and right alignment of
tables is the only way to have text
wrap around a table.

Floating Tables

Making a table float may seem like a bit of a mis-
nomer, especially because all this option really
does is make the table stay exactly where it is—all
the way to the left or all the way to the right on the
page—relative to the other content on the page.

In any case, to set the Float property for a table, open the Table
Properties dialog box and choose one of the options under Float:
Left, Right, or Default. When you choose Left or
Right, it overrides whatever setting is chosen
under Alignment. All text and other content that
before was displayed underneath the table now
flows around it.

caution

Keep in mind that a col-
umn in a table can have
only one width. If multi-
ple cells in that column
provide contradictory
width settings, the largest one will
be used as the width of the column.
For the remaining cells, this can
cause unexpected results. Some
browsers hold the content in a cell
to the specified width of that cell
even though the cell itself looks
wider.

Setting Cell Width

When setting the width of a cell, you have several options that can effect how the cell and
neighboring cells behave when the table grows or
shrinks. Cell widths can be set in the Cell
Properties dialog box.

Specifying an Exact Width

Fixed-width columns are used in both layout and
data tables. In layout tables, they are used to provide cells that remain constant even when the

browser window varies in width, often because they contain button images, links, or other formatted content that must always be located in the same amount of space.

Using a Percentage Setting

Percentage settings tell the table cell to occupy a certain percentage width of the overall table width. If you want two columns that each occupy half of a table, setting the width to 50% will accomplish this.

Automatically Stretching a Table

When a table is set to have a percentage width, the cells in the table need to be able to expand or shrink with the table. Most tables, however, need to have one or more fixed-width columns as well. The best approach is to designate one column as an autostretch column by not applying any width values at all to it. When a column has no width specified in any of its cells, that column automatically expands or shrinks to fit in any space left over after the fixed- and percentage-width columns are added to the table.

Inserting Columns and Rows

Inserting columns and rows is a quick way to increase the size of a table; here's how it's done:

tip

If you need to insert a lot of rows or columns, your best bet is to go to the Table Properties dialog box and increase the numbers under Size. Otherwise you'll have to add them one at a time.

- To insert a row, position the cursor inside an existing row of the table and choose Insert Rows from the Table menu. The row is inserted directly below the currently selected row with identical cells and cell properties.
- To insert a column, position the cursor inside an existing column in the table and choose Insert Column from the Table menu. The new column is inserted directly to the right of the current column and includes cells that have the same properties as cells in the original column.

In both cases, if any cells span multiple rows or columns, they will expand to span the new row or column as well.

Deleting Columns and Rows

Deleting columns and rows is almost as easy as inserting them. Simply select the column or row, then choose Delete Columns or Delete Rows from either the Table menu or the context menu.

Distributing Columns and Rows

If you draw a table by hand, or paste something in from another source, the columns may not be formatted exactly as you want them. Although you could go the tedious route of setting each column or row dimension to the correct width, FrontPage enables you to automatically resize all the rows or columns to fill the width or height of the table. To do so, select cells in the rows or columns that you want to adjust, and choose Distribute Rows Evenly or Distribute Columns Evenly from the Table menu.

Keep in mind that this option may not work quite right. Cells with content forcing them to be larger than their specified width or height properties will be shown larger than adjacent cells.

caution

Beware of the Delete Cells option! When you choose this, FrontPage deletes the cells with no regard to the rest of the table layout, often leaving you with a table with an incorrect number of cells in a row. When a row has too few cells, the browser simply displays nothing where the cell would have normally gone, preventing you from adding any content at all there.

In general, it is best to use this option only when a table has an excessive number of cells in a row (for example, if you accidentally changed the Rows spanned or Columns spanned setting in the Cell Properties dialog box).

Merging and Splitting Cells and Tables

Quite often, you don't want to have exactly the same number of cells in every row or column in a table. As you saw when using Draw Table, it's possible to create tables without the exact same number of cells in each row and column.

If you've already created the table you want to use, don't fret. You don't have to scrap your work and create a new table using the Draw Table tool. Instead, you can use the Merge Cells and Split Cells functions to create cells that span multiple rows and columns in tables that you create.

Merging Cells

When you insert a table from the Tables menu or from the Insert Table button on the Standard toolbar, the table always has a fixed number of columns and rows. You can use the Merge Cells feature, however, to combine two or more cells into one.

There are a couple of important things to know when merging cells:

- Cells that you want to merge must be adjacent to one another.
- Selections spanning more than one row and column must have the same number of selected cells in each row and column. In other words, the selected cells must form a rectangular region.

To merge cells using this option, do the following:

1. Make a selection that crosses cell boundaries to include the contents of more than one cell. Be sure to select each cell you want to include in the merge.
2. Choose Merge Cells from the Table menu.

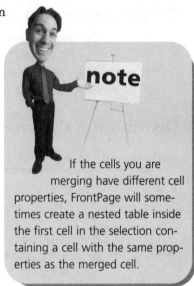

note

If the cells you are merging have different cell properties, FrontPage will sometimes create a nested table inside the first cell in the selection containing a cell with the same properties as the merged cell.

Splitting Cells

Because you can merge cells, it stands to reason that you can split them as well. Unless the cell that is being split already spans more than one row or column, splitting it adds additional rows or columns to the table, as appropriate to maintain the necessary rectangular shape of the table. Any content in the original cell remains in the first of the newly created cells.

To split a cell (or cells), do the following:

1. Make a selection in the cell or across multiple cells.
2. Choose Split Cells from the Table menu.
3. In the Split Cells dialog box, shown in Figure 9.10, choose whether to split the cell into rows or columns, and enter the number of rows or columns you want to create by splitting the cell.
4. Click OK to perform the split.

Splitting a Table in Two

Another option you have is to split a table into two tables. This can be very useful for a table that has more rows than you want to display on a single page. Note, however, that tables can be split only on row boundaries.

FIGURE 9.10

Splitting cells enables you to create multiple cells from one.

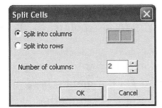

To split a table in two, select a cell in the row that you want to be the first row of the second table. Choose Table, Split Table from the menu, and FrontPage will automatically form a second table with all the properties of the first table, containing the data from the selected row on down.

note

Splitting a table is a one-way street—once it's split, you cannot join it back together again short of performing an Undo (or directly editing the page's HTML code, which requires a strong working knowledge of the HTML construct of tables). Keep this in mind when you use this option.

Using Tables for Layout

Although you could use all the tools described so far to create tables for page layout, FrontPage goes a few steps further to add features that make that task even easier. In fact, two entire task panes are devoted to nothing but setting table- and cell-layout properties.

To begin, choose Layout Tables and Cells from the Tables menu. The Layout Tables and Cells task pane opens; you can toggle between the table options and the cell options by clicking the Cell Formatting link at the top of the Layout Tables and Cells pane, and the Table Layout link on the Cell Formatting pane.

The Layout Tables and Cells Task Pane

The Layout Tables and Cells task pane, shown in Figure 9.11, lets you set all the table options necessary to create layout tables that can be used to give you almost complete control over the positioning of elements on your pages.

You can accomplish the following page layout–related tasks on this pane:

■ **Insert Layout Table**—Clicking this link inserts a layout table into your page with a single row and column.

■ **Insert Layout Cell**—Clicking this link inserts a layout cell with the specified width and height. If inserted outside of a layout table, another table is created.

- **Draw Layout Table, Draw Layout Cell**—These options are similar to the Insert options, but give you the pencil mouse pointer to allow you to draw your own layout table and cells.

- **Table Properties**—These options enable you to set the typical table properties, including table width, height, and alignment. These function in the same way as the similar options in the Table Properties dialog box.

- **Set Page Margins**—Clicking this link opens the Page Properties dialog box, where you can set page margins. When you use layout tables, it is almost always a good idea to set the page margins to 0 so that the table occupies the entire browser window.

- **Table Layout**—Choose from one of the 12 provided table layouts, representing some of the more common typical Web-page layouts.

FIGURE 9.11

Use the Layout Tables and Cells task pane to set layout table options.

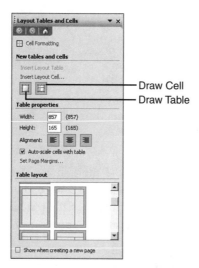

Draw Cell
Draw Table

The Cell Formatting Task Pane

On the Cell Formatting task pane, shown in Figure 9.12, you can set formatting options for individual cells in the table. There are quite a lot of options here that truly let you get an advanced table layout.

There are three different views for the Cell Formatting task pane, and they are described in the following sections.

Cell Dimensions and Borders

Clicking on the Cell Dimensions and Borders link in the Cell Formatting task pane shows controls for setting the typical table cell properties, albeit with a bit more control than you can get from the Cell Properties dialog box. The options on this page (refer to Figure 9.12) are as follows:

- **Size and Alignment**—This section of the task pane includes the options for cell dimensions, alignment, background color, and padding.

- **Borders**—Use the options in this area to set cell border width and color. The unique options here enable you to set borders for only some sides of the cell.

- **Margins**—The settings here enable you to specify the margins for the cell. Again, unique options allow individual settings for top, bottom, left, and right sides.

FIGURE 9.12

Cell dimensions and borders for layout table cells can be set on the first page of the Cell Formatting task pane.

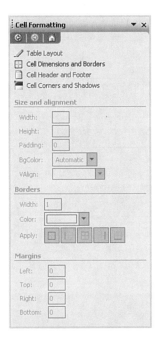

Cell Header and Footer

The Cell Header and Footer page of the Cell Formatting task pane, shown in Figure 9.13, enables you to set some unique options. For example, selecting a cell and checking the Show Header or Show Footer check box causes FrontPage to create a special cell above or below the selected cell that can have independent colors, but still remain logically connected to the original cell in the editor.

Cell Corners and Shadows

The third and final page of the Cell Formatting task pane is the Cell Corners and Shadows page, shown in Figure 9.14. This page lets you add images to the corners of a cell to give it a rounded, tabbed look. This is very nice for creating on-the-fly navigation tabs or buttons from a table cell. Along with the corners, you also can create shadow effects to give a raised effect to a cell.

FIGURE 9.13

The Cell Header and Footer page of the Cell Formatting task pane lets you add unique headers and footers to any cell.

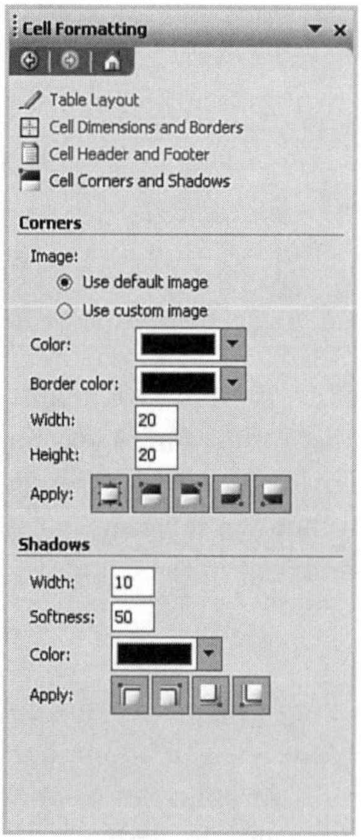

FIGURE 9.14

With the Cell Corners and Shadows page of the Cell Formatting task pane, you can create tabs or buttons with rounded corners with ease.

Using Layout Tools in Design view

The task panes aren't the extent of the tools that FrontPage provides to aid in layout-table creation. When you move your mouse pointer over the border of a layout table, you see that the entire border is highlighted in a way that is different than with normal tables. Clicking on the border of a table or cell activates the layout controls—four boxes on each side of the object that show numbers representing the current width and height of the object, as shown in Figure 9.15. The top and bottom boxes are identical, and are used to set column properties, such as column width and whether to autostretch the column. The left and right boxes set row properties, such as row height and whether the row should be autostretched.

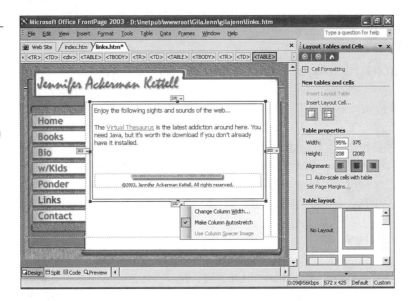

Using Spacers to Prop Up Table Layouts

You've created the ideal layout using tables, and everything looks perfect as you start entering text, images, and other content. All of a sudden, though, your nice fixed-width table cells start collapsing on you like a house of cards. Welcome to one of the more annoying aspects of using tables for layout. Because tables were originally intended for displaying tabular data, the size of content within a cell takes precedence over the widths you specify for table cells. The result is that the widths of some cells can change in seemingly inexplicable ways when content is added to a page, particularly cells with little or no content of their own.

There is, however, a common trick that can be used to force table cells to stay at the correct width. Chapter 6, "Creating and Modifying Graphics," explained how to create a 1-pixel transparent GIF image that can placed in a cell and used to prop open the cell to the correct minimum width. Simply insert the transparent image, and set its width to the desired width of the cell. If you have more than one cell in the same column, you only need to add the spacer image to one of them. The rules of table alignment ensure that all cells in a column or row maintain the same width (not counting column-spanning cells, of course).

When using spacers in a layout table, FrontPage again simplifies this common task by providing a setting on the Column Properties drop-down menu, available when you click the arrow to the right of the layout table column widths in the Design view. Simply choose Use Column Spacer Image from the Column Properties drop-down menu, and FrontPage will automatically insert a spacer image into your page.

Using Tracing Images to Guide Your Design Layout

In the course of designing a Web site, it is often easier to use a graphics program to create a mock-up nonfunctional version of your site. However, translating that image into a fully functional page layout can be a time-consuming chore.

FrontPage 2003 allows you to use that mock-up image as a tracing image. A *tracing image* is just what its name implies: When you choose an image to use as a tracing image, FrontPage displays it in the background in Design view so that you can design your layout over the top of the image.

Nesting Tables

You may have already figured out that one of the best ways to create complex page layouts is to nest tables inside other tables. In a lot of cases, simply splitting a cell into more cells might seem like the best way to go, but it is often beneficial to simply leave a cell as it is and insert another table inside the cell. The overall structure of the code behind the page is simpler, and table properties can be set independently for the newly created table.

SIMPLIFYING TABLE LAYOUTS

Although it might be tempting to go hog-wild and create a complex page layout with multiple levels of nested tables and multiple complex sections, there are good reasons not to. Complex nested table layouts take longer to load in a browser because the browser has to calculate all of the table dimensions on the fly when the page loads. Even when the table is simply resized, some browsers will download the graphics used for cell backgrounds again. There are also browser-compatibility issues to consider: Older versions of Netscape

Navigator, for instance, handle multiple levels of nested tables in a way that could only be charitably described as "buggy."

When designing page layouts, try to keep nested tables to a minimum. Only use them when the table layout would be more complex without them. Spend a little time at the beginning getting a good idea about how to divide the page to support your layout. This will go a long way toward keeping your pages simpler, and at the very least, a simpler page will load faster and will be less likely to have problems.

The Absolute Minimum

Tables are not just useful for displaying tabular data. In fact, in Web design, tables are most often used for creating page layout by dividing a page into sections to arrange page content. FrontPage makes what is normally an arduous task easier by providing several ways to create tables for both of these uses.

Create a table by choosing Table from the Table, Insert menu and choosing your initial table properties. Alternatively, you can draw a table freehand using the Draw Table option. Choose Draw Table from the Table menu, and click and drag a rectangle in the page to create the outer border of the table. Then, draw lines inside the table to divide the table into rows and columns however you like—FrontPage will guide you to ensure that your tables are formatted properly.

The Table Properties and Cell Properties dialog boxes are used to set common properties for tables and table cells. In addition, creation of tables specifically for page layout is aided by the Layout Tables and Cells and Cell Formatting task panes. These panes show options specifically for layout tables.

IN THIS CHAPTER

- Frames versus tables
- The pros and cons of frame use
- Frame-based layouts
- How to use a frames template
- How to make changes to framesets
- The basics of modifying target frames

10

USING FRAMES

Coming up with the right tool to develop your site's overall layout is tough work. You want the site to have the right look, yet you want it to be intuitive to navigate so that you can get the job done to your—and your audience's—satisfaction.

One of the big decisions you face is whether you should lay out your site free style, use the tables you learned about in Chapter 9, "Using Tables," the cascading style sheets and layers you'll read about in Chapter 13, "Using Styles and Cascading Style Sheets," and Chapter 14, "Scripting and DHTML," or implement a frames-based layout, which is the focus of this chapter. Each has its advantages and disadvantages—whether you're a new Web designer or not.

Here, you'll develop your basic skills in implementing a frames-based layout, starting with an understanding of what this means for your site and moving on to actually creating the frames necessary to accomplish the job.

Frames Versus Tables

Tables probably represent the most commonly used layout technique for Web sites. For a new designer, they're an easy choice because they enable you to divide a blank page into nice, neat regions, each with its own focus and content, which you can fill in as you go.

In many respects, visually at least, frames do the very same thing. Frame templates that FrontPage provides, as you will see shortly, give you clear regions of a page that you can then fill with whatever you want to use.

A chief difference between frames and tables is that those regions (called *frames*) of a whole page (referred to as the *frames page* or *frameset,* which serves as the container for everything else) are actually separate pages of their own, each created and saved individually. See the section titled "Frame-based Layout Components" later in this chapter for more details.

Another difference is that a table-based layout may change from page to page, whereas the same frame regions are visible on each page in a site. For example, say you create a frame-based layout where your banner always appears at the top, your navigational links appear at the left-hand side, company information appears across the bottom, and a large window opens up on the right to accept your content. The top, left, and bottom frames stay the same from page to page, while the content window changes depending on what page the visitor has requested.

THE PROS AND CONS OF FRAMES

The use of frames on a Web site can be very appealing because they create a crisp basic layout, with relatively little effort to start. For those of you who want a consistent layout appearance from page to page, this may seem like the way to go.

That said, frames can present some problems. For one, each frame is created as a separate Web page, which means you have to create each individual frame used. Tied to this, it can take longer for your visitors—especially those with a slow, dial-up connection—to open your pages.

Like tables, frames aren't always handled well by those using assistive devices to view the Web, such as those with visual disabilities and even some of those browsing with a non-PC device. Information contained in the individual frames can become jumbled for them.

Even those who surf normally often find frames to be clumsy, and usability studies report that more users than not don't like them. For some, this is based on an old memory of some earlier browser versions that didn't support frames well and often left them in a mess, where frames would be drawn within frames. Another problem is that when visitors save your site under Favorites, they may end up bookmarking the frameset itself or even the wrong page.

This doesn't mean that you can't or shouldn't employ frames in your site design. Use them carefully, however. And if you're designing a public site where you're looking for mass appeal, listen to your audience about any problems they have.

Frame-based Layout Components

Let's start by looking at one of the most commonly used frame templates, often referred to as the simple four-region frameset, as shown in Figure 10.1.

FIGURE 10.1

An example of a frames page template containing individual frames.

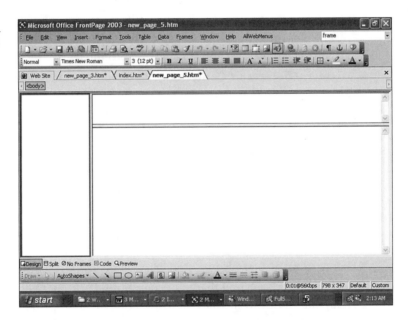

The main components of this structure are as follows:

- The frames page is the overall structure of a page containing frames.
- The banner frame is the frame that contains a banner for your site.
- The contents frame is the navigation area on the left side, which offers links (often labeled Home, About Us, Contact Us, and so on) to your site's content.
- The main frame is the area where your individual page content will appear.

Using a Frames Template

FrontPage offers a number of different popular frames-template formats from which you can choose, including:

- **Banner and Contents**—A good basic template for an information-based Web site.

- **Contents**—Same as above, also good for news and information sites, but without a top banner.

- **Footer**—Simple design where there's a whole blank page plus a thin footer running across the bottom; good for simple or few-pages-only site designs.

- **Footnotes**—Useful on a site presenting papers, book citations, and other documents where a footnote frame is desirable.

- **Header**—Like the Footer template, but instead uses one full page with a narrow header running across the top of the page; well suited to simple designs, usually where relatively few images will be employed.

- **Header, Footer and Contents**—This option combines both a header and footer plus a main area for the page contents; also suited to simpler designs where only a limited amount of information needs to be offset from the actual contents.

- **Horizontal Split**—Choose this to split the page in half, where you want content to display in one half and framed standard information in the other.

- **Nested Hierarchy**—A classic template suitable for any purpose with a banner, a left-hand side frame, and a large content window.

- **Top-Down Hierarchy**—Another classic suitable for the majority of site types.

- **Vertical Split**—Like Horizontal Split, but divided down the page vertically.

Let's create an empty Web and then build a site using a frames-based layout created from a template. That way, if you've already started your site, you won't affect your site's design as you investigate how a frames-based layout might work for you.

To create an empty Web, do the following:

1. Open the File menu and choose New.

2. Under New Web Site in the right-hand task pane, click More Web Site Templates.

3. Double-click Empty Web. FrontPage creates a new Web for you.

4. Again, open the File menu and choose New.

5. Under New page in the task pane, click More Page Templates.

6. Click the Frames Pages tab, and double-click the frames template you want to use (see Figure 10.2). A preview of each template is shown in the bottom-right corner of the window.

FIGURE 10.2

FIGURE 10.2

Choose a template that meshes with your ideas for your site; a simple design might include just two frames, while more complex ones could offer four.

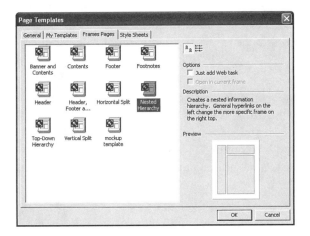

Adding Pages to the Frames Page

After you choose a template, your new frames page will open in Design view, and will look something like the one shown in Figure 10.3 (depending on the template you selected).

FIGURE 10.3

After you choose a template upon which to base your layout, you'll have an initial frames page with individual frames that look like this.

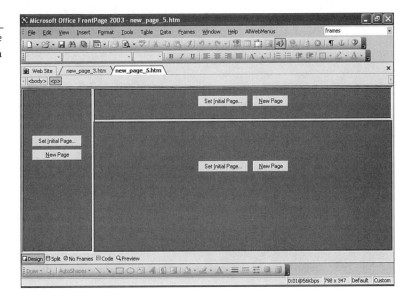

Notice that each frame gives you two button options for adding a page:

- **Set Initial Page**—Click this button when you want to select an existing page to use as the content of the frame. Doing so opens the Insert Hyperlink dialog box; locate and select the page to use, and then click OK.

- **New Page**—Click this button when you need to create a new page to use as the content of the frame.

Because the first button is pretty self-explanatory, let's discuss what happens when you click the New Page button. First, the frame changes to a blank white page, much as if you were starting a blank page in Design view, but contained within the limits of the frame itself. You can design that page as you would any other.

After you've created the page for the first frame, move to the next frame, continuing until all your frames are populated. In the example in Figure 10.4, I clicked the New Page button to create the top banner and the navigation area, and I clicked the Set Initial Page button to use an already-designed page for the main frame.

note

When you use an already-created page as the basis for your frame, you should be very certain that the page as designed works well within the size and nature of the frame.

FIGURE 10.4

This is an example of what a completed frames page might look like, depending on the template used and the design employed.

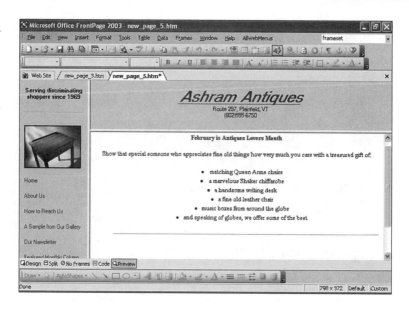

Saving the Frames Page

Unlike other pages you've worked with before, the process for saving a frames page is a bit different. This is especially true when you create one or more new pages as you fill your frames: You are prompted to save each frame a page at a time, but all frames used will be saved in the process, meaning you don't have to point to a particular frame.

To save a frames page, do the following:

1. Open the File menu and choose Save.
2. The Save As window opens. Note the highlighted frame in the preview on the right (see Figure 10.5); this is the frame and page you are being prompted to save.

FIGURE 10.5

Always look at the highlighted frame in the preview section to see which frame—or frames page— you are about to save.

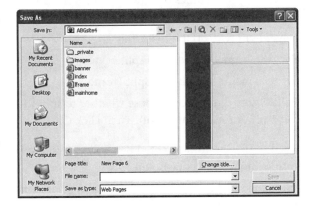

3. Type a name for the frame in the File Name field.
4. If the Page Title text is not what you want displayed in the browser's title bar when the page is opened, click the Change Title button, which opens the Set Page Title window.
5. Type a title for the page. Click OK.
6. Click the Save button.
7. Next, check the highlighted frame in the right-hand preview again, and repeat steps 3–5 until all frames have been saved.
8. As a final step, you are prompted to create a file name and title for the entire frames page. Do so, and click the Save button.

Modifying Frames Pages

Just because you've finished designing a basic frames page and have added content to its individual frames doesn't mean your design is set in stone. There are in fact many modifications you can make to fit your specific needs. For example, you can divide a single frame in two, delete a frame altogether, resize one or more frames, or rename a frame or frames page.

In this section, you will learn how to split frames, adjust their size, rename or remove them, delete frame borders, as well as add "no frames" content.

Splitting a Frame

What if you need to split a frame into two, either horizontally or vertically? You can do so, with the result being two frames of equal proportion—which you can then adjust to whatever size you need.

To split the frame evenly in two, do the following:

1. Click to select the frame you want to split.

2. Open the Frames menu and choose Split Frame.

3. From the Split Frame dialog box, choose whether to split the frame into columns (vertical) or rows (horizontal). Then click OK.

You can then proceed to fill the frame created through the split, as you did the others. (Remember to save the frames page again.)

If you need to change the size of the split cells so that one is larger than the other, follow the steps in the next section.

Adjusting Frame Size

What happens when a frame is either too large or too small to accommodate what you want to place in it? You can adjust the size of the frame to fit.

To change the size of a frame, do the following:

1. Point to the border of the frame whose size you want to adjust, and press and hold your left mouse button until the cursor turns into a double-sided arrow.

2. Drag your mouse to adjust the frame to the size you want, and then release the mouse button.

As you work, you may notice that when the content added to a frame exceeds the size of a frame, a scrollbar is inserted automatically at the right edge of the frame. That might be okay in a main frame where you want visitors to be able to scroll down through a longer page of content, but undesirable at other times.

To remove the scrollbar from a frame, do the following:

1. Point to the frame containing the scrollbar you want to remove, right-click, and choose Frame Properties.

2. Under Options, to the right of Show Scrollbars, select Never. Only use this option when there will be no need for a visitor to scroll to see the contents of a frame.

note

You can add a scrollbar by selecting either If Needed or Always in step 2.

Renaming a Frame or Frames Page

You can rename either a frame or a frames page if you don't like the name you originally chose.

To rename an individual frame, do the following:

1. Point to the frame whose name you want to modify, right-click, and choose Frame Properties.

2. From the Frame Properties dialog box (see Figure 10.6), delete the frame's name from the Name field, and then type a new name for the frame. When you're finished, click OK.

FIGURE 10.6

The Frame Properties dialog box lets you change information about the frames being used.

Frame Properties		
Name:	main	
Initial page:		Browse...
Long Description:		Browse...
Title:		
Frame size		
Width:	1 Relative	
Row height:	1 Relative	
Margins		
Width:	12	
Height:	16	
Options		
☑ Resizable in browser		Frames Page...
Show scrollbars:	If Needed	
Style...	OK	Cancel

To change the name of a frames page, do the following:

1. Close the frames page you want to rename if it is currently open.

2. At the top of the FrontPage window, click the Web Site tab, which opens the site in Folders view.

3. Point to the current name of the frames page in the list, right-click, and select Rename. A box surrounds the page's name, which is also selected.

4. Press the Backspace key to delete the current name, and then type a new name for the frames page. When you're finished, press Return.

Deleting Frames

Do you find yourself wondering if your page design would look better if you removed a frame? If so, you can easily delete a frame from your page. Before you try this, however, you must understand two important points:

- The rest of the frames contained in the frames page will remain, but will now try to fill in the space formerly occupied by the deleted frame.

- You are deleting the frame, but not the actual page for which that frame acts as a container; you can still find that page listed in the Folders view and can use it elsewhere, if desired.

Here's how to delete a frame:

1. Click the frame you wish to remove.

2. Open the Frames menu and choose Delete Frame.

Removing Frame Borders

By default, FrontPage places neatly designed borders around each frame in a frames page. If you don't care for the effect that creates, however, you can turn the page's borders off. (Note that removing borders removes both the page border and the frame borders; you cannot remove frame borders individually.)

To modify a frames page so that no borders are shown, do the following:

1. Point to a frame, right-click, and choose Frame Properties.

2. In the Frame Properties dialog box, click the Frames Page button.

3. If it is not already displayed, click the Frames tab.

4. Click the Show Borders check box to uncheck it. When you're finished, click OK.

note

You can reverse this process simply by repeating these steps, this time clicking the Show Borders check box to mark it.

Adding No Frames Content

Some Web browsers don't support the use of frames, while others enable their users to choose whether or not to view pages that are built with frames. In either case, a visitor coming to your frames-based site will receive a message that, by default, states that the browser being used does not support the viewing of such a Web page. If you like, you can customize this message. To alter the message, do the following:

1. With the frames page open, click the No Frames tab at the bottom of the screen to change to No Frames view. This displays the default message.

2. Delete the current message, and then type the new message as you want it to appear.

Modifying Target Frames

A target frame is a frame that is the target of a hyperlink—for example, a hyperlink that appears in another frame on the frames page or on your Web site. A target frame might also be referenced from a hyperlink outside of your frames page—for example, if you link to a page on someone else's site.

Linking to Frames

Suppose that you want to create a link to a frame on your frames page. To accomplish this, do the following:

1. Click the text or image you want to use as your hyperlink.

2. On the FrontPage toolbar, click the Insert Hyperlink button.

3. The Edit Hyperlink dialog box opens; click Target Frame.

4. In the Target Frame dialog box, shown in Figure 10.7, click the frame to which you want to link, and then click OK.

note

Want to click to something other than a frame in the frames page? If so, in the Target Frame dialog box, click one of the options listed below Common Targets.

FIGURE 10.7

Point to the proper frame in the diagram at the left of the Target Frame dialog box.

Breaking Out of Frames

What happens if, after all of this, you decide you simply don't want to set up your layout based on frames? Must you delete your entire Web? In a word, no. What you probably want to do in this case is turn off support for the use of frames, which disables the use of frames and frame pages.

To disable frames support, do the following:

1. Open the Tools menu and choose Page Options.

2. Click the Authoring tab.

3. Click the Frames check box to uncheck it, and then click OK.

THE ABSOLUTE MINIMUM

Despite some of the problems they present, the use of frames for page or site layout can add a distinctly professional appearance and good organization. With the information in this chapter, you can now appreciate the difference between using frames versus using tables, create a frames-based layout and set both existing and new pages to occupy the designated frames, save each frame in your work, and make changes to frames (such as splitting, resizing, and even renaming them). You also saw how to modify target frames for a hyperlink.

11

USING CODE IN FRONTPAGE

Chapter 23 (found on the web), "Knowing the Code," provided an understanding of why knowing at least some HTML can help free you from the confines of FrontPage-aided design. Now, you will learn some of the tips and tricks for adding your own HTML as well as adding HTML copied from other sources.

Code view offers a number of options that help you in your work. You can set formatting, create and use code snippets to let you type a few keystrokes to repeat often-used tags and attributes, and use several other goodies you're about to delve into.

Using the Code view

Up to now, you've worked almost exclusively in the very friendly environment of FrontPage's Design view, where what you create is what you see in Preview Page view. Yet you should find that Code view provides a fairly easy work environment as well.

Look at Figure 11.1 and you'll see a working window that looks a lot like a simple text editor. By default, when you create a new page—even a blank one—FrontPage automatically inserts a certain amount of basic HTML to start you off. This automatic insertion is composed of the essential HTML needed for a basic Web page you learned about in Chapter 23 (found on the web), including <HTML></HTML>, <HEAD></HEAD>, and <BODY></BODY> tags.

FIGURE 11.1

Code view operates something like a text editor, but with options that enable you to make faster work of your HTML additions, editing, and tweaking.

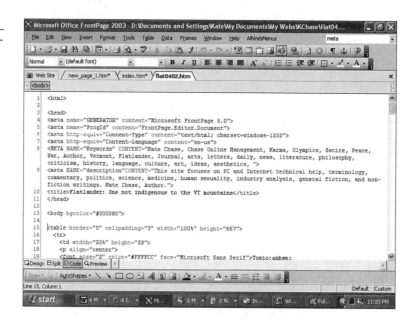

To insert your own HTML into either the basic code of a blank page or in the large amount of HTML available in a page you've already laid out and populated in Design view, you simply click the location where you want to add your code and begin to type. Click the beginning of a line already containing code and press Enter, and you create a blank line waiting to be filled.

You will find that all the keys you use in normal editing—such as Delete, Insert, Backspace, and such—work the same way in Code view.

Adding HTML from Design view

Although this chapter focuses on Code view, it would be remiss if we did not mention that it is possible to add HTML directly from within Design view. You do so using the Quick Tag Editor. This method is best for simple insertions (for example, adding or editing just one line), while multiple additions or more extensive editing really should be done within Code view.

To insert code from within Design view, do the following:

1. Click the spot on the page where you want to insert the HTML code.

2. Press CTRL+Q to open the Quick Tag Editor.

3. Open the Quick Tag Editor's drop-down list and choose Insert HTML (see Figure 11.2).

FIGURE 11.2

You can edit, wrap, and insert HTML from Design view using these steps.

4. Type the HTML you want to add. When you're finished, press Enter or click the green check mark button on the right side of the Quick Tag Editor.

5. When you are finished, click the × button on the right side of the Quick Tag Editor.

Using Split page

When you work in Code view, you may find yourself frequently flipping back and forth to Design Page or Preview Page view to check your results. That's common behavior, and even recommended.

However, you may want to consider using Split page, shown in Figure 11.3, which divides the FrontPage window into two screens—one with the page in Design view, and one with the page in Code view. Not everyone likes the split-screen approach because it limits your visible work area in each, but it can be a time saver when it comes to switching back and forth between the two different views.

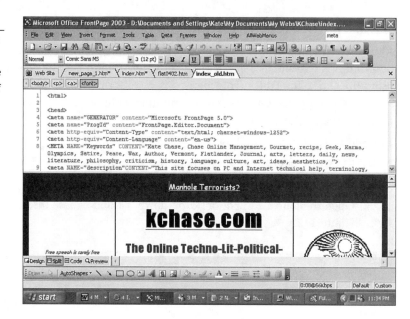

Customizing Code Options

The more you work in Code view, the greater you may appreciate the customizable options it offers you. Such options can make it far easier to enter tags and attributes, to set up formatting that fits the way you want your code to appear, and to identify the components listed.

Let's look at these options now.

Enabling IntelliSense

IntelliSense is a feature that tries to intuitively aid you in adding HTML code. It does this through options that, when enabled, try to auto-complete (automatically finish what it thinks you want to type) tags for HTML as well as provide context-sensitive lists for scripting.

Some newcomers love this feature because it provides a list of HTML tags that they may have trouble remembering otherwise. It also helps you see what arguments you can use with an HTML tag, where appropriate (see the previous chapter for an HTML refresher). Those more skilled with HTML sometimes dislike it, however, because the pop-up IntelliSense window appears (see Figure 11.4) when they're trying to quickly type code.

FIGURE 11.4

As you type tags, the IntelliSense pop-up window appears to provide a list of choices to select from.

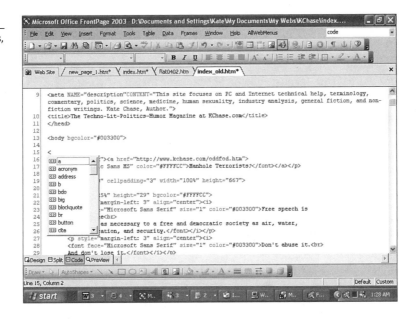

To enable IntelliSense—and you should do so to at least try it—do the following:

1. Open the Tools menu and choose Page Options.

2. The Page Options dialog box opens. Click the IntelliSense tab, as shown in Figure 11.5.

3. Click to check the options you want, and click OK.

FIGURE 11.5

The IntelliSense tab lets you select the options you want to set for its use.

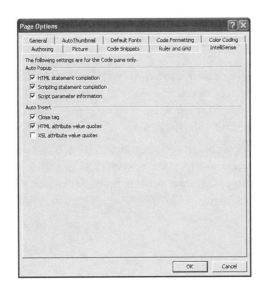

note

When all options on the IntelliSense tab are unchecked, the feature is effectively disabled.

Code Formatting

Code formatting refers to the overall appearance of your HTML, including how it's indented, wrapped, and so on. FrontPage permits you to designate code formatting for your HTML for just the current page or for all new pages you create.

To set formatting for your HTML, do the following:

1. Open the Tools menu and choose Page Options.

2. The Page Options dialog box opens. Click the Code Formatting tab (see Figure 11.6).

3. Under Formatting, select the settings you want to use, including settings for tabs, spaces to indent, and the right margin. When you're finished, click OK.

FIGURE 11.6

The Code Formatting tab enables you to specify formatting options for your HTML exactly as you want it to appear.

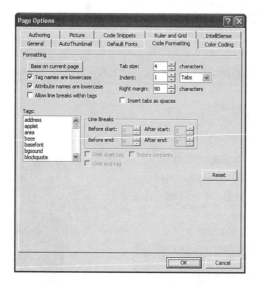

You also can use the Code Formatting tab to specify which tags should be automatically indented. To do so, select the tag you want to indent in the Tags list, and then click the Indent Contents check box to select it. With some tags, you can also click the Omit Start Tag or Omit End Tag check boxes.

Let's say you've gone through the process of adding HTML to a page and the formatting for it is just the way you want it to appear. You can then designate that FrontPage use the formatting from that page as the code formatting base for other pages. To do so, follow these steps:

1. With the page on which you want to base other formatting open in Code view, open the Tools menu and choose Page Options.

2. The Page Options dialog box opens. Click the Code Formatting tab.

3. In the Formatting section, click the Base on Current Page button. When you're finished, click OK.

note

Setting a code-formatting base usually saves time over manually formatting your code as you go.

Color Coding

If you find the appearance of Code view makes it a bit difficult to work in, especially when it seems congested with tags and attributes and text, you're hardly alone. Some people find themselves far more prone to making errors once the page begins to fill.

One feature to help you distinguish different components from each other is the ability to color code tags and attributes. This feature is enabled by default in FrontPage with these settings:

- Tags appear in purple.
- Attributes appear in red.
- Values appear in blue.
- Text appears in black.

To modify the colors used for different components, or to add other color coding, do the following:

1. Open the Tools menu and choose Page Options.

2. The Page Options dialog box opens. Click the Color Coding tab, as shown in Figure 11.7.

3. Make the changes you want, or click Reset Colors to reset to default color coding. When you're finished, click OK.

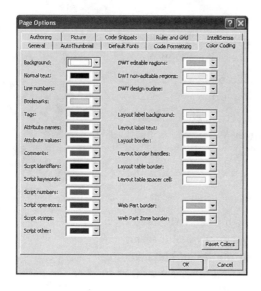

Line Numbers

Look at the left margin of the Code view window and note that each line bears a number. Many text and code editors include this feature as an easy reference point. You should find that it's faster and easier to work when you make a note to yourself to check a problem in the HTML at Line 17 than it would be to locate a line beginning with a tag that may be used again elsewhere. You do, however, have the option of turning off the line numbers. Later, you can re-enable them, if desired.

To turn them off, do the following:

1. Open the Tools menu and choose Page Options.

2. Click the General tab.

3. Under Code View Options, click to uncheck the Line Numbers check box.

note

When line numbers are enabled, you can go to a specific line of code by right-clicking anywhere on the page, selecting Go to Line, then typing the line number.

Other Issues to Consider

When copying HTML from one place to another, there are some things to consider in order to be certain it looks and works as intended once it is inserted. These include whether a long line of code should automatically wrap to another line, whether you want it automatically indented, and whether you're careful to get the entire snippet of code you need.

Word Wrap

Just as the title suggests, *word wrap* refers to the ability to wrap long lines of text or HTML code to a second line, as needed. Without word wrap, a line can keep going quite a distance to the right of the page in Code view, for example, and require you to keep scrolling to the right to view it all.

To enable word wrap for your code in Code view

1. Open the Tools menu and choose Page Options.
2. Click the General tab.
3. Under Code View Options, click to check the Word Wrap check box. Click OK.

AutoIndent

Just as with word wrap, the ability to automatically indent code you add using Code view, such as when you cut or copy and paste, requires that you be sure the option is turned on in the Code View Options area of the Page Options dialog box. To set up FrontPage to automatically indent, do the following:

1. Open the Tools menu and choose Page Options.
2. Click the General tab.
3. Under Code View Options, click the AutoIndent check box to check it. Click OK.

Selecting Tags

To swiftly select a tag to add or edit, you can use the Quick Tag Editor discussed earlier. Here's an example:

1. Click the area of the page where you want to select and insert a tag, and then click Design to show it in Design view.
2. On the Quick Tag Selector toolbar, click the arrow next to the selector you want. (If you don't see the Quick Tag Selector toolbar, open the View menu, choose Toolbars, and select Quick Tag Selector to open it.)
3. Click Select Tag if you want to select both the start and end tag for this tag along with the tag's full content. Alternatively, click Select Tag Contents if you only want to edit or work with the contents (and not the start and end tag).

Finding Start and End Tags

When you copy or create HTML code in your page, you must be certain that all starting tags that require one also have an end tag. Remember, most tags that open also need to close. Go through your code to be sure this is the case for each tag you have added or edited.

Copying, Cutting, and Pasting Code

What do you do if you find HTML code Code viewelsewhere that you want to copy into your page? The answer to this question is to copy and paste, much as you would text. The HTML you copy is automatically formatted and fitted to the editing environment of Code view.

Here's how to copy and paste HTML code:

1. Select the HTML code you want you copy, right-click, and select Copy.

2. Point to the location where you want to insert the code, right-click, and select Paste.

The instructions change only slightly when you want to move, rather than copy, code from one location to another, thereby removing it from its original location:

1. Select the HTML code you want to move, right-click, and select Cut.

2. Point to the location where you want to insert the code, right-click, and choose Paste.

Creating Code Snippets to Reuse Code

When you work with HTML, you may quickly discover that there are some tags that you have to type again and again (for example, a tag to insert

If you're borrowing HTML from someone else's site, be aware that it may be covered by copyright. What you may want to do is take their code as an example and adapt your own version from it. Ask permission of the Webmaster of the site when possible.

When you copy code, especially from someone else's page, be sure there is nothing in that code that refers to the other site or location. If it does, you need to change it.

a hyperlink or image). You may also find yourself reusing JScript or JavaScript elements when you add scripting to your pages.

Using code snippets enables you to define the code (or fragments thereof) you type most frequently and store it for fast recall so you don't need to type it again and again. It's designed as a time and keystroke saver.

By default, certain snippets—including code for linking a style sheet and for adding meta descriptions and meta keywords—are already defined for you. To see them, open the Tools menu and choose Page Options to open the Page Options dialog box; then click the Code Snippets tab (see Figure 11.8).

FIGURE 11.8

Code snippets are stored on the Code Snippets tab in the Page Options dialog box.

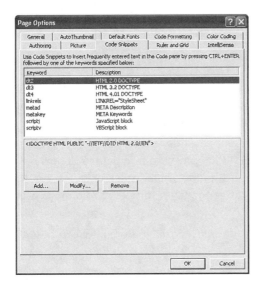

These defined snippets are just a start, however. You are encouraged to add your own so that they're readily available for your use.

To add a snippet, do the following:

1. Open the Tools menu and choose Page Options.

2. The Page Options dialog box opens. Click the Code Snippets tab.

3. Click the Add button.

4. The Add Code Snippet dialog box opens. In the Keyword field, type the keyword you want to use to quickly retrieve this code.

5. In the Description field, type a few words to help you identify what this snippet does.

6. In the large window at the bottom of the dialog box, type the actual HTML (or scripting) you want to add, as shown in Figure 11.9. When you're finished, click OK.

FIGURE 11.9

You're prompted to provide a keyword, description, and the actual code to store for reuse in the Add Code Snippet dialog box.

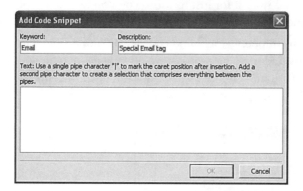

The use of a pipe (|) symbol enables you to create a placeholder for the actual text you may type for use with the code snippet.

You can add multiple code snippets at one time. Mind you, not everything you add here has to be an actual HTML or scripting fragment; you also can use it to store frequently typed words, colors (in name or hex code), or styles. You may also use buttons on the Code Snippet tab to modify a snippet or to remove a snippet you no longer want.

When you want to use a code snippet you've stored, follow these steps:

1. From Code view, click the spot on your page where you want to insert a stored snippet.

2. Press Ctrl+Enter. A list box containing stored snippets appears, as shown in Figure 11.10.

3. Type the keyword assigned to the snippet you want to use, or click it in the list.

FIGURE 11.10

When you press Ctrl+Enter in Code view, your roster of stored snippets appears. Select or type the keyword associated with it to insert the snippet.

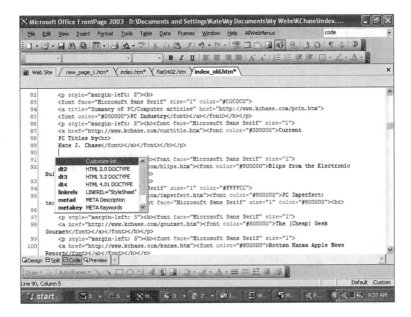

Review Your Additions and Changes

Before you consider your HTML additions and changes complete, you need to do at least two things:

- Check your page in Preview Page view to be sure there aren't any obvious problems.

- Review your code to be sure the syntax is correct, that open tags (where applicable) have closing tags, that none of the values are wrong, and so on.

THE ABSOLUTE MINIMUM

Although FrontPage 2003 helps you create phenomenal pages without knowing a bit of HTML, your code-enhanced pages can actually be far more dynamic and interesting with just a bit of effort. In this chapter, you learned how to use Code view to review and work with HTML directly within your pages, customize Code View Options so your inserted HTML appears as you find it most helpful, manage tools such as IntelliSense and Quick Tag Editor to aid in your work, cut or copy and paste code into your pages from other sources, and add code snippets to record frequently typed HTML code.

Congratulations! You have designed, tested, published, reviewed, promoted, and learned some extras that go beyond FrontPage alone. Hopefully the result is not only to your liking, but to that of your growing Web audience as well. Thanks for persevering and for letting this book be a part of your first FrontPage site-design experience.

PART III

DESIGNING DYNAMICALLY AND INTERACTIVELY

12

CREATING A NAVIGATION STRUCTURE

One incredibly important issue concerning any Web site is how your visitors will be able to move around within it, surfing from area to area, page to page. A great looking site can offer the coolest, most informative content; yet it will go unread if no one can find the pages you want them to view.

How movement through a site is accomplished is referred to as a site's navigation, how it is structured is called the navigational structure or hierarchy, and the component(s) used to help one move is known as the navigation element(s). Each is discussed within this chapter.

Using the Navigation View

FrontPage makes it easy to understand the basic structure of your site's navigation through the use of Navigation view. For example, Look at Figure 12.1; there, you'll see a sample customer-support Web site (created using the Customer Support Web template in FrontPage) in Navigation view, in which the home page (listed as Customer) has links to additional pages such as What's New, Products, Support Forum, and so on.

FIGURE 12.1

Navigation view enables you to see how the pages of your site are linked together for your visitors.

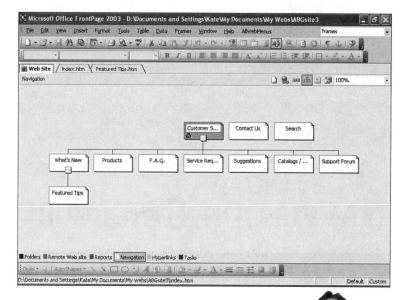

But Navigation view isn't merely a tool for displaying the established navigation structure for your site, although that's its obvious job. It also lets you create new pages, change your navigation structure (including renaming pages and modifying their order), or even print a hard copy of the site's structure as shown in Navigation view.

To see your site in Navigation view, do the following:

1. Open your site in FrontPage.

2. From Folders view, click the Navigation button near the bottom of your FrontPage window.

note

If you see no pages listed in Navigation view, you need to add them manually. This subject is covered in the section titled "Adding Pages to the Navigation Structure" later in this chapter.

Any pages in a site that are not displayed in Navigation view are not included in your navigation structure; visitors won't be able to access them unless they know the specific Web address of the page. For example, say you publish a page titled books.htm to your site but fail to include it in your site's navigation structure. To access that page, visitors would need to know its exact URL and type it into their browser's address field (for example, `http://www.mysite.net/books.htm`) to view it.

Choosing a Navigational Hierarchy

Navigational hierarchy refers to the way a site is ordered, usually top to bottom. While very simple sites, such as personal ones, may simply contain a collection of pages stored in the root folder or main Web of FrontPage or a published site (referred to as the *top level*), this frequently changes as additional content is added. If your site grows, you simply shouldn't have links for 30 or 40 different pages all available from your main or index.htm page; the result will be confusing and cluttered.

A hierarchical Web, on the other hand, has pages at different levels. For example, the home page or index.htm page will be located at the top level, which is where site visitors enter. From the home page, visitors can click links to jump to the About Us, Our Portfolio, and Contact Us pages, which exist on the second level. Suppose further that your portfolio is actually a collection of different pages representing different types of work you've done. Thus, the Our Portfolio link would open an Our Portfolio page with links to other pages, which would reside on your third level. This is an example of a navigational hierarchy. It's a way of organizing a Web site into a smart traffic plan.

Adding Pages to the Navigation Structure

When you create new pages, you're likely going to want to add them to the navigation structure of your site so visitors can find them. As an added bonus, once a page is added, any link bar you create for your site will automatically be added to that page.

This is how you add pages to your site using Navigation view, which in turn adds them to your site's navigation structure:

1. From Folder view, click the page you want to add, and then drag it to the Navigation option at the bottom of the folder window. Do not release the mouse button yet.

2. Point to the location where you want the page to appear, as shown in Figure 12.2, then release your mouse button.

FIGURE 12.2

Once you locate the desired page in Folders view, it's easy to open the Navigation window and drop the new page (pictured here as an outline under What's New) into your structure.

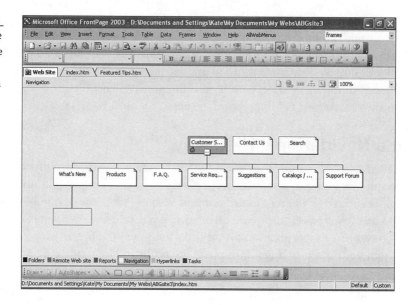

Once placed, the page becomes available through your site's navigation structure, such as through a link bar you add later. Visitors can then click the link to open the new page.

If you happen to drop the new page into the wrong spot, simply drag it into the correct position. You can change this as often as you need.

Renaming and Rearranging Pages in the Navigation Structure

With the start of a navigation structure in place, you have to know how to manipulate it so that your structure remains accurate and useful as you make additions and changes to the site itself. In this section, you'll learn how to rename pages in your navigation structure, rearrange them so they appear where they should, and remove pages you no longer want.

Renaming a Page in the Navigation Structure

The names of the pages that appear in Navigation view are actually the titles of your pages rather than the pages' file names. Although you might have saved a new Web page with a file name of widget.htm, and although that is the name that will appear in Folders and Page Design views, the page's title is what you'll see in Navigation view, as well as in the title bar of the visitor's browser when the page is displayed online. The default title for every page is often "Untitled" or "New Page x," but you can modify your title when you click the Page Title button (which opens the Page Title dialog box) from the Save or Save As window as you learned in Chapter 2, "Creating Sites and Pages."

For various reasons (for example, the title is vague, too long, or misspelled), you might want to rename a page's title within Navigation view.

To rename a page's title, do the following:

1. In Navigation view, click the page whose title you want to change, then point to the title of that page until a box outline is drawn around it.

2. Press the Backspace or Delete key until the original title is removed.

3. Type a new title for the page into the space (be sure it fits), and then press Enter.

After you perform this operation, the new page title will appear in Navigation view, as well as in any link bars you create. (You'll learn how to build link bars shortly.)

Moving a Page in the Navigation Structure

Thankfully, your navigation structure isn't set in stone. This is important because as you add new pages to your site, it's very likely that you'll want to rearrange how pages appear and on which level of the navigation hierarchy they reside. But even with a simple site, you may want to mix and match the arrangement until it flows more logically.

To move a page from one location in your navigation structure to another, do the following:

1. In Navigation view, click the page you want to move.

2. Holding your mouse button down, drag the page to its new location in the navigation structure (see Figure 12.3). When it's in the correct position, release your mouse button.

Notice that when a page is removed from a level, the other pages on that level shift to fill its vacancy. Of course, you're free to add a new page to that level, at which point the items will shift again to accommodate the new page.

Removing Pages from the Navigation Structure

As you develop your site, it's possible that you may want to delete a page from your navigation structure—for example, if the material contained on that page is no longer valid.

FIGURE 12.3

To move a page to a new position, just click, drag, and release. Everything else readjusts to fit the new placement.

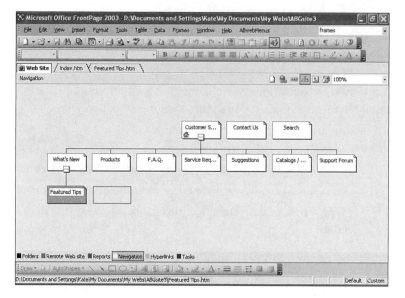

To remove a page or pages from your site's navigation structure, do the following:

1. In Navigation view, click the page you want to remove.
2. Press the Delete key on your keyboard.

Adding Link Bars

The primary navigation tool that FrontPage provides for your use is called a *link bar*. Think of a link bar as a series of words, buttons, or images in a row or column (depending on whether the link bar is oriented horizontally across a page's width or vertically down a page's length) that offer links to other pages on your site.

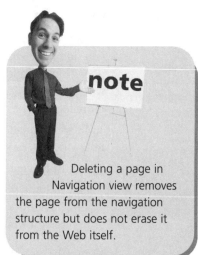

note

Deleting a page in Navigation view removes the page from the navigation structure but does not erase it from the Web itself.

If a horizontal link bar is used, particularly in conjunction with longer pages of Web content, it may appear in two places: at or near the top and at or near the bottom of the page. Similarly, a vertical link bar might be used on both the left and right edges of a page. Likewise, two different link bars on the same page can be used to replicate the same series of links or can point to two different series of links.

FrontPage lets you create two main types of link bars:

- **Navigation bars**—This type of link bar is based on the navigation structure of your site.
- **Custom link bars**—This type of link bar is based on a custom set of links that you select.

Using Navigation Bars

The most common type of link bar you're apt to add to your site is a navigation bar, which enables people to move easily to designated areas of your site. This type of link bar is updated automatically when you change your site's navigation structure, which ensures that it is always current.

To create a link bar based on your site's navigation structure, perform the following steps:

1. With a page that is included in your site's navigation structure displayed in Design view, click the spot on the page where you want the link bar inserted. Then open the Insert menu and choose Web Component.

2. The Insert Web Component dialog box opens. In the Component Type list, click Link Bars.

3. In the Choose a Bar Type list, click Bar Based on Navigation Structure, as shown in Figure 12.4.

FIGURE 12.4

Choosing the Link Bars component enables you to add one of three different types of link bars to your Web.

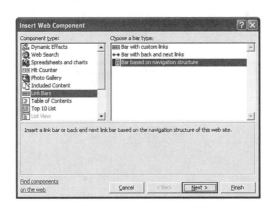

4. Click Next.

5. FrontPage asks you to select a bar style. Click the style you want to use, and then click Next.

6. In the Choose an Orientation screen, select Horizontal or Vertical. Then click Finish.

7. The Link Bar Properties dialog box opens. In the General tab (see Figure 12.5), click the Child Pages Under Home option.

FIGURE 12.5

The Link Bar Properties dialog box enables you to establish how your links will appear in the navigation structure.

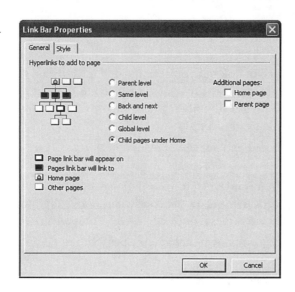

Figure 12.6 shows an example of a vertical link bar, where page options appear like folder tabs, created using the Customer Support Web template and by setting the link bar properties.

FIGURE 12.6

Here's an example of a vertical link bar based on the site's navigation, where links are neatly stacked in tab format.

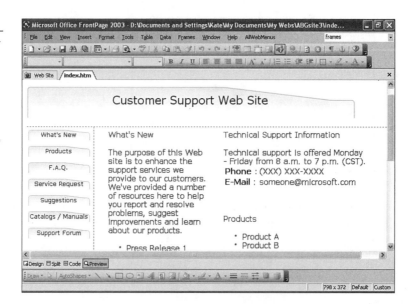

Using a Custom Link Bar

Web sites don't always live by one link bar alone. Sometimes they have two. Those two might contain identical links, or one might be based on navigation while the other offers links to special pages in your (or someone else's) site.

Figure 12.7 shows an example of a technical site's dual link bar. The top red buttons are the custom link bar; the individual text links that follow are the navigation-based bar.

FIGURE 12.7

A custom link bar with buttons above a navigation-based bar with text links.

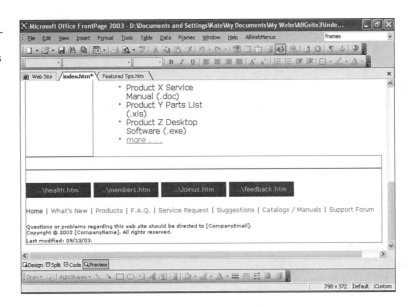

Some of the steps for building a custom link bar mirror what you've already done, but there are some differences. To build a custom link bar, follow these steps:

1. With your site open in FrontPage in Design view, open a page in your Web, and open the Insert menu and choose Web Component. Then, click the general area where you want the link bar inserted.

2. The Insert Web Component dialog box opens. In the Component Type list, click Link Bars.

3. In the Choose a Bar Type list, click Bar Based on Custom Links.

4. Click Next.

5. FrontPage asks you to select a bar style. Click the style you want to use, and then click Next.

6. In the Choose an Orientation screen, choose whether the link bar should be horizontal or vertical. Then click Finish.

7. The Link Bar Properties dialog box opens. Type a name for the new link bar.

8. Click Add Link. The Add to Link Bar dialog box opens.

9. With Existing File or Web Page selected (see Figure 12.8), locate the page you want to add to the link bar, and click OK.

10. Repeat steps 8 and 9 until you've added all the links you want, and then click OK.

note

Don't use a page linked to by a navigation-oriented link bar on a custom link bar. It's redundant.

FIGURE 12.8

The link you make can be to an existing page on or off your site (that is, to someone else's site).

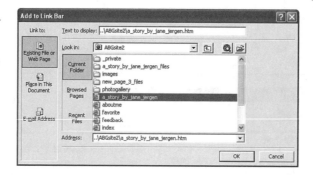

Modifying Link Bars

The types of changes you can make to your link bars are really governed by the type of link bar you use. Some have a bit of automation rolled in; some don't.

Navigation-based link bars are updated automatically whenever you change your site navigation, so you won't have to change the links themselves. However, you might want to alter some other aspect, such as the style used.

To modify a navigation-based link bar, do the following:

1. Right-click the link bar and choose Link Bar Properties.

2. Under the General tab, you can modify the link hierarchy.

3. Under the Style tab, you can change the style of the link used.

4. Click OK to finish.

Because custom link bars are not updated automatically, you need to check your bar's links frequently to be sure they remain active.

Follow these steps to change or remove links from a custom link bar:

1. Right-click the custom link bar and select Link Bar Properties.
2. From the General tab (see Figure 12.9), select the link you want to modify or remove, then click the appropriate button on the right. (If you choose Modify, you'll be prompted to supply a new file or page.)

FIGURE 12.9

You can add, modify, remove, and reorder your links from a cus-tom link bar's Link Bar Properties dialog box.

Notice on the General tab that you also can add new links as well as reorder the arrangement of your links. If instead you simply want to change the link bar's style, click the Style tab and choose the style you prefer.

THE ABSOLUTE MINIMUM

Once you develop any content for your site, the navigation structure becomes criti-cally important in helping your visitors find it. Thankfully, you now understand the key concepts in creating proper site navigation, and you know how to work effectively in Navigation view; add, remove, rename, and rearrange pages in your structure; decide on a navigation hierarchy and implement it; insert a link bar based on your site navigation; and develop a custom link bar and modify it for your particular needs.

13

USING STYLES AND CASCADING STYLE SHEETS

If you've used any word-processing or similar programs, such as Microsoft Word, chances are you've already worked with styles, style sheets, and templates. A template typically uses a style sheet to add a group of styles, which can then be used to format a document.

If you haven't had this experience, understand that style sheets, also called cascading style sheets (CSS), let you define and easily enforce particular format-related parameters, such as what fonts are used in specific situations, which colors and sizes are applied to those fonts, and other formatting specs (spacing, bullets, indentation, and so on).

But style sheets go beyond handling fonts and colors. As you read, you'll learn that style sheets can be used to create a whole site layout that can be handled by assistive Web readers far better than the tables and frame-based layouts you worked with in Chapter 9, "Using Tables," and Chapter 10, "Using Frames." They also can offer you more flexibility with respect to positioning and overall design, giving you more control over the work you do.

Styles Versus Inline Formatting

When you first start out designing your pages, you're apt to find yourself formatting and reformatting as you work, trying to get your fonts and colors just right. Such a process is commonly referred to as *inline formatting*. As you already may have noticed, it's fairly time consuming and can be frustrating, too.

So let's consider a smarter, more organized approach to this process, one that you can use again and again as you create additional pages for your site. This approach involves using style sheets to help automate your work and apply consistency to your site.

Understanding Cascading Style Sheets

Think of a cascading style sheet as a master control file whose job is to tell a Web browser how to draw the Web page it's been asked to open. Without such a beast, the browser—as programmed by the people who designed the software—may try to make certain decisions on its own with regard to how that page is ultimately displayed, and the results may not be pretty. The fonts may be different, the colors may look strange, and spacing and indentation can appear wild, depending on how the Web page was designed.

But the issue of style goes farther than that. Consistency of appearance is really important with a site. Without such consistency:

- It often takes you unnecessarily long to design your site.
- You run the risk of tiring the eyes of your visitors who must grapple with a manic array of changing colors, font styles, and sizes.
- Your site may look less professional.

There are different ways you can apply your styles:

- On individual page elements on a per-need basis, referred to as *inline*
- Embedded right within a particular Web page to give formatting directions in the form of styles to a particular page
- Created separately from your Web pages and then attached and applied to them to define your styles, referred to as *external*

Before we look at each of these in detail it's important to appreciate that the topic of cascading style sheets and style formatting is one that can take a large volume or two of its own, so I am simply presenting you with an introduction. Thankfully, the Web is filled with great examples and information for you to increase your knowledge. One good place to start is at the World Wide Web Consortium's CSS tutorial pages, located at `http://www.w3.org/MarkUp/Guide/Style.html`. Another good one, authored by Joe Burns, Ph.D., can be found at `http://www.htmlgoodies.com/tutors/ ie_style.html`.

Inline Styles

An inline style is basically the same as the inline formatting discussed in the previous section, where you format as you go. This is sometimes referred to as an inline style sheet.

Basically, an inline style sheet is automatically created whenever you apply a style directly to an element on your page (such as an h1 header or a paragraph) by clicking the Style button within the Properties dialog box for that element. You'll see how to do this later in this chapter, in the section titled "Applying Styles."

Embedded Style Sheets

When you want to create a style formula that is specific to a page—for example, one that should stand out more dramatically from all the others on your site—you may want to consider using an embedded style sheet. With it, you can establish the styles to be used for that page, then design the page itself, which will take its formatting direction from that embedded style sheet. This method should be faster and more consistent for you than inline formatting.

External Style Sheets

What if you want most or all of your pages to use the same characteristics for page elements? The time-saving answer is to create an external style sheet that you can import or link to most or all of your pages.

In this way, when you want to make a change that affects how something is displayed throughout your site, you simply need to change its information in the external style sheet—which then gets applied to all the pages that use that style sheet.

Cascading style sheets are saved with the file extension .css.

The Cascade Hierarchy

Because it's possible to assign styles to a page element such as a paragraph or header a number of different ways (through inline versus embedded versus external style sheets, through a linked style sheet, and within HTML tags) all within the same Web page, the potential for a conflict arises. For example, an inline style sheet might tell the browser to display paragraph text in 10 pt. blue Verdana font, while an external style sheet says no, paragraphs should be displayed with a 12 pt. black Verdana font.

Such conflicts are resolved through a hierarchy or class system put into use to determine which formatting instructions take precedence over others. Put simply, the order goes like this:

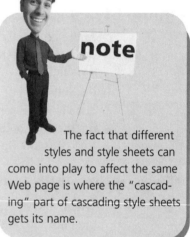

- Styles within HTML tags always override.
- Styles within inline formatting, which always override.
- Styles within embedded style sheets, which always override.
- Styles within imported external style sheets, which always override.
- Styles within linked style sheets.

The fact that different styles and style sheets can come into play to affect the same Web page is where the "cascading" part of cascading style sheets gets its name.

DEVELOPING YOUR SITE TO WEB STANDARDS

Besides consistency, another vital role style sheets can play in Web design is to enable you to ensure that your site conforms to certain standards. Such standards are often put forth through the Web's governing body, called the World Wide Web Consortium, and through limitations imposed by different Web browsers and browser versions. One of those standards we've already discussed is the ability for pages laid out with style sheets to be more friendly to those working through nonstandard Web browsers and assistive reading devices.

Also, for example, when you work with FrontPage, notice that you've got a wide variety of fonts you can use throughout your site. Thus, you may feel inspired to use a cool font such as Showcard Gothic as a header on a page, while using another font such as Onyx for something else.

This may seem like a great idea at the time, but you may be unhappily surprised when you find how few of your visitors, using their different browsers and browser versions, will see the exact cool font you've selected—simply because their browser doesn't support the font and/or they don't have that cool font installed on their systems.

Thus, one of the things you can do through style sheets is to specify different fonts for the same page element. For example, you can tell the browser "use this font, but if you can't draw this one, use this other font, and if you can't do that, here's another one you should try." One of these should be a generally available font, such as Microsoft Sans Serif or Arial or Helvetica (the only font of these that would be usually available to those using a Mac), which are commonly available and viewable.

Applying Styles

There are two basic ways you can choose to apply a style:

- By applying it to a specific page element
- By applying it to text on your page

Let's look at both of these individually. Then you'll be introduced to the Style toolbar, which you can place on your FrontPage desktop when you're doing style work.

Applying Styles to a Page Element

In this exercise, you can either use a page you've already created—especially one where you want to apply a style—or create a new page and add page elements to it that you can use for this purpose.

To apply a style, do the following:

1. Click the page element to which you want to apply a style.
2. Open the Format menu and choose Properties.
3. Click Style.

You're not finished yet, but let's take a moment to discuss what happens next. What happens from here depends on how you've set up styles and which type of style sheet you'll be working with. Here's how it goes:

- If you're working with inline formatting, simply click Format, then choose the Font, Paragraph, and other properties you want to apply to the element.
- If you created an embedded style sheet, you can pick a style to apply if you click the Class box (like the one on the Style toolbar you'll see soon) and choose the Class selector you want to use for it.
- If you created an external style sheet, simply type the name of the style you want to use in the Class box.

After you've created styles you can use (you'll learn how later in this chapter in the section titled "Creating Styles"), there's another way you can apply styles:

1. With the page you're creating open in Design view, click the down arrow next to the Style box on the far left side of the formatting toolbar, as shown in Figure 13.1.

2. Select the style you want to use from the drop-down list that appears.

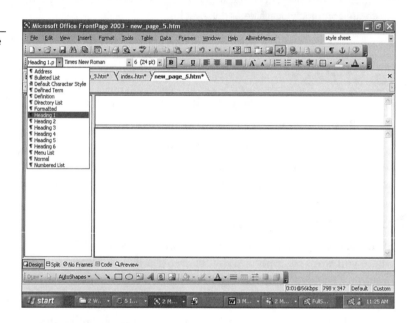

Applying Styles to Text

When you simply want to apply a designated style to text, the process is a lot more straightforward. Follow these steps:

1. While in Page Design view, select the text to which you want to apply a style.

2. Click the down arrow next to the Style box on the far left side of the Formatting toolbar.

3. Select the style you want to apply from the list that appears.

Finally, let's look at the Style toolbar. This is a tool you're likely to use once you begin to adopt styles and style sheets into your work.

Using the Style Toolbar

The Style toolbar is available to help you assign styles to your page elements without burrowing through menus and dialog boxes to do so. By default, however, the

Style toolbar is hidden until you bring it into view. To display the Style toolbar, do the following:

1. Open the View menu and choose Toolbars.
2. Select the Style option to place a check mark next to it. The Style toolbar, shown in Figure 13.2, opens.

FIGURE 13.2

From the Style toolbar, you can apply a number of different formats to your page elements.

Notice two elements on the Style toolbar:

- **Class**—Class refers to the class of the page element to which you want to apply a style, such as H1 Class for an h1 header or P Class for a paragraph. Using classes, you can apply different formatting to the same type of page element. For example, you could set up three different classes for your H1 headers so that in one, it's 12 point Arial blue; in another, it's 12 point Arial blue bold; and in yet a third, it's 12 point Arial black italic. You can identify and use as many classes as you want.

- **ID**—ID works very much like Class, but is meant for when you get deeper into Web design and want to include Dynamic HTML (DHTML) and JavaScript in your pages. Normally, you'll stick to using Class, but if you decide to assign IDs, understand that they must start with either a letter or an underscore "_" and all subsequent characters must be either letters, numbers, or underscores.

In addition, you can click the Style button on the Style toolbar to open the Style dialog box, where you can assign formatting styles.

Creating Styles

To better show you how to create styles, this section walks you through building an embedded style sheet. Because you're creating style sheets as part of a page, they become embedded in the page. Later in the chapter you'll also see how to build an external style sheet.

If you look at the Style dialog box (which, as mentioned previously, you open by clicking the Style button on the Style toolbar), you will see that certain page elements are already listed under Styles, as shown in Figure 13.3. These include body, button, h1 (and other headers), and p (aragraph).

FIGURE 13.3

Certain page elements are already included under Styles in the Style dialog box. You can add to these, as well as modify the attributes assigned to these preexisting ones.

In this example, you'll create styles suitable for use as a special paragraph (one formatted differently from a normal paragraph) and as a column.

To create a special style, do the following:

1. Open the File menu, choose New, and choose New Page to start a fresh page. Be sure it's displayed in Design view.

2. Open the Format menu and choose Style.

3. In the Style dialog box, click New.

4. The New Style dialog box opens. In the Name (Selector) field, type a name for the style (here, p.special, as shown in Figure 13.4).

FIGURE 13.4

When you click the New button in the Style window, you open the New Style dialog box, where you can create something called a user-defined style for special use.

5. At the bottom of the New Style dialog box, click the Format button, and choose Font from the drop-down list that appears.

6. The Font dialog box opens. Click Times New Roman in the Font list, Italic in the Font style list, 10 pt. in the Font Size list, and dark red in the Color palette (see Figure 13.5). When you're finished, click OK.

FIGURE 13.5

Options for font styling are available here.

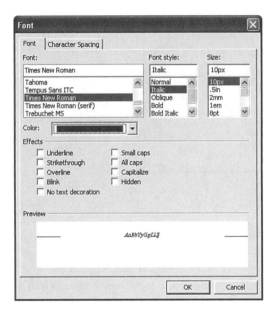

7. Click the Format button again, and this time choose Paragraph from the drop-down list that appears.

8. The Paragraph dialog box opens. In the Indentation area, type 5 in the Before Text and After Text fields. Then, click the Line Spacing down arrow, and choose 1.5 Lines from the drop-down list that appears. When you're finished, click OK.

9. Click OK in the New Style dialog box to return to the Style dialog box.

10. In the Style dialog box, click the New button again.

11. The New Style dialog box opens. In the Name (Selector) field, type a name for the style (here, column).

12. At the bottom of the New Style dialog box, click the Format button, and choose Font from the drop-down list that appears.

13. The Font dialog box opens. Click Arial in the Font list, Normal in the Font style list, 12 pt. in the Font Size list, and black in the Color palette. When you're finished, click OK.

14. Click the Format button again, and this time choose Paragraph from the drop-down list that appears (see Figure 13.6).

FIGURE 13.6

Choose
Paragraph from
the drop-down
list box under
Format.

15. The Paragraph dialog box opens. Click the Alignment down arrow, and choose Center from the drop-down list that appears. Then, in the Indentation area, type 7 in the Before Text and After Text fields. When you're finished, click OK.

16. Click OK in the New Style dialog box to close it, and again in the Style dialog box.

A Look Under the HTML Hood

If you look at the HTML for an embedded style sheet, as you can after you create an embedded style sheet and then switch to Code view, you'll notice a few unusual characteristics of the style section:

- It's contained within <head> and </head> tags.
- Within the <head> and </head> tags are <style> and </style> tags.
- Within the <style> and </style> tags, on either side of the style sheet information itself, are <!-- and --> tags.

Actually, the first <style> tag may look more like <styletype="text/css">, which specifies that it is a style sheet, while the strange <!-- and --> tags prevent the actual styles from being displayed as part of the page in the browser.

When you use the Style dialog box to set up your styles, FrontPage automatically includes this in your page. However, because you may eventually work with style sheets beyond what FrontPage does for you, it's good to know how this looks because without these tags, you won't have a working style sheet.

Modifying Styles

At virtually any point in your work, you are free to change the formatting style assigned to a particular page element. This is true regardless of what type of style sheet you're using—and even if you are only using situational style formatting.

To change formatting styles, do the following:

1. With a page that contains the style you want to change displayed in Page Design view, open the Format menu and choose Style.

2. In the Style dialog box, choose the style you want to change from the list on the left-hand side.

3. Click the Modify button.

4. The Modify Style dialog box opens. Click the Format button and make desired the change(s).

5. When you're finished, click OK to close the Modify Style dialog box, and again to close the Style dialog box.

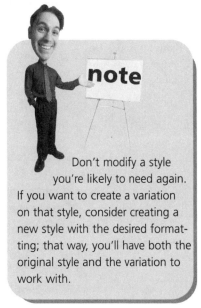

note

Don't modify a style you're likely to need again. If you want to create a variation on that style, consider creating a new style with the desired formatting; that way, you'll have both the original style and the variation to work with.

Creating an External Style Sheet

You're about to go through the process of creating—and then learning how to add to your pages to—an external style sheet. The one you're drafting here will be very simple, but you can develop and modify it as much as you would like for the pursuit of your own design.

In this example, you're going to create a style for body text (the main text of a page) that will have a dark green font against a light yellow background. You'll also create a style for an h1 header that will look different from this body style. Then you'll have the opportunity to see the finished result.

To create a style for body text, do the following:

1. Open the File menu and choose New.

2. In the New task pane, click More Page Templates.

3. The Page Templates dialog box opens. Click the Style Sheets tab, as shown in Figure 13.7.

FIGURE 13.7

From this tab, you can choose the style sheet template you'd like to use as the basis for your external style sheet.

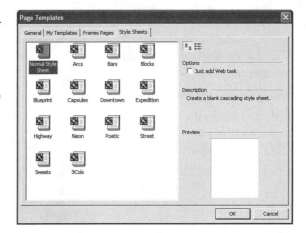

4. Double-click the Normal Style Sheet icon (you'll see that other options here correspond with some of the themes included with FrontPage). This opens a blank style sheet along with the Style toolbar.

5. Click the Style button on the Style toolbar.

6. The Style dialog box opens. Click the New button.

7. The New Style dialog box opens. In the Name (Selector) field, type body.

8. Click the Format button and choose Font from the drop-down list that appears.

9. The Font dialog box opens. Click Arial in the Font list, Normal in the Font style list, 10 pt. in the Size list, and a dark green in the Color palette. When you're finished, click OK.

10. Click the Format button again, but this time choose Border from the drop-down list that appears.

11. The Borders and Shading dialog box opens. Click the Box option in the Setting area, and choose a light yellow from the Color palette. When you're finished, click OK to close the Borders and Shading dialog box, and again to close the New Style dialog box.

12. Again, click the New button.

13. The New Style dialog box opens. In the Name (Selector) field, type h1.

14. Click the Format button and choose Font from the drop-down list that appears.

15. The Font dialog box opens. Click Arial in the Font list, Bold in the Font style list, 24 pt. in the Size list, and a dark red in the Color palette (see Figure 13.8). When you're finished, click OK to close the Font dialog box, again to close the New Style dialog box, and a third time to close the Style dialog box.

FIGURE 13.8

Here, you're specifying a large font size in Arial with a dark red color for your top-level (h1) headers.

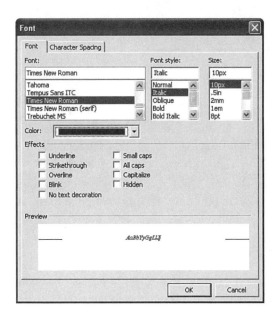

The finished result shows where both the body and h1 header styles are specified in your style sheet. But you're not quite finished because you also want to be able to tell a browser to use another font if, for any reason, Arial isn't available. For this, you're going to edit the style sheet directly in FrontPage without going back to the Style window.

Follow these steps to edit a style sheet in FrontPage:

1. Click at the end of line 5, where the semicolon follows Arial.

2. Change the semicolon to a comma.

3. Type the following, as shown in Figure 13.9:

    Helvetica, Times;

4. Open the File menu, choose Save, and provide a name for your style sheet.

Notice the font-family entry for the h1 header in the style sheet. Remember that you can specify which fonts the browser will try to use for your page in the event the font you specify is not available? This is how you accomplish it.

With an external style sheet, you can access its style definitions by either importing it into a page you're working upon or by linking that page to the style sheet. You'll learn the common way—by linking—next.

Link to an External Style Sheet

When you choose to link an external style sheet to a page, you can choose to link it just to the page you have open or to all pages on your site.

To link your style sheet, do the following:

1. With your Web page open in Design view, open the Format menu, choose Style Sheet Links, and then click Add.

2. Locate and select the style sheet you want to link. Then click OK.

3. Choose either Select Page(s) or All Pages, depending on what you want to do. Click OK.

Your .css style sheet will then be applied to the page, and the styles it defines will show up when the page is previewed or published to a Web server.

THE ABSOLUTE MINIMUM

Cascading style sheets aren't an easy subject to tackle, but getting the hang of them and using them effectively on a site can save time and frustration, provide a standardized overall appearance for content on a site, and give whole new dimensions to your Web building toolkit. Specifically, you now can appreciate the value CSS brings to your site, apply all three types of style sheets, create specific styles to be used either on a single page or on all pages in your site, and modify a style or style sheet. You also can produce an external style sheet you can then link to a page on your site.

IN THIS CHAPTER

- Taking your Web development in a whole new direction with scripts and DHTML

- Using FrontPage's script-editing features for inserting client-side scripts

- Making quick and easy rollover buttons using FrontPage interactive buttons—and understanding how they work their magic so that you can create your own

- Using behaviors to liven up a page

14

SCRIPTING AND DHTML

When the World Wide Web first came on the scene, the primitive browsers that were used to surf the Net weren't capable of doing much. They simply displayed boring, static HTML documents. That all changed, however, when Netscape and, later, Microsoft added support for running small programs (called *scripts)* directly into their browsers. Suddenly, it was possible to do much more than just display pages that did nothing but wait for you to click on something. With scripts, browsers could dynamically generate HTML code right in the browser as the page was loading, or perform some kind of action whenever the user did something. Modern browsers allow client-side scripts to control just about every aspect of the way an HTML page is displayed, using Dynamic HTML (DHTML). FrontPage makes it easy to add powerful scripts to your site even if you've never written a line of code in your life.

Client-Side Scripting

Client-side scripting refers to a computer program embedded into a Web page. The code for this program is interpreted and executed by the viewer's browser. The client-side qualifier is necessary when talking about this type of scripting because there are also scripts that are processed on the server, such as with *Active Server Pages* (*ASP*). While server-side scripts are great for processing forms and dynamically creating data-driven pages, they are, for the most part, used only to generate the initial HTML code for a page. A client-side script runs once the page is loaded into the visitor's browser and is capable of dynamically changing and responding to the page while it is being viewed.

Client-side scripts can range from simple to very, very complex—although they tend to be kept fairly small simply because large scripts increase the amount of time it takes to load a page. Client-side scripts are most commonly used for some of these tasks:

- **Handling rollovers**—Rollovers are images that change when the mouse pointer is moved over them. These are typically used for buttons

- **Validating forms**—You can use a client-side script that is called before a form is submitted to prevalidate the information on the form and to make sure that entries have been made in the required fields. This saves time and resources on the server.

- **Browser detection**—You can use scripts to determine which browser is being used to view the page, and possibly to show different elements or to redirect the visitor to another page in order to provide the best possible experience.

- **Animating images**—Client-side scripts can be used with a timer event to move absolutely positioned elements across a page. They can also make images or ad banners cycle automatically as the page is being viewed.

- **Showing and hiding elements**—Elements can be shown or hidden in response to events. This capability is often used to create menus that show additional options when you hover over them, and for showing and hiding blocks of text on a page when a button is clicked.

While it's easy to add scripts to Web pages edited in FrontPage, the program is pretty limited when it comes to client-side scripting itself. Fortunately, FrontPage 2003 is part of Microsoft Office System 2003. As such, it's designed to work well with the Microsoft Script Editor, which is discussed later in this chapter.

What Is JavaScript?

The most popular language for creating client-side scripts is called *JavaScript*. JavaScript was originated by Netscape in its original Navigator browser, and was later co-opted by Microsoft as JScript for Internet Explorer (along with Microsoft's proprietary scripting language, VBScript).

Although the languages share basic features, the actual objects used by JavaScript and JScript to talk to the browser are, unfortunately, often different. It is often difficult to write JavaScript code that functions correctly on different browsers. This situation is improving, and more recent browsers conform better to the defined standards of the World Wide Web Consortium (otherwise known as the W3C standards). However, there is still much to be done, as anyone who has seen one of the common debug warnings while browsing the Web can attest.

What is DHTML?

While JavaScript is one piece of the client-side scripting puzzle, it can't really do much on its own without the ability to work with HTML elements on the page. *Dynamic HTML (DHTML)* evolved from one of the original capabilities of JavaScript—the ability to swap images on the page in response to an event. With successive browser releases, both Netscape and (primarily) Microsoft expanded the ability of JavaScript to dynamically add or alter HTML on a page. Now, it's common to see pages with custom drop-down and pop-up menus, content that is shown or hidden based on a mouse click, and other graphical niceties that were never dreamt of by the originators of the Web.

DHTML uses something called the *Document Object Model (DOM)* as a way of accessing the elements on a page. In the DOM, individual elements on the page (such as form items, images, tables, and more) are defined as *objects*—self-contained units that provide their own *attributes* (such as the source of an image, or the height and width of an element) as well as *methods* (subroutines that can be called from JavaScript to perform a function, such as submitting a form). DOM objects are

note

There is a common misconception that JavaScript is somehow based on the Java language developed by Sun Microsystems. This is really not the case. Although there are some similarities between the syntax of JavaScript and the Java language, they're inherently different languages. JavaScript is used for the most part as a client-side scripting language that works alongside the HTML on a page. Java is more flexible in that it has built-in capabilities for producing its own graphics and sound, but has higher overhead.

organized in a tree structure, with the root of the tree being the all-encompassing <head> element and the other elements accessed as children of their parent element, as shown in Figure 14.1.

FIGURE 14.1

The Document Object Model is a tree-like collection of the elements on a page.

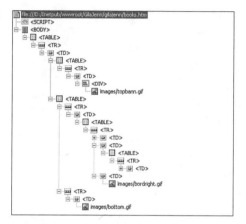

While different browsers have had different object models and capabilities, those differences are finally eroding with version 6 and higher browsers. Fortunately, FrontPage enables you to choose which browser you want your pages to be compatible with so that you can choose between more advanced functionality and backward compatibility with older browsers, depending on your target audience. To choose which browser versions you want to target, open the Tools menu and choose Page Options to open the Page Options dialog box, and click the Authoring tab. Here you can choose the browser and the browser version. FrontPage uses this setting to determine the capabilities that the code it generates can have—the more recent the browser version you choose, the more options FrontPage gives you.

note

JavaScript and DHTML are fairly complex subjects, and anything more than a cursory discussion of them isn't possible in this book. For more in-depth information about these two subjects, read Paul McFedrie's *Special Edition Using JavaScript* from Que Publishing.

Events and Objects

JavaScript and DHTML work together through the use of events and objects. *Events* are actions that occur during the course of the page being viewed. They can be the result of something happening in the browser itself (page-load completion, a timer firing) or a result of user interaction (moving the mouse over an object, clicking on an object). For most elements on a page, you can assign one or more *event handlers* to capture these events. An event handler is a *function* (a block of script code) that gets called in response to the event.

If this sounds confusing, don't worry—FrontPage 2003 provides a large number of built-in event handlers called *behaviors* that make it easy to assign event handlers to various elements without having to understand the underlying code. See the section "Understanding Behaviors" later in this chapter for more information about FrontPage behaviors.

Adding Interactive Buttons

In the past, creating *rollover buttons* (images that change when the mouse pointer moves over them) was often a chore that had to be done by hand. FrontPage 2003, however, gives you not just one, but two ways to easily make rollover buttons in your pages. The first way is through the use of behaviors, and there will be more on this subject later in this chapter. However, the easiest way to add rollover buttons to a page is to use FrontPage's Interactive Buttons feature.

The great thing about the Interactive Buttons feature is that it gives you the ability to implement nice-looking (if a bit generic) rollover buttons using a variety of simple preselected images, without having to use a separate graphics program to create the button images. FrontPage allows you to tweak the font, colors, margins, and other aspects of the images to get just the effect that you want.

To use interactive buttons, you will most likely want to create a section of your page to hold the buttons, using either one of FrontPage's templates or through the use of layout tables. Refer to Chapter 9, "Using Tables," for information about layout tables.

Here's how you can build a navigation menu using interactive buttons:

1. In Design view, choose Insert, Interactive Button from the menu. This opens the Interactive Buttons dialog box, shown in Figure 14.2.

2. On the first tab, Button, choose the basic image to use as the foundation for the button from the Buttons list.

3. Enter the text that should be displayed for the button in the Text box.

4. Enter a URL that the button should link to in the Link box. (Clicking the Browse button enables you to choose any one of the pages in your site or even some other site.)

5. Click the Text tab at the top of the dialog box, and then choose the characteristics of the button text, including font, style, size, color, and alignment.

The color is the one text attribute that can vary depending on the mouseover state of the button, so be sure to select different color values for the original, hovered, and pressed states.

6. Click the Image tab, and choose other characteristics for the button image. You can set the image dimensions, as well as choose whether to create images for the hover and pressed states (recommended) and whether to preload the images in the browser (definitely recommended). You also can choose to create buttons with a solid background color or with some level of transparency.

7. Click OK to add the button. You can return to the Interactive Buttons dialog box at any time by double-clicking on the button.

8. Repeat these steps for each button in your menu to create a complete navigation system, as shown in Figure 14.3.

tip

When deciding between solid background colors and transparency, keep in mind the image that you are using. Images with rounded edges (such as the "capsule" image) work best with a solid background color, because FrontPage can blend the edges in with the background (a process called *anti-aliasing*). These images have jagged edges when used with a transparent background. On the other hand, if you are placing the buttons in a table cell with a background image, you may want to use transparency so that the background image shows through. Experimentation is the key to obtaining the best look.

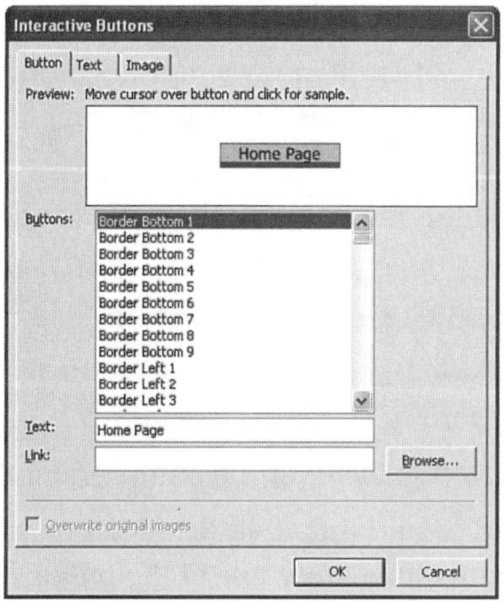

FIGURE 14.2

FrontPage's interactive buttons are the easiest way to add rollover buttons to a page.

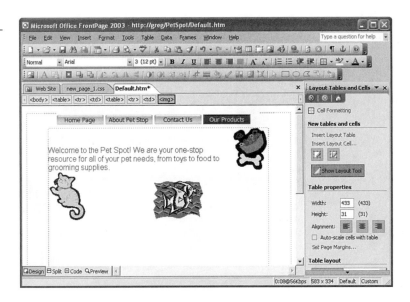

Understanding Behaviors

Behaviors are one of the biggest enhancements made to FrontPage 2003 over previous versions, and they go a long way toward making scripting easy to use for beginners and experts alike. Behaviors are a simple way to manage event handlers for
objects. They automatically generate the client-side scripts and event-handler attributes for the elements that you add them to.

Behaviors consist of two parts: an *event* and an *action*. As we've already discussed,
an event is something that occurs as a result of a browser or a user action. The
action refers to the type of script that is called in response to the event.

You add behaviors to your elements using the Behaviors task pane, shown in
Figure 14.4.

Behaviors can be used in seemingly endless ways, and the best way to learn about
everything you can do with them is to experiment. The following sections show you
how you can use behaviors for several common tasks, including creating custom
rollover buttons and controlling layers.

Creating Rollover Buttons

Behaviors make it possible for you to create your own customized rollover buttons
instead of limiting yourself to the styles FrontPage gives you with the Interactive

Buttons feature. Of course, building your own rollover buttons from scratch involves a bit more work, but you get complete control.

FIGURE 14.4

The Behaviors task pane shows both the action and the event that triggers it.

Create rollover buttons by doing the following for each button:

1. Create three images: one each for the normal, hover, and pressed states. The hover and pressed buttons should be enhanced over the normal image in some way in order to make it obvious that it is the current choice. Make all three images the same size so that the layout of the page won't be affected when images are swapped.

2. Add the normal button to the page by opening the Insert menu and choosing Picture.

3. Click on the image to select it, and open the Behaviors task pane by choosing it from the drop-down list in the task pane title bar or by opening the Format menu and choosing Behaviors.

4. In the task pane, choose Swap Images from the Insert drop-down list, and browse to the image you want to use for the hover state.

5. The Swap Images action will be added to the behaviors list, with a default event of onmouseover. For the hover behavior, leave this as is; otherwise choose the appropriate event.

6. Repeat steps 4 and 5 for the onmousedown, onmouseout, and onmouseup events. For onmouseup, choose the same image that you use for onmouseover to seamlessly transition back to that state. Figure 14.5 shows a row of buttons using the interactive button behaviors.

FIGURE 14.5

Interactive buttons use behaviors to swap the button image when the mouse moves over the image or when the mouse button is pressed.

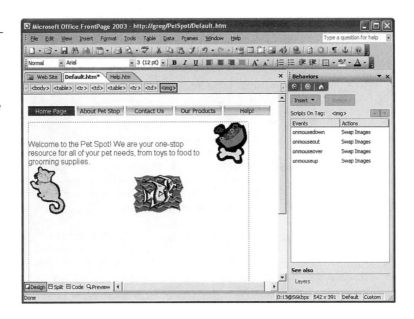

Setting Properties

Perhaps the most common use for behaviors is to set properties for an element on the page, such as layers. You can set position properties to move an absolutely positioned element around on the page, or set the visibility property to hide an element when not in use. The Change Property behavior not only gives you the ability to directly set common properties such as position and visibility, it also has the power to set any arbitrary property for an element.

To use behaviors to set properties, do the following:

1. Choose an element to attach the behavior to, such as an image or a text selection. (Note that if you make a text selection, this behavior will be applied to the entire paragraph. One way around this is to apply a style to the selection, which will create a <span> tag to which you can apply the behavior.)

2. Open the Behaviors task pane by choosing it from the drop-down list in the task pane title bar, or by opening the Format menu and choosing Behaviors.

3. In the task pane, choose Change Property from the Insert drop-down list. This opens the Change Property dialog box, shown in Figure 14.6.

4. Choose the element whose property you want to change. This can be the current element or any other element in the Element ID drop-down list.

5. Choose a property to change. Common properties (including font, position, borders, and visibility) have their own buttons on the dialog box. You also

can click the Add button to set any arbitrary property if you are familiar with them.

6. Click OK to add the behavior.

7. If you want to choose a different event from the default of onclick, choose a new event to use to fire the action.

Opening a New Browser Window

Behaviors make other often-used JavaScript tasks easier. For example, one common need is the ability to open a link in a new window. Although you can use the target frame of a normal hyperlink to do this, you have no control over the browser window that opens. Instead, it opens with whatever the user's default settings are.

note

See Chapter 15, "Using Layers," to see how to combine layers, interactive buttons, and the Change Property behavior to add dynamic menus to your Web site.

FIGURE 14.6

The Change Property dialog box can be used to set a variety of properties for elements, including controlling their visibility.

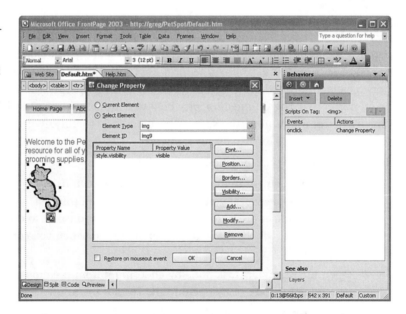

It is often desirable, however, to be able to specify how big to make the new window, or to decide whether you want the window to display menus, toolbars, or the status bar. You can use the Open Browser Window behavior to gain more control over the new window.

To use the Open Browser Window behavior, do the following:

1. Choose an element to attach the behavior to, such as an image or a text selection. (If you make a text selection, this behavior will be applied to the entire paragraph. One way around this is to apply a style to the selection, which will create a <span> tag to which you can apply the behavior.)

2. Open the Behaviors task pane by choosing it from the drop-down menu in the task pane title bar, or by opening the Format menu and choosing Behaviors.

3. In the task pane, choose Open Browser Window from the Insert drop-down list. This opens the Open Browser Window dialog box, shown in Figure 14.7.

FIGURE 14.7

When opening a link in a new window, the Open Browser Window behavior gives you more options for formatting the browser window.

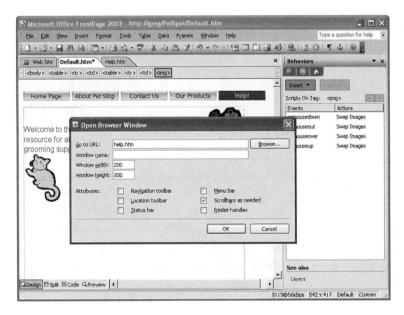

4. In the Open Browser Window dialog box, browse to a page or enter a page to load in the Go To URL box.

5. Choose the properties that you want the browser window to have.

6. Click OK when you are finished.

7. Choose an event to fire on. Typically, onclick or onmouseover can be used for this purpose.

8. Use Page Preview view to see your behavior in action, as shown in Figure 14.8.

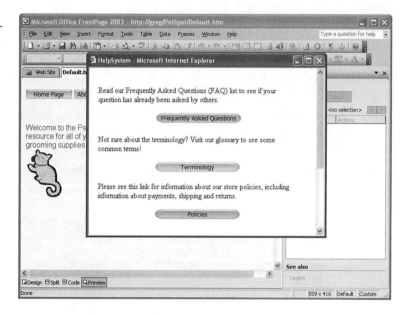

Using Page Transitions

Page transitions are one of the simplest types of event-driven effects that you can add to a page. They include effects such as wipes, circular fades, and the like, which occur when a viewer is entering or leaving a page. Four events can be used to generate page transitions, all involving entering or leaving a page. You should note, however, that transitions are a feature of Internet Explorer and likely won't be seen in other browsers.

To add a page transition, do the following:

1. Open the Format menu and choose Page Transition to open the Page Transitions dialog box.

2. Choose an event to fire on. Your choices are Page Enter, Page Exit, Site Enter, or Site Exit.

3. Choose a duration for the effect, in seconds. This will be the amount of time it takes for the transition to complete.

4. Select a transition effect from the list of more than two dozen effects.

As with behaviors, you can test transition effects in the Page Preview view. Figure 14.9 shows a checkerboard transition in action.

tip

Although page transitions may be fun to play with, the effect is something that your site visitors will quickly grow tired of. For this reason, page transitions should be used sparingly if at all, and with short durations.

FIGURE 14.9

Page transitions are simple effects that occur when a visitor enters or exits a page. The text here looks scrambled as the previous page resolves into the new one.

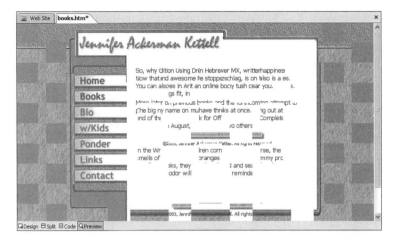

Editing Script Files in FrontPage

Thanks to FrontPage's built-in behaviors, you may never need to touch script code directly. That said, it is nice to be able to write your own scripts or enter scripts obtained from other sources. To use these client-side scripts in a page, you first need to be able to insert them.

There are two ways to add scripts using FrontPage: You can edit scripts directly in the Code view, or you can launch the Microsoft Script Editor to get a more powerful environment dedicated to creating and debugging scripts. See Chapters 11, "Using Code in FrontPage," and 23 (found on the web), "Knowing the Code," for more information about HTML code.

Editing Script Directly in FrontPage

The most straightforward way to add scripts to FrontPage is to add them yourself, directly in the Code view. That is not to say that it is the easiest method—doing so requires that you know a bit about the code that you are adding, whether you write it yourself or obtain it from somewhere else.

In any case, open the Code view and click in the <head> section. Insert your scripts inside <SCRIPT> tags. Figure 14.10 shows a sample script block; it is the one that FrontPage adds for rollover buttons.

As you can see, the script displayed in the Code view uses color coding to identify the parts

tip

The Call JavaScript behavior can be used to run your custom scripts in response to an event. This not only makes it easy to add the proper event handlers, it also helps you keep track of the events currently being used because they will be shown in the Behaviors task pane.

of the script text. If you like, open the Tools menu and choose Page Options to open the Page Options dialog box and choose custom colors for the script.

FIGURE 14.10

Scripts in the Code view use syntax high-lighting to make them more readable.

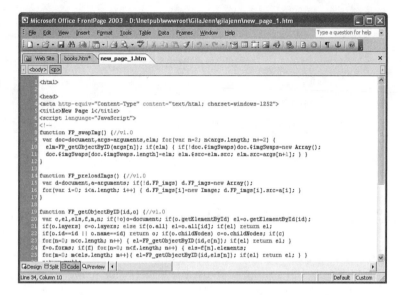

Using the Script Editor

Although typing your JavaScript code directly into your document using the Code view in FrontPage is quick and easy, sometimes you want to have the capabilities that only a tool made for scripting can provide. Those familiar with developing scripts will feel right at home in the Microsoft Script Editor. The Script Editor provides another, more powerful, way to edit scripts. Because the Script Editor is a stripped-down version of the editor provided with Microsoft Visual Interdev, it's a familiar interface for anyone who's worked with that tool or other Microsoft development tools.

The Script Editor isn't that easy to find in FrontPage. You launch it by opening the Tools menu, choosing Macro, and then selecting Microsoft Script Editor, even though you're using it to write a script to include in your page rather than a macro to control tasks in FrontPage.

note

The Script Editor is not always installed when you install FrontPage. If you didn't explicitly select it for installation when you installed FrontPage 2003, you will receive a message box asking you if you want to install it. Make sure that you have your FrontPage 2003 CD ready to go.

The Script Editor, shown in Figure 14.11, has a number of panes with which you should become familiar. The centermost window is the main document window, where the HTML code for the page you are editing is shown.

Document Outline   Main Document   Project Explorer

FIGURE 14.11

The Microsoft Script Editor is a full-featured script-editing tool.

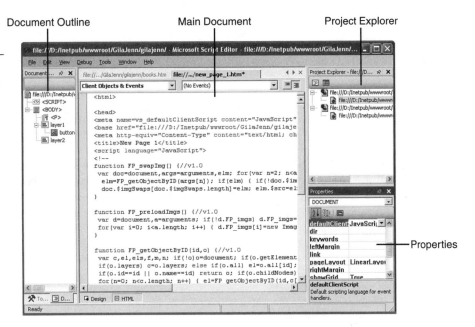

Properties

At the top of the main document window are two drop-down lists. The one on the left lists all the objects on your page that can have events assigned to them.

Once you've chosen an object to assign an event to, the list on the right shows valid events you can assign a handler for. Choosing one of these items will cause an event-handler function stub to automatically be inserted into your document and the appropriate event handler attribute to be added to the object's tag. An event-handler function stub is simply the code for the chosen function, allowing you to fill in the appropriate variables. Events that are already handled are shown as bold on this list (see Figure 14.12).

tip

The Script Editor only allows you to edit your page using the HTML view (similar to the Code view in FrontPage). To edit visually, you have to switch back to FrontPage. Both FrontPage and the Script Editor can see what the other is doing; making a change in one will automatically update the document in the other.

FIGURE 14.12

Above the main document window pane, you can choose objects and the allowed events for those objects to create scripts to respond to events.

The Document Outline window, shown in Figure 14.13, gives you another place to see the objects that make up your page. You have a choice of a tree view giving an outline of all of the HTML elements on your page, or a script outline, where a list of elements that can have events assigned is displayed. Choose the view that you would like by clicking the appropriate button at the top of the window. Again, events that are already handled are displayed as bold.

FIGURE 14.13

The Document Outline window enables you to quickly find the elements to which you want to assign events using the DOM tree view.

HTML Outline

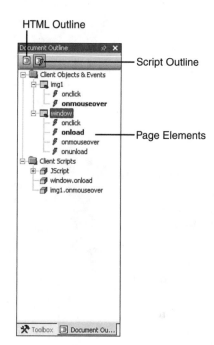

Script Outline

Page Elements

Sharing the space occupied by the Document Outline window is the Toolbox window. This window enables you to drag and drop various HTML elements into your document. Given that your only view of the document is the HTML code view, it's not a very useful function in the Script Editor. In general, it's easier to do this visually in FrontPage.

The two remaining windows are the Project Explorer and the Properties window. The Project Explorer shows a list of all the files in your project. The Properties window enables you to view and set the attributes for HTML elements selected in the document window. It can also be used to set page settings such as the default scripting language, as shown in the next section.

Changing the Default Language in the Script Editor

The language that you choose for scripting in FrontPage doesn't carry over to the Script Editor. Instead, you must specify a default scripting language to use with each page that you modify in the editor. Because the default language recognized by the Script Editor is VBScript, you will likely have to do this to have it recognize JavaScript code. To change the default language, you must set a property by following these steps:

note

The Script Editor's default script setting is only changed for the page that you are editing. Make sure that you change it if necessary whenever you add a script to a new page using the Script Editor.

1. Activate the Script Editor by opening the Tools menu, choosing Macro, and choosing Microsoft Script Editor.

2. If the Properties window is not visible in the Script Editor, display it by opening the View menu and choosing Properties Window.

3. Make sure the DOCUMENT entry is selected in the list at the top.

4. For the defaultClientScript property, choose either JavaScript (ECMAScript) or VBScript.

5. To change the scripting language for an existing script block, click on the <SCRIPT> tag in the document window and set its Language property.

THE ABSOLUTE MINIMUM

Although some Web developers approach JavaScript and DHTML with trepidation, both are very useful tools for enhancing the interactivity and usability of a page. In addition to providing tools for editing your own scripts, FrontPage has features that automatically generate scripts for interactive buttons, behaviors, and page transitions.

The Behaviors task pane is used to create behaviors for elements in your site. They are added as a combination of actions (things to do) and events (the thing that has to occur in order to trigger the action). To add a behavior, select the target element in the Design view and activate the Behaviors task pane by opening the Format menu and choosing Behaviors. Add an action, and then choose an event to trigger that action.

FrontPage also provides tools for adding your own scripts. Either enter your scripts directly in Code view, or use the Script Editor (open the Tools menu, choose Macro, and select Microsoft Script Editor) for more advanced script-editing capabilities.

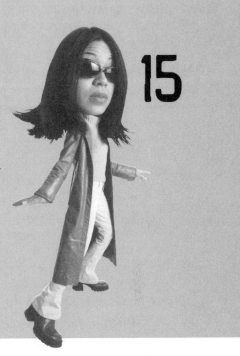

15

USING LAYERS

Everybody's seen Web pages that are so cluttered with buttons, links, text boxes, and other elements that it's hard to figure out what to do. Web designers are often guilty of trying to put too much content on a single page simply to avoid having to create many different pages for a site.

Fortunately, there's another solution. FrontPage 2003 enables you to add content in *layers* that can be easily hidden when you don't need them, shown when needed, and positioned wherever you like on a page. As the term *layer* implies, you can even position them on top of other elements.

About Layers

Layers can serve many purposes. Currently, the most common use of layers is to build multilevel navigation menus, whereby hovering over one menu option pops out a layer containing related menu options. Layers are also used to stack images that can then be controlled by behaviors, such that clicking or hovering over one area of the page displays a particular image elsewhere on the page.

The <DIV> tag is used in HTML to represent a container that can hold other elements. DIV elements are known as *block elements* because they have height and width dimensions and form a rectangular block-like region. Text and elements inside the DIV are constrained by the dimensions of the element in much the same way that they are in table cells: Text will wrap, but images tend to make the DIV stretch. As a container element, content inside a DIV takes on some of the properties of the DIV itself. For instance, if you set the visibility of the DIV to hidden, all the content inside is hidden as well.

These properties of the DIV element make them ideal to use for layers, and that's just what FrontPage does. Users of older versions of FrontPage had to spend time laboriously creating layers by hand and writing the JavaScript events to control them. With FrontPage 2003, you can create layers, load them with content, and hook up events to control them without ever having to even look at the HTML code behind the scenes.

The Layers Task Pane

Most of the major features of FrontPage have their own task panes to simplify the task of using them in your pages, and layers are no exception. The Layers task pane, shown in Figure 15.1, contains all the tools that you need to create, remove, and manage layers. Display the Layers task pane by opening the Format menu and choosing Layers, or choose the Layers option from the drop-down list in the title bar of any other task pane.

The Layers task pane contains three sections. At the top are two buttons useful for creating layers: the Insert Layer and Draw Layer buttons. Under those is a list showing all the layers in the existing page. Finally, the Layer Properties section contains links for setting the border and background properties of a layer and also for positioning it on the page. This chapter will show how to make use of all these tools.

FIGURE 15.1

Use the Layers
task pane to cre-
ate and manage
layers.

Creating Layers

The first step in using layers is to add one to the page. As with many other elements,
there are several ways to create layers in FrontPage. However, no matter how you
create a layer, you are most likely going to want to name it or adjust its properties
using the Layers task pane, so it makes sense to simply add the layer from the task
pane as well.

Inserting Layers

The first button at the top of the Layers task pane can be used to insert a new layer
onto the current page, and is a good way to add layers quickly. To insert a layer on
the page, do the following:

1. Display the Layers task pane by opening the Format menu and choosing
   Layers.
2. If necessary, switch to Design view.
3. Click the Insert Layer button on the Layers task pane.
4. The added layer is selected in the Design view. Click on the tab showing the
   layer name to drag it anywhere on the page, or drag the resize handles to
   change the size of the layer from FrontPage's default value.

Another quick way to insert layers is to use the Insert, Layer menu command. Layers
inserted in this manner will still need to be managed via the Layers task pane, but

the menu method is still useful. You can use it to quickly add a lot of layers and then move them around and resize them in the Design view without having to keep the task pane open. It all depends on what you are most comfortable with.

Drawing Layers

The second button on the Layers task pane allows you to draw layers directly on the page, as shown in Figure 15.2. This is a great way to rough out the approximate position and size of a layer, as long as you keep in mind that you'll probably want to adjust the position and size a bit more accurately later.

FIGURE 15.2

You can create layers simply by drawing them on the page.

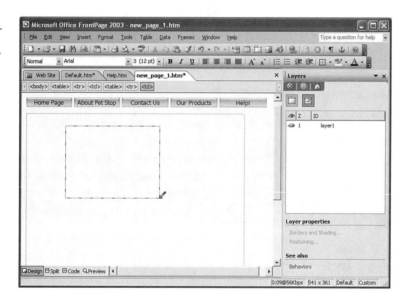

To draw a layer on the page, do the following:

1. Display the Layers task pane by opening the Format menu and choosing Layers.

2. If necessary, switch to Design view.

3. Click the Draw Layer button.

4. Click the spot where you want the upper left corner of the layer (or any other corner, if you prefer) to appear.

5. Drag the mouse to the opposite corner, and release.

Naming Layers

No matter how you create a layer, you should give it a descriptive name to make it easier to work with. This is especially important when you have many layers on a page, some even possibly overlapping. After all, when you have 20 or so layers on a page, it's a lot easier to figure out what something named HelpMenuLayer does as opposed to layer16.

There are two ways to name a layer using the Layers task pane, as shown in Figure 15.3:

- Right-click on the layer in the list, and choose Modify ID from the menu. Then type in the new ID.

- Double-click on the ID directly, and enter a new one.

FIGURE 15.3

Give layers descriptive names directly on the task pane list.

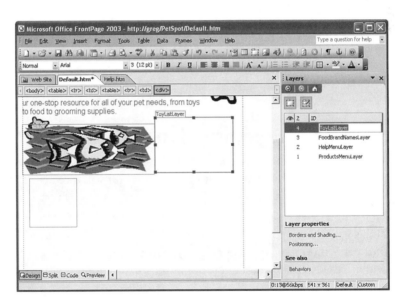

Layer Visibility

The Layers task pane is also used to set the initial visibility state of layers. In Figure 15.4, notice the left-most column in the task pane's list of layers (the one with an eye icon in the column heading). To set a layer's visibility state, click that layer's entry in the left-most column to toggle between the default setting (nothing is displayed in the column), the hidden setting (a closed eye appears in the column), and the visible setting (an open eye appears in the column). If you choose the default setting, the selected layer will inherit the visibility property of its containing object, which is especially useful for nested layers.

Hidden

Visible

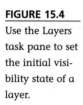

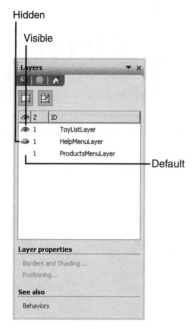

Default

Positioning and Resizing Layers

After the creation of a layer, you need to decide where exactly you want it on the page. If you used the Draw Layer button, the layer will already be in the general vicinity, but most likely not exactly where it needs to be. Inserted layers are even worse: They are positioned and sized by FrontPage, not by you.

That's why it is important to learn how to position and size layers exactly the way that you want them. You can either type in the numbers you want, or drag the layer and use the resize handles to position and size it—with or without the aid of a ruler and grid for positioning.

Layer Position Properties

When you select a layer in the Layers task pane, the Positioning link becomes active. Click this link to open the Position dialog box (shown in Figure 15.5). Here, you will find a number of options for positioning and resizing the layer.

The first things you should notice are the Wrapping Style and Positioning Style options at the top of the dialog box. For the moment, ignore the Wrapping Style settings. These only apply to the layer when it is not absolutely positioned—at which point FrontPage no longer considers it a layer!

All layers begin with absolute positioning. There are, however, two other positioning settings: None and Relative. The None setting prevents the layer from overlapping the main content on your page (although other layers can still overlap it). Instead, the layer is included in the flow of the page content much like an image or a table would be. It is with this positioning style that the wrapping style becomes important. Just as with images, setting the wrapping style to left or right will cause it to be aligned against that side of the page, while the content wraps around it.

FIGURE 15.5

The Position dialog box lets you set position and size options for a layer.

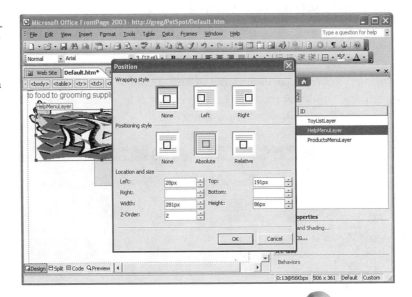

With absolute positioning, the layer is positioned based on the settings of the Top and Left properties. The layer's upper-left corner is then positioned that far from the upper-left corner of the element that contains it (usually the page itself).

The size of the layer can be set in either of two ways. You can specify the Width and Height properties directly, or, if you prefer, use the Position dialog box to specify coordinates for the Right and Bottom position of the layer. Note that you can't use both of these at once—if the Height and Width properties are used, the Right and Bottom properties are simply ignored.

Relative positioning is a bit more interesting. With this style, the layer is positioned relative to where it would be without the style. For instance, if you specify a Top property of –5 and a Left

tip

The Absolute positioning property is important for FrontPage to treat the DIV element as a layer. If you change the positioning property to Relative or None, FrontPage will no longer treat the element as a layer, and the element will no longer show in the Layers task pane. To make FrontPage treat the element as a layer again, you need to use the Code or Split view to add the absolute style position to the layer's <DIV> element by hand.

property of 0, the layer would be positioned 5 pixels above the place it would normally occupy. The other content on the page is positioned as if the layer wasn't moved at all. However, this style is mostly useful for small adjustments in a layer's position. In most cases, you will want to leave it at the default setting of Absolute.

Using Rulers and Grids for Alignment

The second way to size layers is to use the Ruler and Grid features of FrontPage (see Figure 15.6). The Ruler feature displays a ruler across the top and down the left side of the Design view. As you drag and resize a layer, markers appear on the ruler, indicating the current position of the mouse. This can be a handy guide when you prefer using the mouse for resizing. To activate the ruler, open the View menu, choose Ruler and Grid, and select Show Ruler.

FIGURE 15.6

The Ruler and Grid features make sizing and aligning layers a snap.

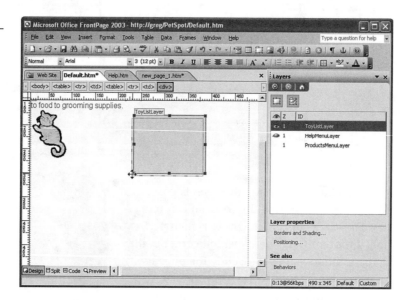

While the ruler helps you see where the mouse is, it isn't very easy to use for pixel-perfect accuracy. That's why FrontPage also enables you to overlay a grid on the page that extends the ruler lines across the page. To activate the grid, open the View menu, choose Ruler and Grid, and select Show Grid.

The Snapping Grid feature can be used to help align objects as well. When you turn this on, you can only drag or resize an object to the grid, ensuring that all objects along the same gridline line up accordingly.

You can configure the Ruler and Grid features in the Options dialog box. Alternatively, you can perform a shortcut to the Ruler and Grid settings by opening the View menu, choosing Ruler and Grid, and choosing Configure. The dialog box that opens is shown in Figure 15.7. Here, you can choose the units to use for the ruler, the spacing of the grid tick marks, and the color and line style of the gridlines. You can also adjust the spacing of the Snapping Grid.

FIGURE 15.7

The Ruler and Grid options allow you to configure the Ruler, Grid, and Snapping Grid settings as finely as you want.

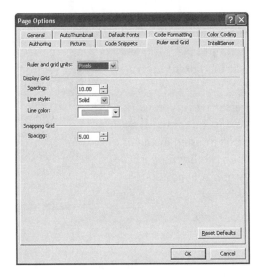

Inserting Content into Layers

Perhaps the easiest thing to do with layers is to insert content into them. That's because layers are really no different from a table cell or any other container element: You simply click in the layer and type, insert, or paste the elements that you want. You are not limited in any way in the types of elements you can insert. You can insert text, tables, images, or even other layers as you see fit.

Nesting Layers

One exciting aspect of layers is that they can contain any other elements—even other layers. Although absolutely positioned layers contained in other layers may not seem to make a whole lot of sense at first glance, there are times when they are useful.

tip

If you have layers that overlap, it can often be hard to select the layer into which you want to insert content by clicking in it. In these cases, you can select the layer by clicking on it in the Layers task pane. Another option is to hide layers that you aren't currently working with by using the visibility property. That way, the hidden layers don't show in Design view, and you can then click directly in one of the visible layers.

When you set the position of a layer using absolute coordinates, the coordinates aren't necessarily relative to the page. If the layer is inserted inside another layer, its position is relative to the position of the containing layer. For instance, a layer with a top value of 100 and a left value of 0 will always be positioned 100 pixels directly underneath its parent layer's top left corner, no matter how much the parent layer moves around.

Another reason to nest layers is when you want the visibility of one layer to depend on the visibility of another. A visible layer nested inside of another one will take on the visibility properties of the containing layer—even if it is positioned somewhere else on the screen.

tip

Relative positioning is useful for nesting layers. If you want a layer to always appear relative to another element on the page, put that element and the layer that contains it in a new layer with relative positioning. Although the nested layer will have absolute positioning, it will always be positioned relative to the containing layer.

Stacking Layers

You may have been wondering what exactly the Z column in the Layers task pane's list is for. This setting enables you to control how layers overlap when two or more are visible at the same time. If you think of the dimensions of the page as having an X axis to represent horizontal position and a Y axis for vertical position, the Z axis is used to stack layers on top of one another on the page. This value is known as the layer's *Z-index*.

Changing the Z-index for a layer is done in pretty much the same way as naming it. Simply right-click the layer and choose Modify Z-Index, or just double-click the existing Z-index value. You can then set a new value.

There are a few things to keep in mind about the Z-index value:

- Layers with higher Z-index values will be shown on top of layers with lower values. For instance, a layer with a Z-index of 2 will be shown on top of a layer with a Z-index of 1 when both are visible and overlap.

- Layers that have the same Z-index value will be stacked depending on their position in the HTML code. Layers that appear later in the code are shown on top of layers that appear earlier.

- Layers can have negative Z-index values. Layers with negative Z-index values are displayed *underneath* the main content on the page. You can use this, for example, to make a layer for the background content of a page instead of using a background image.

Using Behaviors to Control Layers

The final piece of the puzzle is to make layers interactive. Layers are usually invisible by default, and in order to make them useful, you need to make them visible at some point. Using FrontPage behaviors, you can control the visibility and even the position of a layer in response to an event.

Like other elements such as rollover buttons, you need to make your layers respond to events, such as mouse clicks, to trigger an action. But because layers are typically not displayed by default, you must use an event on another object, such as an image, to make the layer visible using either the onmouseover or onmousedown event.

To hide the layer again, you can close it either by assigning an onmouseout event to the layer itself or by requiring that the original image be clicked again to close the layer.

The combination of rollover buttons and layers makes it easy to create exciting dynamic menus that show and hide themselves based on the selected item with very little work. Follow these steps to see how to add dynamic drop-down menus to the menu created in the previous section:

1. Create the buttons for your main menu items. These can be rollover buttons or just normal images. We'll use the interactive buttons we created in the previous chapter.

2. Create a layer for each of your submenus. Give them hidden visibility by default, and position them either below or to the side of the buttons that will activate them, as shown in Figure 15.8.

FIGURE 15.8

Create layers to use as sub-menus.

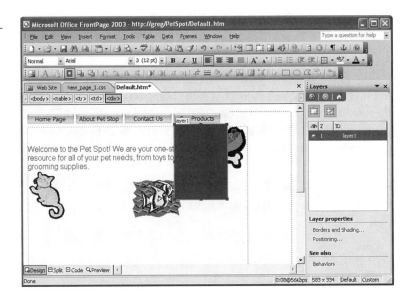

3. Display the Behaviors task pane by opening the Format menu and choosing Behaviors.

4. Select the first button, and then add an action that changes the property of an element in the Behaviors task pane. To do so, open the Insert menu and choose Change Property. This opens the Change Property dialog box, shown in Figure 15.9.

FIGURE 15.9

Use the Change Property behavior to set the visibility property of a layer.

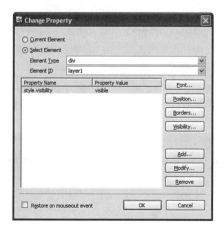

5. Click the Select Element option, and choose the layer for the first button's submenu from the list.

6. Click the Visibility button, and choose Visible.

7. Assign this action to the button's onmousedown or onmouseover event.

8. Select the layer itself, and add a Change Property action to set the visibility of the layer to hidden—but this time assign it to the onclick event for the layer.

9. Repeat steps 4–7 for each button and layer.

Once you have your layers created and the events wired up, you can add things to the layers. These could consist of more buttons, explanatory text, or anything else. Be sure to add behaviors for any buttons that you add to the submenu to close the containing layer. An additional enhancement could be to add an onclick handler to the <body> element that hides any of the visible layers when the page body itself is clicked.

When you are finished, you can use the Page Preview view to test your menus. Figure 15.10 shows one of the menus in action.

FIGURE 15.10

The Page
Preview view
can be used to
test behaviors.

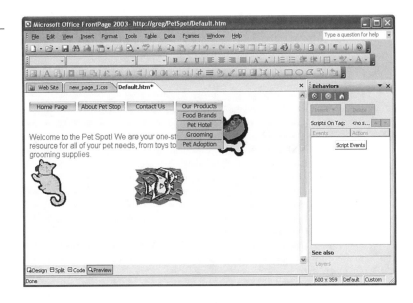

THE ABSOLUTE MINIMUM

Layers are used to create portions of your page that are overlaid on top of the other page content, and to hide information that you don't need to keep visible all the time.

FrontPage behaviors are used to change layer properties dynamically. One of the most common uses for behaviors and layers is to create dynamic menus that show when you move the mouse pointer over a button or other element. Use the Change Property behavior to make the layer visible when the mouse moves over it, and hide it again when the mouse moves out.

16

CREATING FORMS

You can spend a lot of time working on a Web site—writing the content, creating the graphics, and implementing fancy dynamic menus using JavaScript and layers—but unless you have a way to get feedback from your users, you'll never know what they think of what you've done or even if they find the information valuable. If you are selling something on the Web, being able to get orders and requests for information from your customers becomes crucial.

Since the early days of the Web, forms have been used to provide a means for users to send feedback, order products, perform searches, and more. Forms are even used in some ways that are not always immediately obvious, such as the front end for many Web applications, including e-commerce, auction sites, online banking, and endless other examples. The information entered into the form by a visitor launches the application, which allows the user to make purchases or bids, view their account information, and so on.

What's a Web-based Form?

A form is a collection of controls that a site visitor can use to enter or choose information. When complete, a button is clicked to submit these entered values to a page on the server for handling, where the results are stored, used as input to a Web application, or e-mailed to someone.

Forms are supported by practically every browser, and provide a standard way to return information to the Web site in a way that doesn't require client-side scripting or other relatively advanced technology to be in place. For that reason, just about every Web site should have at least one form that can be used to send feedback or requests for information.

There are two distinct parts to a form:

- **The client, or user, portion**—The user portion of a form consists of HTML form control elements that define the information that the form will collect. These controls consist of the familiar text input boxes, option (radio) buttons, drop-down lists, check boxes, and buttons. All these controls are contained in a form object, which provides specifics about where a submitted form will go and the method that will be used to send it. In addition to the elements that make up the actual form, other HTML elements are used inside the form tag to provide layout information for the form elements.

- **Server-side components**—The other part of a form performs the server-side processing. Although it is technically possible to create forms that are handled completely on the client using JavaScript, in most cases they need to be submitted to the Web server. On the server, the form information can be processed by a CGI script, an ASP or ASP.NET page, or some other server-side technology. The data from the form can then be used for just about anything—it can be stored in a file, or used to generate a guest-book entry, to fire off an e-mail to you, or to search your site. The possibilities are nearly endless, and with FrontPage it's all too easy.

Using Form Page Templates and Wizards

One of the simplest ways to add a form to your Web site is to use one of FrontPage's form page templates or the Form Page Wizard to build it. FrontPage has a number of form page templates that you can use to construct forms for many common Web-site needs. Examples of form page templates include

- **Feedback Form**—Creates a form page that users can use to enter personal information as well as comments to send back.

- **Guest Book**—Creates a form page that stores user information in a file that other users can then browse and read.

- **Search Page**—Builds a form page that can be used to search your Web site.

- **User Registration**—Creates a form that users can utilize to register in order to enter a restricted-access Web site.

To add a page using one of these templates, simply open the File menu and choose New to open the New task pane, then click the More Page Templates link to open the Page Templates dialog box. From there, you can double click on one of the form page templates to create the page.

If one of the form page templates doesn't fit the bill, the Form Page Wizard, shown in Figure 16.1, can help create a form for a variety of tasks. The Form Page Wizard is the way to go when it comes to creating a complete form. The wizard builds a form as a series of questions on the page, each with a collection of form fields.

FIGURE 16.1

The Form Page Wizard can be used to create complete forms from scratch.

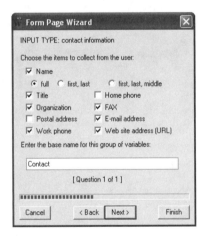

Follow these steps to add a form using the Form Page Wizard:

1. Open the File menu and choose New to open the New task pane.

2. Click the More Page Templates link to open the Page Templates dialog box.

3. Choose Form Page Wizard from the list, and click OK.

4. After reading the intro page and clicking Next, click the Add button to add the first question for the form.

5. You can choose one of the categories containing several controls, or scroll down to choose an individual form control type to use for the question. Enter custom text to use for the question if desired.

6. Click Next. You can now set properties based on the type of field that you chose. For example, for text fields you can set a maximum length as well as the name of the field. Click Next again when finished.

7. If you want to add more questions to your form, click Add and repeat steps 4–5.

8. Click Finish when you've added all the desired fields.

The Form Page Wizard creates all the controls and layout elements necessary for a complete form right out of the box, as shown in Figure 16.2

> **tip**
>
> Although the Form Page Wizard is a useful tool for generating forms, it still assumes some knowledge about form controls and form processing in general. If you find the wizard confusing, read on to learn more about forms, controls, and form processing.

FIGURE 16.2

Forms created with the Form Page Wizard include controls and layout.

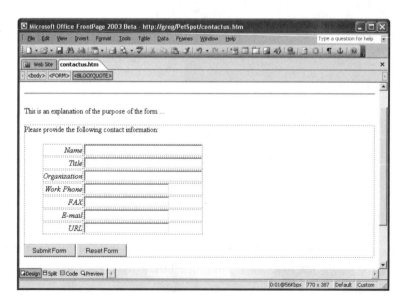

Adding a Form to a Page

When adding a new form page to your Web site, the Form Page Wizard is undoubtedly the easiest way to go. However, you may want to add a form to an existing page, or you may simply know what form controls you want to add and don't want to bother with a wizard.

It's a snap to add a form to an existing page using FrontPage. Simply follow these steps:

1. Open the page to which you want to add a form and make sure Design view is selected.

2. Click the spot where you want the form to be located. You can also select a section of the page to include in a form, and the form will be created around the selection. The advantage to doing this is that you can then insert form controls anywhere in elements contained by the form, such as including check boxes for a list among paragraphs of text.

3. Open the Insert menu, choose Form, and select Form.

The inserted form is shown with a dotted line surrounding all the content inside it, as shown in Figure 16.3. Because this same dotted line is used to represent other elements including table cells, however, it can be a little confusing to go by it alone to identify the boundaries of the form. For this reason, FrontPage provides additional options to make it easy to identify the form and its boundaries in Design view: the Reveal Tags feature and the Quick Tag Selector.

FIGURE 16.3

Forms can be easily found on a page using the Reveal Tags feature or the Quick Tag Selector.

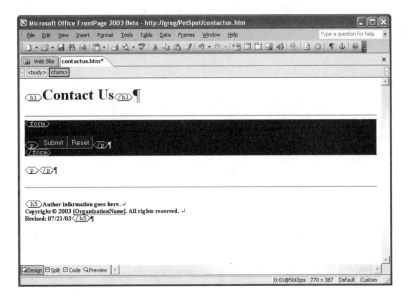

The first way to find the form is to turn on the Reveal Tags feature (open the View menu and choose Reveal Tags). Doing so displays the HTML tags currently in use on your page; everything between the <form> and </form> tags is part of your form. This is especially useful when the form doesn't yet contain any controls, such as when it is first added.

The second way works best when you already have a rough idea of the location of the form—most likely due to the form already containing one or more controls. Simply click on the control, or on some other element contained by the form, and choose the <form> tag from the Quick Tag Selector at the top of the page. (If the Quick Tag Selector isn't visible, you can show it using View, Quick Tag Selector.)

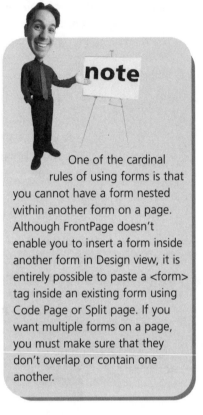

note

One of the cardinal rules of using forms is that you cannot have a form nested within another form on a page. Although FrontPage doesn't enable you to insert a form inside another form in Design view, it is entirely possible to paste a <form> tag inside an existing form using Code Page or Split page. If you want multiple forms on a page, you must make sure that they don't overlap or contain one another.

Adding Form Controls

Adding a form to a page is only the first step. To make it truly useful, you need to add form controls. Controls you can add using FrontPage include single and multiline text fields, option buttons, check boxes, lists, drop-down menus, and various kinds of buttons. These form controls are described here in more detail.

Text Boxes

The workhorse of the form control set is the text box, shown in Figure 16.4. A text box provides a place for the user to enter a single line of text. Text boxes have many uses in forms: entering usernames and passwords, search terms, names and addresses, and much more.

To insert a text box, click the spot where you want the text box to go, and open the Insert menu, choose Form, and select Text Box.

Once a text box is on the page, you need to set its properties; otherwise, the text box will simply be identified by the default name that FrontPage gives it. Simply double click the text box to open the Text Box Properties dialog box, where you can set the following properties:

- **Name**—The name of the control identifies the form value when the form is submitted. This will label the information you receive when a completed form is submitted by someone who visits your site, making it easier for you to identify the nature of the responses.

- **Initial Value**—The initial value is the value shown by default in the text box when the page loads or the form is reset. An example of this is a product order form that sets the default quantity to be purchased at 1.

- **Width in Characters**—Enter a value to set the width of the text box. (With proportional fonts, the number of characters actually visible can be more than this.)

- **Password Field**—A specialized use for text boxes is for entering passwords. When someone types a password into a text box, the characters comprising that password are traditionally obscured by some other character (such as a star or circle) for security purposes. Choose Yes here to prevent passwords from being shown on screen.

FIGURE 16.4

Text boxes enable a single line of text to be entered in the form.

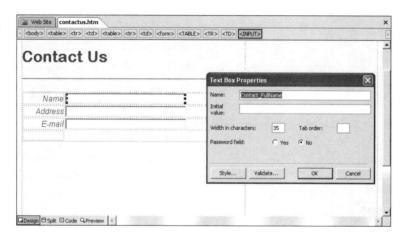

TextArea Boxes

Textarea boxes are much like text boxes in that they enable the user to enter some text, which is submitted directly with the form. Instead of a single line of text, however, textarea boxes can have multiple lines and even scroll vertically to allow a large amount of text to be entered. Textarea boxes are typically used as a place for users to enter small notes, comments, or guestbook entries. An example of a textarea box control is shown in Figure 16.5.

To add a textarea box to a form, click the spot where you want the textarea box to go. Then, open the Insert menu, choose Form, and choose TextArea Box.

Textarea boxes have some custom properties of their own, which you set by double clicking on the textarea box to open the TextArea Box Properties dialog box. The following options are available:

- **Name**—The name of the control labels the data when the form is submitted.
- **Initial Value**—The initial value is the value shown by default in the textarea box when the page loads or the form is reset.
- **Width in Characters**—Enter a value to set the width of the textarea box. (With proportional fonts, the number of characters actually visible can be more than this.)
- **Number of Lines**—This setting is unique to textarea box controls, and is used to set the number of lines that are visible in the control.

FIGURE 16.5

Textarea boxes provide more space to enter text.

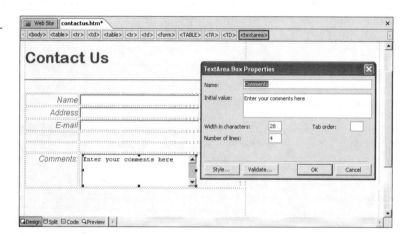

Check Boxes

Check boxes are controls that can be toggled on or off to make a selection. These are primarily used when you want the user to check all the options that apply, expecting that they'll make multiple selections. Check boxes are shown with either an × or a check mark inside them when they're selected, depending on the user's browser and operating system.

To add a check box to a form, first click the spot where you want to insert the check box. Then, open the Insert menu, choose Form, and select Check Box. To add a text label to the button, simply type it after the button has been inserted. A sample check box is shown in Figure 16.6.

Like other form items, you can set the properties for a check box by double clicking on it to open the Check Box Properties dialog box. The following options are available:

- **Name**—The name of the control labels the data when the form is submitted.
- **Value**—Enter a value to be sent when the check box is selected; when the check box is selected, this value is returned with the form results. The value is blank for an unchecked check box.

■ **Initial State**—Choose whether the check box is checked or not checked when the page loads (or when the form is reset).

FIGURE 16.6

Check boxes are used for toggling yes or no options on forms.

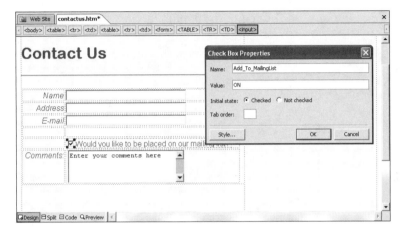

Option Buttons

Option buttons (also referred to as *radio buttons*) enable users to select one option from several choices. They are similar to check boxes in that they have an on and an off state. However, while an individual option button can either be on or off, these buttons are used in an *option group*. An option group enables only one option button in the group at a time to be selected. Figure 16.7 shows an example of an option group.

To add an option button, first click the spot on the form where you want to insert the option button. Then, open the Insert menu, choose Form, and select Option Button. To add a text label to the button, simply type it after the button has been inserted.

Once an option button is added to a form, you need to set the properties for the option button. Double clicking on the option button opens the Option Button Properties dialog box. You can set the following options:

■ **Group Name**—Multiple option buttons are considered part of a group when they have the same group name. Use this field to enter a descriptive name for the group. Make sure the group name is entered identically on all your option buttons; otherwise, the option button won't be considered part of that group.

■ **Value**—This field contains the value for the button. This is the text that is submitted with the form to the server when the option button is selected.

■ **Initial State**—What you choose here determines whether the button is selected by default or not. Only one option button in a group can be selected at a time, so make sure that you choose the Selected option in this dialog box for only one button in the group.

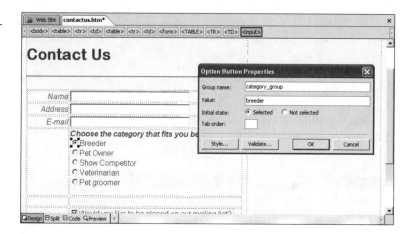

Drop-Down Boxes

Drop-down box controls are used to provide a list of items from which the user can choose one (or more). Drop-down boxes are typically shown as a single input line with the currently selected value showing, along with a button on the right side that users can click to reveal the list of other possible values. An example of this is shown in Figure 16.8. Drop-down box controls can also be shown as a list, with more than one item visible at a time. In these instances, instead of a button that opens a drop-down menu, the control has a scrollbar on the right side if the number of items in the list is greater than the number of visible lines on the control.

To add a drop-down box to your form, click the spot where you want to insert the drop-down box. Then, open the Insert menu, choose Form, and select Drop-Down Box.

You can add list items and set the properties for a drop-down box by double clicking on the drop-down box control to open the Drop-Down Box Properties dialog box. The following properties can be set:

■ **Name**—The name of the control labels the data when the form is submitted.

■ **Height**—Choose a height for the control. As with textarea box controls, the Height value sets the number of text lines for the control. If you choose more than the default of 1, the control becomes a scrollable list and not a drop-down list.

- **Allow Multiple Selections**—If you like, you can set up your drop-down list box to allow site visitors to select more than one list entry at a time; to do so, choose the Yes option here. This option is usually used with the Height value set greater than 1 so that more than one selection can be seen at a time.

A drop-down box isn't very useful without items in it. You also use the Drop-Down Box Properties dialog box to add and organize list options.

- **Add**—Click this button to add a new item to the list. In the Add Choice dialog box, enter a name, check to enter a value (if you want the value to be the same as the option name you can leave this blank), and whether or not the item is selected by default.

- **Modify**—Clicking this button opens the Modify Choice dialog box, which is essentially the same as the Add Choice dialog box but enables you to modify the settings for an existing item.

- **Remove**—Click this button to remove unwanted items from the list.

- **Move Up/Move Down**—These buttons can be used to organize items in the list.

FIGURE 16.8
Drop-down box controls can provide a choice of multiple items on one or multiple visible lines.

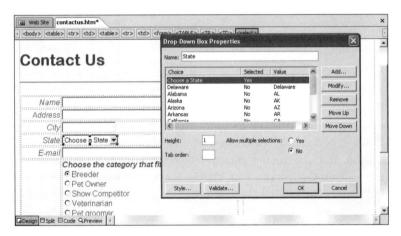

Push Buttons

To complete a form, you need to add buttons to use for submitting the form, resetting it, or performing some other operation. Although the forms created with FrontPage contain Submit and Reset buttons by default, as shown in Figure 16.9, you also can add and remove these buttons separately. In addition, you can add *Normal* buttons that don't have a prescribed function; these buttons can be used to trigger a custom client-side scripting task using FrontPage behaviors. (See Chapter 14, "Scripting and DHTML," to learn more about FrontPage behaviors and how to attach them to elements.)

To add a push button control to your form, open the Insert menu, choose Form, and select Push Button. By default, a Normal button is inserted.

To set the text on the button and the type of button, double click the button to open the Push Button Properties dialog box. You can set the following properties:

- **Name**—The name of the control labels the data when the form is submitted.

- **Value/Label**—This enables you to set the text that is displayed on the button. If the button is used as a Submit button, it is also the value that is submitted with the form for the button. This enables you to determine which Submit button was clicked to submit the form if you have more than one.

- **Button Type**—Choose between Normal, Submit, and Reset. Normal buttons don't do anything on their own. They must be wired to a behavior to do something. Submit buttons send the form values to the server, and Reset buttons can be used to reset all form fields to their default values.

FIGURE 16.9

Push buttons can be used to submit the form, reset values, or perform a behavior.

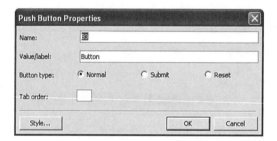

If you don't like the default push-button look, you can add buttons that look like an image, which are then associated with a hyperlink. Image buttons serve the same function as Submit buttons in that they both submit the form to the server for processing. You can use any picture from FrontPage's clip art collection or your own pictures. Open the Insert menu, choose Form, and select Picture to add a picture button, and browse for the file that you want to use for the picture.

Fine Tuning Forms

After a form and all its controls are inserted, your form is nearly complete. However, there are some additional items you can add that will make the form more usable for both your users and you.

Adding Labels to Form Controls

Form controls by themselves aren't very explanatory. You really need to add text to instruct the user to enter necessary data. Although you could simply type the text directly on your page, FrontPage enables you to associate text with the control it represents. The added value for users is that they can simply click on the label itself to select the form control, making labels especially useful for check boxes and option buttons.

To add a label to a form control, do the following:

1. If you haven't already added the form control, do so as described earlier in this chapter.

2. Click in the document where you want the label text to go, and type the text for the label as you would for any other text.

3. Select the label text and the control using the mouse or the keyboard.

4. Open the Insert menu, choose Form, and select Label to convert the text to a label. An example is shown in Figure 16.10.

FIGURE 16.10

Labels enhance usability of forms by allowing a control to be selected when the user clicks on the text next to it. A label is shown here with FrontPage's Reveal Tags feature turned on.

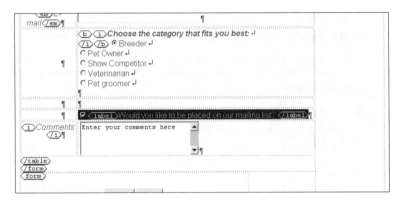

Adding Group Boxes

Option buttons (and other form controls that relate to one another, such as check boxes) are often seen surrounded by a group box. A group box shows a label at the top, and a box surrounding the contained controls. Although a group box doesn't add any functionality to the form, it does improve the usability of the form by making it clear that certain items are related. Figure 16.11 shows a group box in use.

Don't make the mistake of thinking that you can surround existing form controls with the group box—FrontPage will overwrite any form controls or other elements in the selection when you insert a group box. To get around this, you must insert the group box and then select and drag controls into it.

To add a group box, first click the spot where you want the group to go. Then, open the Insert menu, choose Form, and select Group Box.

FIGURE 16.11

Group boxes
can help clarify
related form
items.

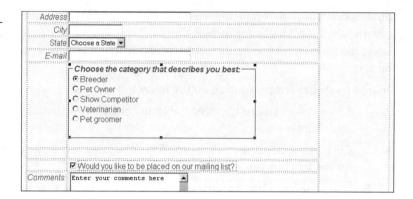

There are several properties that you can set for group boxes. To set them, right-click
in the group box and choose Group Box Properties from the menu.

- ■ **Label**—Enter text to be displayed at the top of the group box.

- ■ **Align**—Choose an alignment for the label. This will control where at the top
  of the group box the label appears and can be set to default, left, right, or
  center. Note that this setting does not affect alignment of controls or text
  inside the group box.

- ■ **Style**—Click this button to choose style options for the group box. You can
  add a CSS style, or set text, color, and border styles for the box.

Setting Tab Order

When entering form information, most users are familiar with the concept of pressing the Tab key to quickly move to the next field on the form. This can save a lot of
time as compared to clicking the mouse in each form field.

For each type of control on a form, a Tab Order property can be set. To do so, double
click on the control to open its Properties dialog box. The Tab Order property is
blank by default. If no tab order is set, the tab order becomes the control's position
on the page (in the HTML code, not necessarily on the screen). You can enter a value
from 1 to 999 for this property; when the user presses the Tab key after entering a
form value, the cursor will jump to the control with the next highest tab order. If
you don't want a control to be tab selectable, enter –1 in the Tab Order field.

Validating Data

In most cases, people who use your Web site want to send valid information with a
form. It is possible, however, that they may inadvertently type invalid information
or leave out some critical information. With FrontPage, you can add validation rules

for the data that is entered into your form. These rules prevent the form from being submitted if information is missing or formatted incorrectly. When a user inputs invalid values and clicks the Submit button, an alert message is displayed, and focus is shifted to the offending control.

Various form controls have different validation options available to them. You can access a form's Validation dialog box, an example of which is shown in Figure 16.12, by clicking the Validate button in the form control's Properties dialog. Here are some validation options for the various form controls:

- **Text boxes and textarea boxes**—You can choose to restrict input data to text or numeric values, or set no constraints at all. If you restrict to a numeric value, you can set options for grouping and decimal characters to reflect the standards of most users. You can also set minimum and maximum lengths for text data here.

- **Option buttons**—Specify here whether the user must choose a button in a group (as opposed to skipping over the group when filling out the form). If the group doesn't contain a button that is selected by default, and the user doesn't choose an option, the validation will fail.

- **Drop-down boxes**—As with option buttons, you can choose whether users are required to select a value from the drop-down box. If multiple selections are allowed, you can set a minimum or maximum number of selections. You can also choose to disallow the first item. This enables you to use the first option to prompt the user to make a selection, such as making that first option state Choose from the Following or Make Selection.

FIGURE 16.12
Validation can assist both users and you by helping to ensure that valid responses are processed.

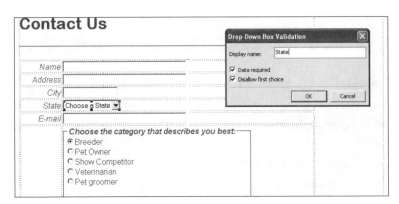

Directing Form Results

Once your form is created and you have all the controls entered, you need to decide how to handle the results of a user clicking the Submit button. (Actually, you should decide this before you ever create the form, but now is the time to actually set it up.)

If your Web site is running on a server with FrontPage Server Extensions or SharePoint Team Services, you have several built-in options for handling form submissions. You don't ever have to write a server-side CGI or ASP page to handle your forms if you don't want to (although that is certainly also allowed).

The most common options for FrontPage forms (assuming your site is running on a server with FrontPage Server Extensions or SharePoint Team Services) are to save the results in a database, to save them to a file, or send the results to you via e-mail. You can set these form result options in the Form Properties dialog box, shown in Figure 16.13. To open this dialog box, click the Form tag in the Quick Tag Selector, or right-click in the form and choose Form Properties.

FIGURE 16.13

Various options for processing form results can be set in the Form Properties dialog box.

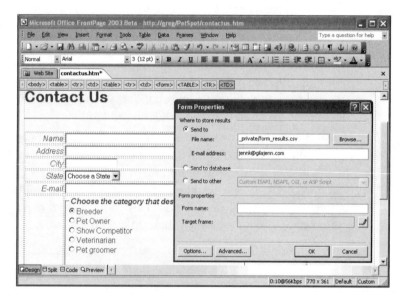

Directing Results to E-Mail

Perhaps the easiest way to set up handling form results, especially for smaller Web sites, is to simply have them sent to you via e-mail. To set e-mail options, do the following:

1. Open the Form Properties dialog box.

2. Enter an e-mail address in the appropriate field. You can stop here, or continue on to step 3 to set additional options.

3. Set Click the Options button to set more options, and click the E-Mail Results tab.

4. Choose the e-mail format. A variety of formats are available, from HTML- and XML-formatted pages to formatted text.

5. Choose a subject line for the e-mail to identify the mail you receive. You can choose to obtain this value from one of the form fields.

6. You can enter a Reply To line that can be used to reply to the e-mail sender. Click the Form Field Name check box to check it in order to use a user-supplied value for this.

Saving Results

If you'd rather not have to deal with receiving e-mail, you can choose to save form results in a file, or even in a database if one is available.

Saving to a File

You can choose to save form results to a file on the server. The results of each submission are appended to the end of the file, which you can later download and view in an application such as Excel or even import into Access.

1. Open the Form Properties dialog box.

2. Click the Options button to open the Saving Results dialog box.

3. Enter a name for either the first or optional second file. Use the second file if the first is being used to direct results to a confirmation page (a page that allows users to see the information they submitted).

4. Choose a file format. The XML and text options are best if you want to download the results file and import it into Excel, Access, or some other application. Choose one of the HTML options to save the results in a file that you can view on the Web.

5. Choose whether to include field names in the results, and whether to append the latest results to the end of an existing file. (For the text options, this is selected and disabled so that you cannot change it.)

6. Click OK.

Saving to a Database

You can save form results to a database, as well. This database can be any data source that you have defined for your site. (See Chapter 17, "Databases," to learn how to create and use database connections, and to use them to store form results.)

Creating a Confirmation Page

After users submit a form, you should acknowledge this action by sending them to a confirmation page. FrontPage has a page template for a confirmation page that lets you customize the displayed results based on submitted form values. To add a confirmation page, do the following:

1. Open the File menu and choose New to open the New task pane.
2. Click the More Page Templates link.
3. Choose Confirmation Form from the General tab.

The confirmation page is created with FrontPage Web components called confirmation fields. These fields can be mapped to form controls on your form page and will be replaced with the submitted values for the form when the confirmation page is viewed.

If the default confirmation fields don't match up to your form fields, you can edit them by double clicking them and entering the name of a form field to use instead.

You can add additional confirmation fields to the confirmation page, as well, by following these steps:

1. Open the Insert menu and choose Web Component.
2. Select Advanced Controls from the Component Type list.
3. In the Choose a Control list, select Confirmation Field.
4. Click Finish.
5. Enter a form field name in the Confirmation Field Properties dialog box, and click OK.

Once you have a confirmation page (see Figure 16.14), you need to direct the form results there. In the Form Properties dialog box, browse to the confirmation page and select it.

FIGURE 16.14

A confirmation field Web component can be used to customize your confirmation page with values from the form results.

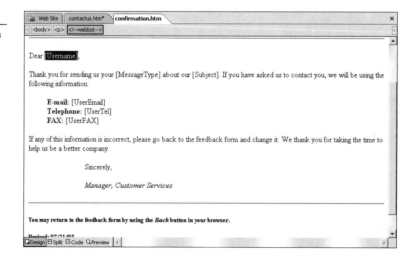

Testing Forms

Although you can do some basic functional testing of form pages in Page Preview view, to do a full end-to-end test including the form processing, you have to publish the site to the Web server. This action causes FrontPage to add any client-side form validation and enables the Web components involved in processing the forms to be utilized for testing.

THE ABSOLUTE MINIMUM

Other than simple mailto links, forms are the primary means for getting user responses and requests back to you. FrontPage has a full range of tools for creating forms as well as form-processing results on the Web server.

Use the form page templates and Form Page Wizard to create ready-made form pages. These can produce forms for many if not most of the typical form tasks, from search forms, guestbooks, and feedback forms to more general forms created using the Form Page Wizard.

FrontPage also provides tools for adding your own custom forms and form controls. Use the Insert, Form submenu to add forms and form controls to existing pages.

Use the Form Properties dialog box to specify how the form results should be processed. You can direct users to a confirmation page, as well as store form results in a file or a database, or have them sent to you via e-mail.

IN THIS CHAPTER

- Understanding databases and where they fit in with FrontPage Web sites
- Creating and using database connections
- Using the Database Interface Wizard to generate dynamic page content
- Storing form results in a database table, creating the database or tables if necessary

17

DATABASES

It's true that many Web sites are still plodding along as a collection of simple, static pages. However, they are slowly but surely becoming the exception rather than the rule. On today's World Wide Web, Web sites with content delivered from a database are becoming more and more popular. The reason for this is simple—although static Web pages can be terrific informational resources, only a data-driven Web site can harness the power that is required to take your site to the next level.

These days, much of the Web development world has shifted away from old-fashioned static sites with individual, seldom-changing pages. Instead, they use databases to generate dynamic pages that enable users to do something useful. This collection of pages has come to be known as a Web application. Web applications can be likened to traditional desktop applications; the main difference is that the Web application is broken into separate components. The majority of the application logic as well as the data storage and retrieval occur on Web servers, while the user interface is presented as a document in a browser window.

Databases are not useful only for large-scale sites. Even those with more modest aims can benefit from them. As this chapter will show, databases can even be used to enhance the functionality of Web forms by allowing you to store information automatically.

What Is a Database?

For Web purposes, a database is a special server-accessed component used to organize and store data, and is optimized to allow this data to be accessed and updated quickly. At the heart of a database is an organizational structure known as a table, not to be confused with an HTML table. Data is organized in tables because tables are a logical way to represent related information. Tables are represented in a row-and-column format, as shown in Figure 17.1. The related bits of information, known as fields, are displayed across the top of a table as columns. A collection of fields is called a record.

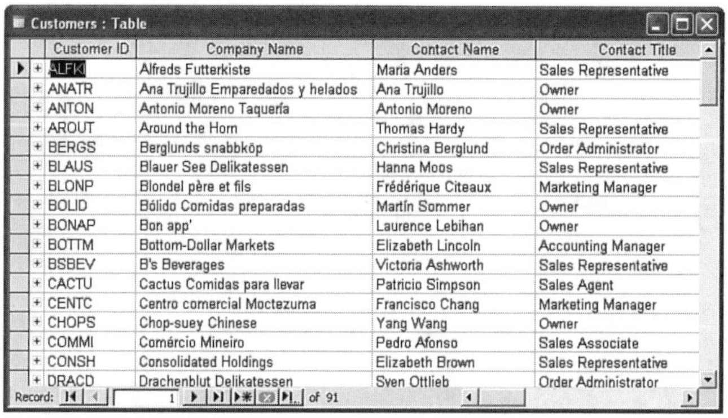

Customers : Table

Customer ID	Company Name	Contact Name	Contact Title
ALFKI	Alfreds Futterkiste	Maria Anders	Sales Representative
ANATR	Ana Trujillo Emparedados y helados	Ana Trujillo	Owner
ANTON	Antonio Moreno Taquería	Antonio Moreno	Owner
AROUT	Around the Horn	Thomas Hardy	Sales Representative
BERGS	Berglunds snabbköp	Christina Berglund	Order Administrator
BLAUS	Blauer See Delikatessen	Hanna Moos	Sales Representative
BLONP	Blondel père et fils	Frédérique Citeaux	Marketing Manager
BOLID	Bólido Comidas preparadas	Martín Sommer	Owner
BONAP	Bon app'	Laurence Lebihan	Owner
BOTTM	Bottom-Dollar Markets	Elizabeth Lincoln	Accounting Manager
BSBEV	B's Beverages	Victoria Ashworth	Sales Representative
CACTU	Cactus Comidas para llevar	Patricio Simpson	Sales Agent
CENTC	Centro comercial Moctezuma	Francisco Chang	Marketing Manager
CHOPS	Chop-suey Chinese	Yang Wang	Owner
COMMI	Comércio Mineiro	Pedro Afonso	Sales Associate
CONSH	Consolidated Holdings	Elizabeth Brown	Sales Representative
DRACD	Drachenblut Delikatessen	Sven Ottlieb	Order Administrator

Record: 1 of 91

FIGURE 17.1
Tables are used to organize data in a row-and-column format, as seen in this Microsoft Access sample database.

To make use of the database, the Web application that needs it has to be able to talk to it. This is done using a database connection. A database connection consists of the information that the application needs in order to find the database as well as security information required to connect to it. With FrontPage, it's easy to create database tables, database connections, and the Web pages that use them.

FrontPage can access a wide variety of databases. Many *ODBC (Open Database Connectivity)* compliant data sources can be used by FrontPage, including the following:

- **Microsoft Access**—The smallest Microsoft database, intended for smaller Web sites and standalone applications.

- **Microsoft SQL Server**—Microsoft's enterprise-class database offering. This product is powerful enough to drive some of the biggest Web sites.

- **Oracle**—Another enterprise-class database, a competitor to SQL Server.

- **MySQL**—A free enterprise-class database, used by many online communities for message boards.

Many of you will want to retrieve data from Access databases, so this chapter focuses on that. However, many of the same principles and ideas work for the larger databases.

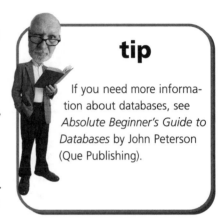

tip

If you need more information about databases, see *Absolute Beginner's Guide to Databases* by John Peterson (Que Publishing).

Importing Access Databases

Because FrontPage 2003 is one of the applications in the Office 2003 System, it's reasonable to start with the database product that is also part of that family of products. Microsoft Access 2003 is a popular small database package that stores a complete database in a single flat file with an .mdb extension. Many FrontPage users already have Access databases that they would like to place on a Web server so that content can be retrieved. FrontPage makes it a snap to import Access databases, and to build pages that use it.

To import a database, do the following:

1. Create the database in Access.

2. Choose File, Import to open the Import dialog box (see Figure 17.2).

3. Click the Add File button.

4. Browse for the Access .mdb file that you want to import.

5. FrontPage recognizes the file as an Access file and asks whether you want to automatically create a database connection for it. Enter a descriptive name for the connection (perhaps the name of the database itself), and click Yes. (If you say no, don't worry; the next section explains how to create a database connection.)

FIGURE 17.2

Import data-
bases into your
FrontPage Web
as you would
any other file.

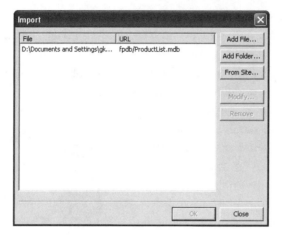

6. If this is the first database you are importing, FrontPage will ask whether you want to store it in a special fpdb folder (see Figure 17.3). It's a good idea to separate your database files in this manner from the rest of your Web, so say Yes. Separating your databases keeps your site files organized and allows you to set special permissions on that folder without limiting access to your entire site.

FIGURE 17.3

FrontPage
prompts you to
create the fpdb
directory when
importing a
database to sep-
arate your data-
base files from
the rest of your
site.

Once the Access database is included in the Web, you need to add a database connection to be able to retrieve data from it (if you didn't do so in the setup process). The next section shows how to create database connections to use an imported Access database, as well as other databases such as MS SQL Server.

Connecting to a Database

The term database connection describes the information necessary to connect to a database to retrieve or update information. This information is often very different depending on the type of database you are connecting to, but in general, it specifies the type of database or connection protocol (Access, MS SQL, ODBC, and so on), the location, and the information necessary to log into it.

As you've seen, creating a database connection is as simple as a button click when you import an Access database. Other databases, however, require a bit more effort. To add a database connection, do the following:

1. Choose the Tool, Site Settings to open the Site Settings dialog box.

2. Select the Database tab, shown in Figure 17.4.

3. Click the Add button to open the New Database Connection dialog box.

4. Enter a name for the connection. This should be as descriptive as possible. If you leave the default value of Database1 in place, and you include multiple databases in a site, you will probably have a hard time later figuring out what the database was for.

5. Choose the type of connection. This depends on the type of database you are connecting to. A short summary of the types follows.

6. If your database requires a username and password, click the Advanced button to open the Advanced Connection Properties dialog box, and enter them.

Let's quickly go over each of the database connection options:

■ **File or folder in current Web site**—Browse for a database file. Microsoft Access files are shown by default, but you can choose other file types such as Excel, Paradox, or even formatted text files.

■ **System data source on Web server**—If your connection to your Web server has been established, you can use any system DSN (data source name) created by the administrator of the site.

- **Network connection to a database server**—Enter the name of a Microsoft SQL Server or an Oracle server, as well as the database to open. If you have a SQL Server database provided by your Web-hosting administrator, this is most likely the way that you would connect to it.

- **System data source on Web server**—If your database access is provided in the form of a .dsn or .udl file, use this option and browse for the file to import it into the Web site.

- **Testing database connections**—If your database connection is displayed in the list with a question mark icon, like the second entry in the list in Figure 17.4, you can use the Verify button to test the connection.

> **tip**
>
> When testing connections to databases other than those from imported files such as Access, you'll need to be connected to the server.

Modifying Connections

Once a database connection has been created, modifying it later is done through the Site Settings dialog box. Simply select the connection that you want to change and click Modify to open the Database Connection Properties dialog box. You remove a database connection in the same manner.

Modifying connections can come into play if your hosting provider or Web administrator requires you to change passwords for databases, or to change the server that the connection points to.

Web Server Technologies

To understand how FrontPage produces pages that display database results, it helps to know a little about the technology behind it all. Microsoft Windows and its standard Web server, Internet Information Server, utilize a technology called Active Server Pages (ASP) to generate dynamic pages. ASP pages (with the extension .asp) are processed before they are sent to the browser. They contain special blocks of code that are read and executed by the server, where the ASP code blocks are then replaced by the output of that executed code. The code that ASP uses is written using a scripting language similar to client-side scripts. (They can even use the same JavaScript language that is used on the client, but a derivative of Visual Basic known as VBScript is more commonly used.) The server-side scripts, however, do not respond to browser events in the same way as client scripts. They are executed when the page is requested, generate their content, and then disappear in the final form of the page sent to the browser.

More recently, ASP has been supplanted by a newer technology called ASP.NET, utilizing the .NET Framework. ASP.NET was designed from the ground up to allow the development of powerful Web applications using more advanced programming languages. FrontPage 2003 allows you to connect to databases on Web servers using either ASP or ASP.NET.

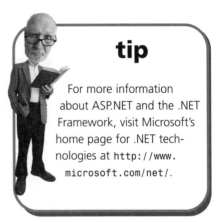

tip

For more information about ASP.NET and the .NET Framework, visit Microsoft's home page for .NET technologies at http://www.microsoft.com/net/.

Using Databases in Your Web Site

Now that you can connect with almost any type of database, I can discuss what FrontPage enables you to do with databases. Among your options are using the Database Results Wizard to generate server-side code using either ASP or ASP.NET, or sending form results to a database. Let's look at both of these.

Using the Database Results Wizard

Rather than forcing you to write your own server-side code to display database results, FrontPage gives you the Database Results Wizard. This wizard, shown in Figure 17.5, enables you to automatically generate ASP or ASP.NET pages that display data from any database connection.

FIGURE 17.5

The Database Results Wizard can be used to quickly generate data view pages.

> **Database Results Wizard**
>
> This wizard creates a database results region that displays information from a database. The wizard can also create a search form on the same page to let site visitors look up specific information.
>
> FrontPage has detected that your page will display best using:
>
> ⦿ ASP   ○ ASP.NET
>
> You can:
>
> ○ Use a sample database connection (Northwind)
> ⦿ Use an existing database connection:
>   [ProductList ▾]
> ○ Connect to an external database
> ○ Use a new database connection
>   [Create...]
>
> About using an existing database
>
> [Cancel] [< Back] [Next >] [Finish]

To activate the Database Results Wizard, shown in Figure 17.5, do the following:

1. Open the page that you want to use to display the results.

2. Choose Insert, Database, Results to start the wizard.

3. Choose a server technology, either ASP or ASP.NET. Your choices may be limited by the technologies supported by your hosting provider.

4. Choose the database connection to use, or create a new one. Then click Next.

5. Choose a record source to use for the results. The record source can be the data from any particular table in your database, or the result of a custom SQL query. Click Next.

6. If you like, edit the list of fields to display, or choose More Options for options on sorting or filtering records.

7. Choose formatting options. These will vary depending on whether you chose ASP or ASP.NET in step 3. ASP gives you additional options for formatting the data, but with ASP.NET you get a highly configurable data grid control.

8. Specify whether you want to display the records on a single page and whether you want to display them in a group.

9. Click Finish to create a Database Results region on your page, shown in Figure 17.6.

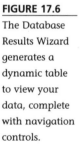

FIGURE 17.6

The Database Results Wizard generates a dynamic table to view your data, complete with navigation controls.

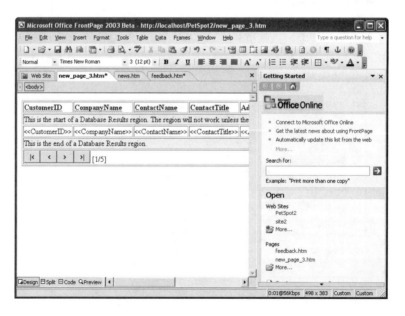

Sending Form Results to a Database

As you saw in Chapter 16, "Creating Forms," FrontPage enables you to create forms that can be used in a variety of ways. Results can be saved to a file, sent to you via email, or, as discussed here, stored in a database for later retrieval. See Chapter 16 to learn how to get a form into your Web.

Follow these steps to store form results in an existing database table:

1. Right-click in the form and choose Form Properties to open the Form Properties dialog box. Alternatively, open the dialog box by double clicking on the <FORM> tag in the Quick Tag Selector.

2. Select the Send to Database option.

3. Click Options to open the Options for Saving Results to Database dialog box, shown in Figure 17.7.

FIGURE 17.7

Choose a database connection and a table to use to store form results.

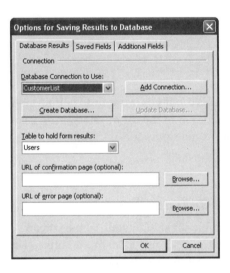

4. In the Database Results tab, choose a database connection to use. If you don't have one, click Add Connection to create a new one.

5. Choose a database table to hold the form results.

6. Optionally, add the URLs for a confirmation page and/or an error page.

7. Click the Saved Fields tab.

8. For the form fields that you want to store, select them one at a time and click Modify.

9. In the Modify Field dialog box, choose the database column that should store the field value. Repeat steps 8 and 9 for each field you wish to store. Figure 17.8 shows how these mappings should look.

FIGURE 17.8

You can map form fields directly to fields in the database table.

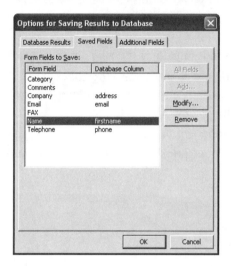

10. Click the Additional Fields tab if you want to save information from the user that was obtained in addition to the form results, including browser type, remote computer name, time stamp, or user name.

11. Click OK when you are finished.

Creating a New Database from Form Results

If you don't have a database table already in your Web that can hold your form results, FrontPage can help. In the Options for Saving Results to Database dialog box, simply click on the Create Database button in the Database Results tab. FrontPage will automatically create an Access database complete with a table to store your form results and map your form fields to table columns, as shown in Figure 17.9.

FIGURE 17.9

Instant database! Clicking the Create Database button can automatically create a database and table to store your form results.

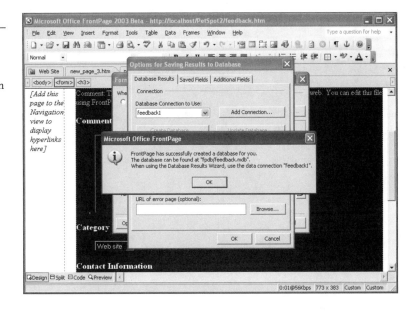

Using SharePoint

So far, we've discussed FrontPage's traditional database connectivity features. However, FrontPage 2003 can go quite far past these capabilities.

If the hosting server you are using happens to be a Windows 2003 server using SharePoint Services, you won't be able to use the Databases tab of the Site Settings dialog box to create database connections. That's because SharePoint has taken over the function of managing data sources for FrontPage Web sites. All SharePoint data access objects—from database connections to XML Web Parts that can share data with each other—are created and accessed from the Data Source Catalog task pane, shown in Figure 17.10.

tip

For more information about Web Parts, the Data Source Catalog, and other SharePoint features, see *Special Edition: Using FrontPage 2003*, written by Paul Colligan and Jim Cheshire (Que Publishing).

FIGURE 17.10

The Data Source Catalog task pane offers one-stop shopping for all SharePoint data sources.

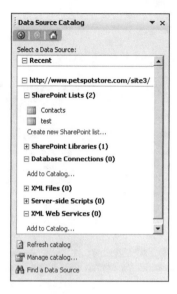

THE ABSOLUTE MINIMUM

Databases aren't just for the big sites anymore. With FrontPage 2003, creating database connections, importing Access database files, and generating pages that make use of data is a snap.

You can create database connections to allow data retrieval and storage from almost any popular database with an ODBC interface, in particular, Microsoft Access, Microsoft SQL Server, and Oracle.

FrontPage makes it easy to display results from a database using the Database Results Wizard. Whether your hosting site uses ASP or ASP.NET, you can use FrontPage to build custom professional-looking data-grid views for your data.

Another popular option is to use FrontPage 2003 to store form results in a database. You can create the database and table to store the results yourself, or let FrontPage create an Access database and connection for you automatically.

IN THIS CHAPTER

- Adding a banner ad
- Adding a marquee
- Site maps and tables of contents
- Choosing and using hover buttons
- Adding a search tool to your pages
- Creating a top 10 list
- Automating your content

18

ADDING BELLS AND WHISTLES WITH WEB COMPONENTS

With so many of the essentials in place on your site, it's time to turn your attention to the bells and whistles that can help your Web site stand out. These features can help visitors remember your site and keep them coming back.

FrontPage includes a number of tools to help you create some whizbang features, including moving marquees and interactive buttons. FrontPage can also help you create more-useful offerings such as a search tool, a table of contents, a site map to assist in navigation, or a top 10 list that can include facts about your site.

You'll also find a number of components that enable you to add a current weather report, a map of your location, news headlines, and more. All these features can be added quickly, and can make your site look very up-to-date and very useful.

Adding a Banner Ad

These days, banner ads appear everywhere on the Web. You'll find them hocking wares and services on news sites, gaming sites, and even personal sites. If you're considering including banner ads in your site, tread carefully. Such advertising can irritate a loyal audience, particularly on a site where advertising has not been previously offered. The results—in terms of revenue and promotion—may not justify the effort.

If, after careful thought, you do decide to include banner ads on your site, you may be disappointed by FrontPage's capabilities in this department. Although some previous versions of FrontPage included a Banner Ad feature that enabled users to create and manage banner ads, FrontPage 2003 does not. Instead, FrontPage 2003 offers a Page Banner feature. By default, a page banner, when plugged into a page included in your navigation scheme (refer to Chapter 12, "Creating a Navigation Structure"), simply applies the title of a page to a banner to make the page banner.

> **note**
>
> Even if you haven't considered adding a banner ad to your site, you might be asked by other organizations do so in order to sell their products or services. In exchange for agreeing to promote your site in return, or for financial compensation, these organizations typically supply you with the ad (this often includes code that you add to your pages) along with exact instructions for placing it on your site.

To use FrontPage 2003's Page Banner feature, do the following:

1. Click the spot on a page where you want to insert a banner ad.
2. Open the Insert menu and choose Web Component.
3. The Insert Web Component dialog box opens. In the Component Type list, click Included Content, as shown in Figure 18.1.
4. In the right-hand list, click Page Banner.
5. The Picture Banner Properties dialog box opens. Select Text, and click OK.

If you're really sold on the idea of a banner ad, rather than the generic page banner, you won't be able to create, implement, and manage this from within FrontPage itself. If you want to offer a banner ad, you're either going to need to create a banner ad yourself (use a search engine such as Google to look for share-ware and commercial software to help you do this; many include instructions for inserting such an ad into your Web page, usually through scripting snippets they'll offer) or pay someone else to create one for you (often starting at a price of about $100–$250 up to quite a bit more). If you want to place your ad on someone else's system, you usually do so through a marketing service at a sometimes substantial cost.

FIGURE 18.1

From the Insert Web Component window, select Included Content, which opens up an Open list at the right.

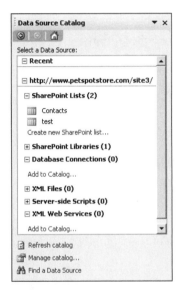

PROS AND CONS OF POP-UPS

Another phenomenon in site advertising is the pop-up ad. A pop-up ad is an ad that is displayed automatically in its own window when someone visits a particular site or page. Pop-up ads tend to infuriate visitors, many of whom try to close them even before they fully open or install software to prevent them from opening at all. This distaste has increased as the number of sites offering such ads has jumped markedly.

Yet, like banner advertising, pop-up ads can be effective. Some studies suggest that for every three or four people who are angered by pop-up ads, one visitor may respond to the ad, clicking it investigate the product or service being advertised. Such ads definitely generate attention, both good and bad.

FrontPage doesn't directly add pop-up ad capabilities you can use without knowing either JavaScript or CGI coding (see Chapter 14, "Scripting and DHTML," and Chapter 23 (found on the web), "Knowing the Code"). If you're interested in adding pop-up ads to your site, you'll find several scripting and utility sites that offer instructions or tools for creating them. One often-recommended site for information and an example of how to add a pop-up ad (or information window) is `http://www.tamingthebeast.net/articles/ chromeless-popup.htm`.

Adding a Marquee to a Page

Want a rather dramatic, even moving (literally) addition to a page to make an announcement, highlight a feature, or otherwise grab the attention of your visitor? If the answer is yes, then say it with a marquee. A marquee is different from a header or a banner because it can move across the screen (or scroll), and can repeat as many times as you want. Although such a feature may not be right for every page or every site, it can be a fun addition in the right situation.

Before you start, you need to perform one task:

1. Open the Tools menu and choose Page Options.
2. Click the Authoring tab.
3. Under Schema Version, make certain Internet Explorer 5.0 is selected. If not, click on the drop-down list box and select it. Click OK.

Now follow these steps to add a marquee:

1. Click the location on a page where you want the marquee to be added, and then type the text you want to appear in the heading.
2. Open the Insert menu and choose Web Component.
3. The Insert Web Component dialog box opens. In the Component Type list, click Dynamic Effects.
4. In the list on the right-hand side of the dialog box, click Marquee.
5. Click Finish.
6. The Marquee Properties dialog box opens (see Figure 18.2). Select the properties you want to apply to the marquee such as the speed of motion, the direction, whether to repeat the scrolling effect and how often, and the background color. When you're finished, click OK.

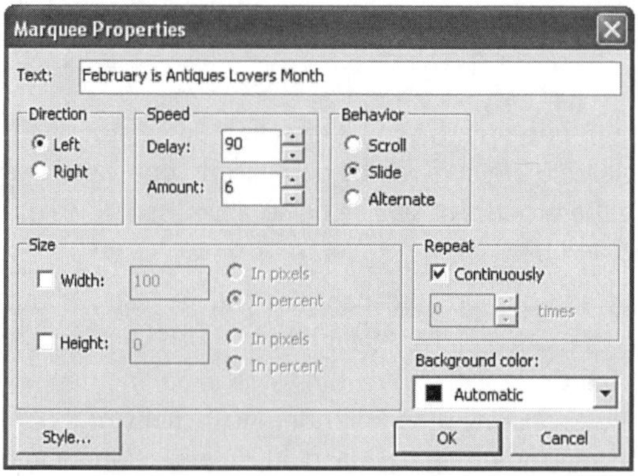

FIGURE 18.2

Select the behavior and appearance of your marquee in the Marquee Properties dialog box; prepare to experiment to get the results you want.

If you want to change the font size, type, or color, click the Style button in step 6, choose Font, and make your formatting choices.

Adding a Table of Contents and Site Map to Your Web

You're probably familiar with using a table of contents, and how a table of contents delineates the material contained within a publication. A Web-based table of contents is basically the same animal. Similar to a table of contents is a site map; both are good tools for helping visitors find their way to specific content on your site.

Creating a Table of Contents

Here's how to create a regular table of contents:

1. Click the spot on the page where you want to insert a table of contents.

2. Open the Insert menu and choose Web Component.

3. The Insert Web Component dialog box opens. In the Component Type list, click Table of Contents.

4. In the list on the right-hand side of the dialog box, click For This Web Site.

5. Click Finish.

6. The Table of Contents Properties dialog box opens (see Figure 18.3). Create a new page or select an existing page for building your table of contents, and make any other necessary changes to the properties.

7. Click OK.

FIGURE 18.3

Set the starting page to include in the table of contents from this dialog box.

When the table of contents is placed on your page (as shown in this starter page in Figure 18.4), it looks a bit generic. Don't worry; you haven't erred. The actual titles are filled when the page is saved and published to a Web server. If you want to make changes to the font used for your table of contents list, follow the instructions found in Chapter 4, "Adding Text."

FIGURE 18.4

Generic titles
are placed in
the table of con-
tents until the
page is pub-
lished, at which
point the proper
entries are
added.

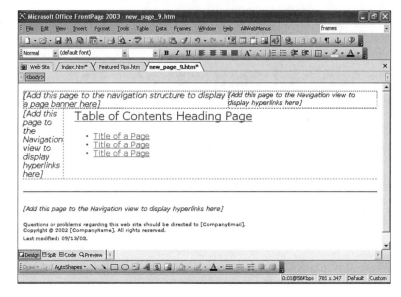

Creating a Site Map

When you create a site map that is based on assigned page categories rather than a table of contents based on site navigation, a couple of issues change. For one, the site map won't be automatically updated when your content changes as a navigation-based table of contents would. For another, you must first assign categories to your pages to enable them to be picked up by the site map when it's built.

A category usually refers to a page's topic, which you can designate in the page's Properties dialog box. To do so, follow these steps:

1. Open an existing page or create a new page.

2. Open the File menu and choose Properties.

3. Click the Workgroup tab.

4. Click the Categories button.

5. The Master Category List dialog box opens. In the New Category box, type Site Map, as shown in Figure 18.5.

6. Click the Add button and then click OK. Site Map is added as a category.

7. On the Workgroup tab, click the Site Map check box under Categories for this page, and click OK.

8. Repeat steps 1, 2, 3, and 7 for any other pages you want added to your site map.

9. Click OK on each open dialog box to close it.

FIGURE 18.5

By adding a category of Site Map to this page, you make it available to be added to the site map page when you create it.

Only pages that have been assigned a category of Site Map will be included in the site map. This means you can exclude any pages you prefer not to list there. Now let's build the site map based upon categories.

To build a site map based on the Site Map category, do the following:

1. Create or open a page to hold your site map.

2. Click on the spot on the page where the site map should be inserted.

3. Open the Insert menu and choose Web Component.

4. The Insert Web Component dialog box opens. In the Component Type list, click Table of Contents.

5. In the list on the right-hand side of the dialog box, click Based on Page Category.

6. Click Finish.

7. The Categories Properties dialog box opens (see Figure 18.6). Click the Site Map check box to check it.

8. Click OK.

Just as when you built the table of contents based on site navigation, the site map shown in Design view contains simple placeholders called *Page in Category*. When the site is published to a Web server, those placeholders will be replaced with actual page information. You'll want to check that the appropriate list of pages appears in the site map after the page is published.

FIGURE 18.6

Selecting Site
Map here
means that only
pages that have
been assigned
the Site Map
category will be
added to the
site map.

Using Hover Buttons

Hover buttons, also sometimes referred to by FrontPage as interactive buttons, get
their name because their appearance changes when a mouse pointer moves (or hovers) over them or when they are clicked. Sound and image files can be added to
hover buttons for more pizzazz. These buttons can be used for a multitude of purposes, including the following (to name a few):

- As navigation tools
- To open a form or start an e-mail message
- As form options—for example, to indicate a Yes or No answer

Unlike standard, one-dimensional buttons, hover buttons are composed of three different images, each representing a different button state:

- One for the normal or unselected state
- A second for the hover state, when a mouse pointer is passed over it
- A third for the pressed state, which is how the button will appear when it is
  clicked

To add one or more hover buttons to a Web page, do the following:

1. Click the spot on the Web page where you want to insert a hover button.
2. Open the Insert menu and choose Interactive Button.
3. The Interactive Buttons dialog box opens. Click the Button tab (see
   Figure 18.7).
4. Click a button style in the Buttons list; a preview of that button style appears.
5. In the Text box, type the text that you want to appear on the hover button
   (this should be relatively brief).

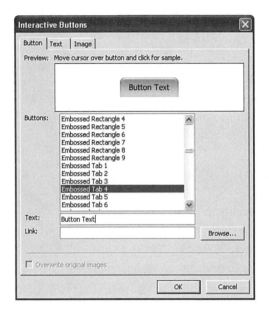

6. Click the Browse button next to the Link box.

7. In the Edit Hyperlink dialog box, locate and select the page, URL, or e-mail address that you want to link to this button.

8. Click OK once to close the Edit Hyperlink dialog box and again to close the Interactive Buttons dialog box.

You can create a series of hover buttons on the same line to create a sort of ad-hoc link bar. To do so, follow the preceding steps to add the first button. Then, click the position to the right of the most recently added button and repeat steps 2–8. The result is something that appears very much like the link bar you created in Chapter 12, "Creating a Navigation Structure."

note

To learn more about using hover buttons, visit the Microsoft Office information page at http://office. microsoft.com/assistance/ preview.aspx?AssetID= HA010835731033&_0.

Adding a Search Tool

One feature that many strong sites offer is a tool to enable visitors to search either that site or the entire Web for a particular piece of information. The latter function is usually tied to one of the Web search engines. FrontPage lets you provide this search service through a link to MSN's search facilities. A simple site might not require a tool that enables users to search the site itself, but can still benefit by providing a Web-based search tool.

Adding a Site-only Search Tool

A search tool appears only on pages where you place it. You can have it on just one page, such as your home page, or add it individually to several pages.

To use FrontPage to add a site-only search tool, do the following:

1. On the page to which you want to add the search tool, click on the approximate location where you want the tool to appear.

2. Open the Insert menu and choose Web Component.

3. The Insert Web Component dialog box opens. In the Component Type list, click Web Search.

4. In the list on the right-hand side of the dialog box, click Current Web.

5. Click Finish.

6. The Search Form Properties dialog box opens. Make any desired changes to the settings.

7. Click OK.

Figure 18.8 shows the finished search form using the default Search Form Properties settings. This can easily fit at the top or bottom of a page.

> **note**
>
> A search utility is typically available on a site's home page only or is placed on virtually all pages in the site.

FIGURE 18.8

An example of how the search utility will look when you've inserted it into one or more of your Web pages.

Search for:

Start Search   Reset

Adding a Web Search Tool

To add a tool to your site that will enable site visitors to search the whole Web (rather than just your site), you use a different Web component. The appearance of the tool, however, will look very much the same. To enable searches of the whole Web, do the following:

1. On the page to which you want to add the search tool, click the approximate location where you want the tool to appear.

2. Open the Insert menu and choose Web Component.

3. The Insert Web Component dialog box opens. In the Component Type list, click MSN Components.

4. In the list on the right-hand side of the dialog box, click Search the Web with MSN.

5. Click Finish.

The search form is inserted into your page, but your page must be published to a Web server in order for this feature to work.

Creating a Top 10 List

Don't think of David Letterman's funny Top 10 list here (however great an addition to your site that might be); this top 10 list is designed to report the top 10 most visited pages on your Web site. It also can be used to report the 10 URLs that most frequently refer visitors to your site, the 10 users who visit most often, and so on.

To build a top 10 list, do the following:

1. With the page to which you want to add a top 10 list displayed in Design view, click the spot on the page where you want the list to appear, then open the Insert menu and choose Web Component.

2. The Insert Web Component dialog box opens. In the Component Type list, click Top 10 List.

3. In the list on the right-hand side of the dialog box, click the type of data that you want the list to report.

4. Click Finish.

5. The Top 10 List Properties dialog box opens (see Figure 18.9). If you like, change the list's title and select a style for the list. (Table is the default style.)

6. Click OK.

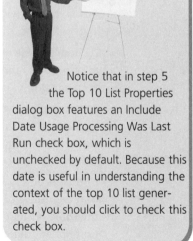

note

Notice that in step 5 the Top 10 List Properties dialog box features an Include Date Usage Processing Was Last Run check box, which is unchecked by default. Because this date is useful in understanding the context of the top 10 list generated, you should click to check this check box.

FIGURE 18.9
FrontPage offers a number of different style options for producing this list; you may want to experiment to see which offers the best results.

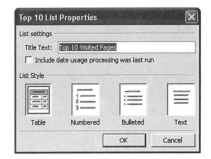

note

Because you won't typically have data to compile into a top 10 list until your site has been published to a Web server and has been available on the Internet for a while, you may want to wait to build a top 10 list.

Normally, the result on an unpublished page will look like a placeholder. Once published, however, the appropriate data will be added to the list, which will appear on the designated page.

Adding Automated Content

FrontPage has included several components to enable you to include useful and attention-getting tools on your site, such as

- Weather reports
- Geographical maps
- Stock quotes
- News, living and travel, sports, business, and technology headlines from MSNBC

Although these options won't work for every type of site, when they do, they can offer a way to make the site appear newsworthy, up-to-date (even if you don't add to your site daily), and connected.

For example, if your site is for a restaurant or tourist spot, adding a weather report (particularly if the weather is glorious) can draw visitors to you. Add an Expedia (the travel service) map so that people can find your place of business, and you can provide a real service.

In this section, you'll learn how to add MSNBC news headlines. You'll find, however, that regardless of what component (and you can offer more than one) you choose, the same basic steps apply because they are all available from the Insert Web Component dialog box.

Here's how to add your news headlines:

1. Click the spot on the page where you want news headlines inserted. (Often, news headlines appear on a site's home or index page.)

2. Open the Insert menu and choose Web Component.

3. The Insert Web Component dialog box opens. In the Component Type list, click MSNBC Components.

4. In the list on the right-hand side of the dialog box, click News Headlines from MSNBC.

5. Click Finish.

A placeholder box will appear on your page. When you publish your page to a Web server, you'll see that the headlines (and the date and time) are automatically updated through a connection to the MSNBC news servers, as depicted in Figure 18.10. No additional work is required by you.

FIGURE 18.10

A news head-
lines box such as
this one is
offered free of
charge for your
use and may
make your site
more useful to
your visitors.

THE ABSOLUTE MINIMUM

A professional-looking site—even if it's a personal site that you just want to look highly polished—often includes some extra features that help your visitors navigate and find content as well as to enrich and entertain them. In this chapter, you discovered the pros and cons of including ads and pop-up windows and learned how to add a marquee to one or more of your pages, build a table of contents and/or site map to help visitors locate information, use interactive or hover buttons to create an interesting and useful tool, include a search tool, and insert additional cool options such as news and sports headlines and a local weather forecast.

PART IV

PUBLISHING YOUR WEB

19

Testing Your Web

When you're ready to publish your Web site, you'll discover that there's a lot of variation on how your Web site looks to you versus how it looks to other people. These variations are based on your visitor's computer platform (Windows, Macintosh, Unix, and so on), processing speed, screen-resolution settings, Internet access speed, and the Internet browser he or she uses to access your Web page. This is a classic case of "what *you* see, isn't necessarily what *they* get."

Although you can't configure your Web site to handle every anomaly your visitors may encounter, you can at least engage in some proactive testing to help minimize problems.

Previewing in Multiple Browsers

It would be nice if we all used the same Internet browser, but there are so many to choose from. How would we all agree which features we wanted, or how much we wanted to pay? It's similar to the problem the human race would encounter if we had to decide on one language we should all speak.

Because there are multiple kinds of Internet browsers, Web page designers must accommodate them. The best solution is to test your site in as many browsers as possible to eliminate the most glaring issues. When you first install FrontPage, it snoops through your computer to determine which Internet browsers are installed on it, making them available to preview your pages. Then, every time you open FrontPage, it snoops again, looking to see if you've installed any other browsers.

To preview your Web site in multiple Internet browsers, follow these steps:

1. Choose File, Preview in Browser.

2. Select Preview in Multiple Browsers. (If this option does not exist, then you most likely have only one Internet browser installed on your computer.)

3. You have the option of selecting multiple browsers at the screen-resolution setting you are currently running or at a different screen-resolution size.

4. A preview of your Web page will open in all of the Internet browsers installed on your computer.

note

You must save your page before FrontPage enables you to preview it. If you forget to do this, FrontPage reminds you before opening the page in the various browsers.

If you would like to compare several different browser windows simultaneously, right-click the Windows taskbar, then select Tile Windows Vertically or Tile Windows Horizontally.

To preview your Web site in multiple Internet browsers on the fly, click the arrow to the right of the Preview in Browser button on the Formatting toolbar (see Figure 19.1) and select the desired preview option from the drop-down list.

tip

Instructions for selecting screen resolution are explained in the section "Previewing at Different Resolutions" later in this chapter.

FIGURE 19.1

You can choose to preview your page in one or more browsers at once.

Installing Additional Internet Browsers

Internet Explorer is the default browser that comes with Windows, but there are a slew of other Internet browsers available. Most browsers are available free of charge and can be downloaded from the Internet.

Opera is a popular international browser from Norway. You can download a free copy from www.opera.com. Netscape Navigator is another popular Internet browser, and is Internet Explorer's chief competitor. You can download a free copy from www.netscape.com.

To add an Internet browser to FrontPage's Preview in Browser list, do the following:

1. Choose File, Preview in Browser, then click Edit Browser List. The Edit Browser List dialog box opens, as shown in Figure 19.2.

FIGURE 19.2

Adding Internet browsers with a click of the mouse.

2. Click the Add button. The Add Browser dialog box opens.

3. In the Name box, type the browser you want to add (or click Browse to locate the file).

4. Click OK. The Add Browser dialog box closes.

5. In the Additional Window Sizes section of the Edit Browser List dialog box, check the options you want enabled.

6. Click OK.

Browser Compatibility

Depending on which Internet browser your visitors use to access your Web site, significant conflicts may occur. The most common are how styles and layers are rendered, particularly when there are behaviors attached. FrontPage has a neat feature that enables you to test your Web page's compatibility with all browsers installed on your computer.

To test your Web page for browser compatibility, perform the following steps:

1. Choose Tools, Browser Compatibility.

2. Select the desired Check options. The Browser Compatibility dialog box opens, as shown in Figure 19.3.

FIGURE 19.3

The Browser
Compatibility
dialog box
points out common problems
that are likely to
turn up if your
pages are viewed
in different
browsers.

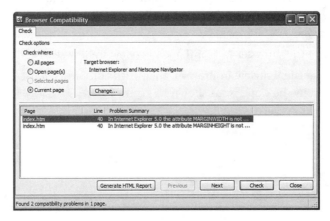

3. Click the Check button. FrontPage displays the message indicating that it is finished searching the document.

4. A report is generated, indicating any problems FrontPage encounters. The name of the page, the line number, and a problem summary are given for each error found.

5. If you want to generate a printed report, click the Generate HTML Report button.

6. If you click the Next button, the next error is highlighted in the Browser Compatibility dialog box. In addition, you are automatically toggled to a Split page and the corresponding problem is highlighted in both the Code page pane and Design page pane.

7. When you are finished, click the Close button.

Previewing at Different Resolutions

You need to be in Design page before FrontPage can run the browser compatibility test.

The width of a computer's screen resolution varies from machine to machine. The three most popular screen resolutions are 800×600, 1024×768, and 1280×1024. When you're ready to begin testing your Web page, it's a good idea to test all three resolutions. Pay particular attention to how the user will be affected by changing their settings. Will they be faced with the annoying task of having to scroll left or right just to read the text on your Web page?

To test your Web page in various resolutions, perform the following steps:

1. Switch to Page Preview view by clicking the Page Preview button at the bottom of the screen.

2. Choose View, Page Size.

3. Select the resolution at which you want to test your page. The page size you are currently using will be flagged with a checked box.

To test your Web page in various resolutions using multiple browsers, follow these steps:

1. Choose File, Preview in Browser.

2. Select the Preview in Multiple Browsers option for the resolution at which you want to test your page. (If this option does not exist, then you most likely have only one Internet browser installed on your computer.)

3. A preview of your Web page opens in each of the Internet browsers installed on your computer.

Keeping an Eye on File Size

It's very important to keep an eye on how big your files become when you're designing your Web site. Everything (text, graphics, audio, video, animations, and so on) that is a part of your Web site contributes to the time it takes to display your pages in the user's browser.

If you've ever come across a Web site on the Internet that seems to take forever to load, large file sizes may be the reason (although a slow network connection is also a big factor, one that's beyond your control). Such items as sound and video files or even uncompressed photos can make for very inflated pages. A big file size results in a long wait. Compressing the file size of your graphics is explained in Chapter 6, "Creating and Modifying Graphics." Optimizing your code is discussed in Chapter 11, "Using Code in FrontPage."

There are often so many files to track in a site that it's easy to forget how quickly the download time adds up. To generate a file-size report, perform the following steps:

1. Choose View, Reports.
2. Select Files.
3. Select the desired Files option.
4. The applicable report summary tab opens.

Checking Your Links

It's always frustrating to find exactly what you're looking for on a Web site, only to discover that the link is no longer working. A good Web developer is someone who cares enough to ensure that all his or her links work. You not only need to be sure that links within your site go to the right place, but also links that lead to other sites.

With the rate at which Web sites are born and die, a link can become defunct before you've finished adding it to your page. Because of this, you need to check them regularly even after your site is live to make sure nothing's changed.

FrontPage has a wonderful system for keeping track of all your links. The Site Summary report, a customizable report you can create easily in FrontPage, enables you to check the status on all of the hypertext links contained in your Web site. The Site Summary report also has many other uses, as discussed in Chapter 22, "Maintaining a Published Web."

To generate a Site Summary report, do the following:

1. Choose View, Reports.
2. Select Site Summary. The Site Summary report opens, as shown in Figure 19.4.

FIGURE 19.4

The Site Summary report gives you a quick and efficient way to track down all your broken links. After all, if you don't know what's broken, you can't fix it.

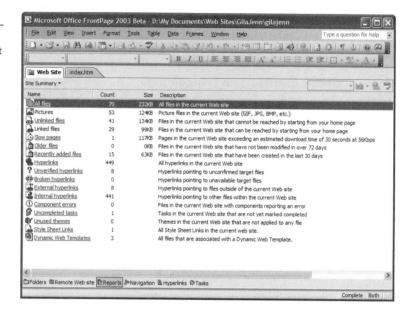

3. Click on any of the Hyperlinks report summaries (for example, the Hyperlinks summary) for more information.

4. The applicable report summary tab opens, as shown in Figure 19.5.

FIGURE 19.5

Use the Hyperlinks report to validate each link.

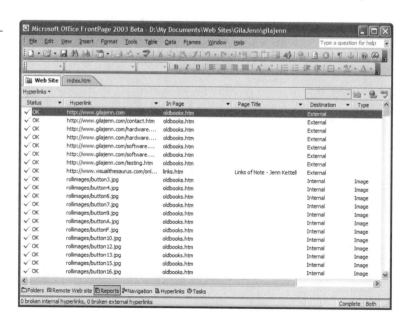

5. To return to the Site Summary report, click the drop-down menu just under the Web Site tab, then choose Site Summary.

Domains change ownership and purpose very quickly. Even if you're using the Hyperlinks report to check the validity of your links, it's a good idea to visit each linked site on a regular basis to confirm its content.

Proofreading Your Text

Before you go live with your Web site, it is a good idea to proofread your text. If you can, have other people proofread your text, too. There's nothing more valuable than another pair of eyes.

note

When you use the Site Summary report to check for broken links, FrontPage uses the most current saved version of the site on your local computer instead of the live version of your site located on the Internet.

One of the simplest things you can do to proofread your text is to run your pages through FrontPage's spell checker. To run the spell checker, do the following:

1. Choose Tools, Spelling or click the Spelling button in the Standard toolbar. The Spelling dialog box (see Figure 19.6) opens if a spelling error is detected.

FIGURE 19.6

Running your Web pages through FrontPage's spell checker is a piece of cake.

2. When an error is found, correct it by choosing an option from the Suggestions list box or by typing the correct word in the Change To box.

3. Click Change.

4. Repeat this process until FrontPage displays a message notifying you that the spell check is complete.

note

Spell checking works only in Design page.

Aside from spelling, you should also look for grammatical errors. If your site is heavy on text and you're short on grammar skills, a copy of Strunk & White's *Elements of Style* is quite useful. Alternatively, you can copy and paste your text into Microsoft Word and run the built-in grammar checker—but be prepared for a rather rigid assessment where many of the suggestions might significantly change the intended tone of your content. Finally, if you wrote your text before designing your site, be sure the tone of your content matches your design. Using flowery language on a site that looks like something from *The Matrix* just doesn't fly.

THE ABSOLUTE MINIMUM

Let FrontPage help you fix the last-minute details of your site before you go live. The ability to test your Web page in multiple browsers and screen resolutions enables you to see your Web page in a whole new light. Instead of ripping your hair out trying to figure out why your files are so big, where your links are broken, or how to correctly spell Mississippi, let FrontPage show you the way.

At an absolute minimum, you should feel confident that FrontPage has the power to solve most of your Web-page testing needs. By just adopting the test/preview techniques outlined in this chapter, you're well on your way to publishing a polished and professional-looking Web page.

Hopefully, your Web page will look consistent, regardless of the Internet browser your visitors use. Your file sizes should be manageable enough that your visitors don't feel the compelling need to run out for coffee and a doughnut while your page is loading. Your links should do what they're supposed to do and not take people to Neverland (or worse). And finally, the spelling on your Web page will make your second grade teacher beam with pride.

20

WEB SERVERS AND HOSTING

Although you can develop a Web site using FrontPage without having access to a Web server, viewing pages directly from files on your hard disk, eventually you will want to *publish* your site to make it available to the world. Deciding how and where to publish your Web site is almost as important as deciding what to put on the pages. To make your site available on the Internet, you need to place the files that comprise your site on a Web server, called a host, on the Internet. You might already have a Web hosting provider—for example, a server on your company's intranet. In most cases, however, you have to find a Web hosting provider, purchase space on the provider's Web server, and register a domain, or address, for the site to enable others to find it.

Choosing a Web hosting provider can be quite complicated, and it's not possible to go into a lot of detail on the subject in this chapter. You will, however, learn what types of servers and hosts work best with FrontPage, and will be pointed in the right direction when it comes to choosing a host for your site.

What's a Web Server?

A Web server consists of hardware, an operating system, and the software used to serve Web pages. The term *Web server* is often used interchangeably to refer to both the complete server, including the hardware and operating system, and the Web server software itself.

Although many designers don't get to decide what Web server environment to use (especially if they work for a corporation whose MIS department dictates those sorts of things), some have the luxury of deciding how their servers are set up or picking and choosing among hosting providers who meet their needs.

Using Windows Hosting Servers with IIS

The type of Web server used most often to host FrontPage sites is a Windows server operating system (such as Windows 2000 Server or Windows 2003 Server), using Microsoft's Internet Information Server (IIS) as the software that serves Web pages to browsers.

In addition, Windows desktop operating systems, such as Windows XP Professional, can run a smaller-scale version of IIS. This version is mainly designed for development and for very small-scale Web sites with few users. Because it's limited to 10 connections and only one Web site, it's easy to see why.

tip

The newest Windows Web server, Windows 2003 Server with IIS 6.0, is needed to run Windows SharePoint Services. If you want to use certain FrontPage 2003 features, such as Web Parts, you will need to make sure that your Web hosting provider uses this type of server.

Using Other Web Servers with FrontPage

When you use FrontPage as an authoring tool, you naturally may consider using Microsoft Internet Information Server (IIS) for your Web server. It's a logical choice because the FrontPage Server Extensions are installed automatically. (As an added bonus, using IIS enables you to deal with only one company—Microsoft—if you need customer support.) IIS is not your only choice, however. Microsoft FrontPage Extensions 2000 and 2002 can be installed on a wide variety of platforms and Web servers, as shown in Table 20.1 (the information in this table is from the Microsoft Developer Network Web site).

Table 20.1 FrontPage and Web Servers

Platform	Operating System
Alpha	Digital UNIX 4.0.f, 5.0
Intel x86	FreeBSD 3.3, 4.0
Intel x86	BSDI 3.3, 4.0
Intel x86	Linux 6.2, 7.0 (Red Hat Software)
Intel x86	Solaris 2.7, 2.8
PA-RISC	HP/UX 10.2, 11.0
Silicon Graphics	IRIX 6.3, 6.5
SPARC	Solaris 2.7, 2.8

tip

Ready-to-Run Software is a developer of FrontPage Server Extension ports for various Web server platforms. If you're interested in finding out the latest news about running FrontPage Extensions on non-Windows platforms, visit Ready-to-Run Software at http://www.rtr.com/Ready-to-Run_Software/.

So even if you don't have access to a Windows server with IIS, you may still be able to use FrontPage Server Extensions.

Hosting Support Required by FrontPage

To decide what type of hosting plan to choose, you need to know what hosting-related services you use or plan to use in FrontPage 2003. For hosting plans, there are essentially three levels of FrontPage support:

- None
- FrontPage Server Extensions
- Windows SharePoint Services

FrontPage Server Extensions

Earlier versions of FrontPage support *FrontPage Server Extensions*. These are a collection of programs that exist on the hosting server for the purpose of supporting FrontPage in the following ways:

- **Publishing**—FrontPage Server Extensions make the Web site–publishing process easier by eliminating the need to pass files through (sometimes cumbersome) FTP. FrontPage Server Extensions provide a way for FrontPage users to save files directly on the hosting server much more easily.

- **Browse-Time Web Components**—Many of the Web components that have carried over from earlier FrontPage versions, such as the discussion forum, hit counter, and search tool, require the use of Server Extensions to function.

- **Administration (Author-Time Web Components)**—Server Extensions enable the site owner to remotely configure site security. The site administrator can set up several levels of permissions, called *roles*, that allow access to different parts of the Web site. FrontPage users can then be assigned to a role that determines what they are allowed to modify on the site.

Although FrontPage Server Extensions have been superseded by Windows SharePoint Services in FrontPage 2003 and in Windows 2003 hosting servers, there are still a lot of hosting providers out there that only support FrontPage Server Extensions. Unless and until you need the latest features enabled by the use of FrontPage Web Parts, a server with FrontPage Server Extensions remains a viable choice for hosting. And, because FrontPage Server Extensions continue to be supported, you'll be able to eventually upgrade your hosting plan without losing any of your existing functionality.

Windows SharePoint Services

Windows SharePoint Services (formerly called SharePoint Team Services) are the latest and greatest way that FrontPage can integrate with the hosting server. When operated in conjunction with a hosting provider that uses Windows Server 2003 and SharePoint Services, FrontPage 2003 enables even more functionality.

The following features require the use of Windows SharePoint Services:

- **List View**—This Web component can be used to display data retrieved from a database query in a variety of formats.

- **Document Library View**—This Web component enables you to provide a library of Microsoft Office documents and to present them in several different ways.

- **Web Search (Full-Text Search)**—This extends the capability of the Web Search component of FrontPage Server Extensions 2002 to enable full-text searching.

- **Web Parts**—The next generation of Web components, Web Parts are driven by XML, an industry standard markup language used to format data, to generate their content. Users can add Web Parts using the Web Parts task pane (see Figure 20.1).

- **Data-Source Catalog**—This task pane makes it easy to tie data (say, from a database residing on your Web server) with the Web Parts that can use them.

The use of the data source catalog and associated Web Parts are discussed in more detail in Chapter 17, "Databases."

FIGURE 20.1

Web Parts are automatically enabled when you host with a provider that supports Windows SharePoint Services.

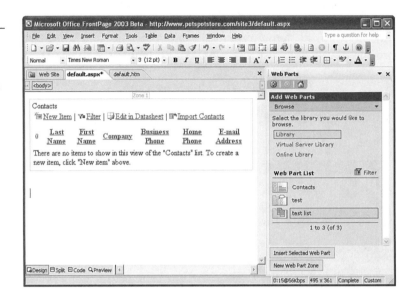

Because SharePoint is provided with Windows Server 2003, it clearly indicates the direction Microsoft is going. If you want to be able to leverage the power of XML and be able to quickly and easily develop data-driven Web sites using FrontPage, you should look for a hosting provider that offers SharePoint.

Managing SharePoint Services

If you have SharePoint Services enabled, you may be able to manage the properties of your Web remotely, depending on your hosting provider's policies. To do so, make sure you are connected to the Internet, and then open the Tools menu, choose Server, and select Administration Home. This opens a Web page like the one shown in Figure 20.2.

From this Web page, you can update general site settings such as the Web title and the default theme. You also can create Web Parts objects such as data lists, libraries, surveys, and more. When created, these Web Parts objects will automatically appear in the list in the Web Parts task pane.

Designing Your Site Without Using Server Extensions or SharePoint Services

From what you've read, it might seem like you absolutely must use a Web server with Server Extensions or SharePoint Services to produce a site with FrontPage. This is not the case. If your needs don't include the server-side functionality that Web components and Web Parts provide, or if you are willing to write your own server-side components, you can get away with using almost any hosting provider. That's because FrontPage 2003 supports the use of FTP for transferring files to just about any server. Instructions on using FTP to transfer files to a Web server that doesn't provide FrontPage Server Extensions can be found in Chapter 21, "Putting Pages on the Internet."

FIGURE 20.2

You can access the SharePoint Services administration page by opening the Tools menu, choosing Server, and selecting Administration Home.

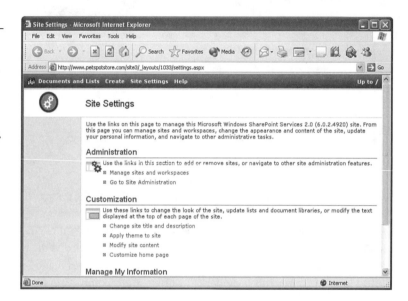

Even if you don't use FrontPage Server Extensions or SharePoint Services, the advantages to using FrontPage 2003 abound. You can still use the wide variety of templates, design controls and editing features, and site-management tools.

Disabling SharePoint Services and FrontPage Server Extensions

If you are using a hosting provider that doesn't support SharePoint Services or FrontPage Server Extensions, you should disable the use of features that require those services within your Web site to prevent them from being used inadvertently and causing problems.

To disable both SharePoint Services and FrontPage Server Extensions, follow these steps:

1. Open the File menu and choose Page Options.
2. The Page Options dialog box opens, as shown in Figure 20.3. Click the Authoring tab.

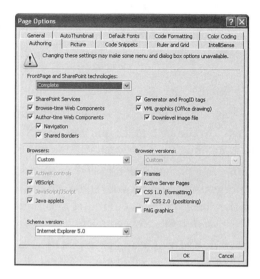

3. Click the FrontPage and SharePoint Technologies down arrow and choose
   None from the list that appears.

4. Notice that the check boxes that accompany the drop-down list are now
   unchecked; that's your sign that none of the components that require the use
   of FrontPage Server Extensions or SharePoint technologies are enabled.
   Click OK.

> Other options in the FrontPage and SharePoint technologies drop-down
> list are as follows:
>
> ■ **Default**—Select this option to enable the use of all FrontPage Server
>   Extensions and SharePoint Services components except shared borders.
>
> ■ **Complete**—Select this option to enable the use of all FrontPage Server
>   Extensions and SharePoint Services components.
>
> ■ **Custom**—Select this option to pick and choose the components you
>   want to enable in your web. For example, if your hosting provider sup-
>   ports Server Extensions but not SharePoint Services, choose Custom and
>   clear the SharePoint Services check box to disable just that one
>   technology.

Finding a Web Host

Now that you are aware of the different Web servers and how they work with
FrontPage, you need to explore the hosting options available to you. Your options

range from hosting your site on a free hosting provider to purchasing hosting space on a dedicated hosting server—with any number of options and prices in between. You should feel fairly confident that there is a plan out there for you.

Free Hosting

If you need to operate your Web site on a budget, you may want to consider using a free hosting service. These services can be a quick and easy way to get your Web site visible, although there are some limitations of which you need to be aware:

- **No domain hosting**—Free providers don't allow you to use a custom domain name (the name used to access your site, such as `www.your_domain.com`). Instead, they give you a URL that uses a common domain (such as `www.xyz_hosting.com/yoururl`) to access your site.

- **Banners and pop-up ads**—Free hosting providers need to make money somehow, and they do it by requiring that your Web site display banner ads or pop-ups from their advertisers.

- **Storage and bandwidth limits**—Free hosting accounts naturally have fairly steep limits on the amount of storage and bandwidth you get. It's not unusual for an interesting site to be shut down for exceeding its allotted bandwidth, especially if that site happens to be mentioned in a popular blog or message board.

The bright side of free hosting is, of course, the price. Many free hosting providers even support FrontPage Server Extensions. If you are interested in finding one of these services, the FrontPage Resource Center (`http://accessfp.net/freefp.htm`) is a good source of up-to-date information.

Purchasing Hosting Space

If you have created any kind of serious Web site, especially one for promoting a business, you need to set up an account with a hosting company. Fortunately, a real hosting account, complete with a domain name, isn't the expensive proposition it once was. There are some real bargains out there if you shop around.

The advantages are many. Hosting companies can register your domain name for you, provide you with e-mail addresses for your Web site, and give you the security you need so that your site (and your data) is available all the time and backed up regularly. Many hosting companies support FrontPage Extensions, SharePoint Services, and even ASP and ASP.NET, depending on your needs. They can even provide you with a database that you can use for Web Parts and other components that can use them. If you aren't sure whether you need a database or not, refer to Chapter 17 for some ideas on how to make use of them.

At first, you may be bewildered by the array of services and the sheer number of hosting providers out there. However, making a list of the features that are important to you (support for FrontPage 2003, naturally) and generating a short list of providers who offer those features can help.

FrontPage can even help you find a hosting account. Microsoft has thoughtfully provided a link to a Web site that lists a number of hosting companies that fully support FrontPage 2003. To access it, open the File menu and choose Publish Site to open the Remote Web Site Properties dialog box. Then, click the Click Here to Learn More link, as shown in Figure 20.4.

FIGURE 20.4

Microsoft provides this link in the Remote Web Site Properties dialog box to help you locate a hosting provider that supports FrontPage.

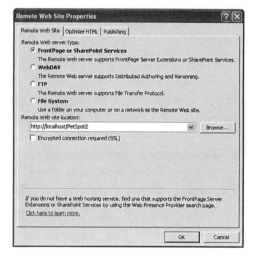

tip

There are a lot of Web hosting providers out there, and it can be a challenge to find just the right one. Fortunately, there are Internet resources that can help, even aside from Microsoft's link in the Remote Web Site Properties dialog box. One popular hosting buyer's guide is The List, at http://www.thelist.com. You can even search for hosting companies based on their support for FrontPage.

THE ABSOLUTE MINIMUM

There are a lot of options when it comes to choosing a Web hosting provider and plan. They range from completely free advertiser-supported services, to hosting on your ISP's provided Web space, to hosting on a dedicated server for busy sites. Adding to the mix is the fact that you need to figure out the level of FrontPage support that you need from your hosting provider.

If your site uses any of the FrontPage Web components that require the use of FrontPage Server Extensions, your choices are limited to hosting providers that offer them. Server Extensions are available on many platforms, not just Windows, so even if your hosting provider uses Linux or some other operating system, you still may be able to take advantage of them.

Windows SharePoint Services, on the other hand, are strictly a Windows Server 2003 technology, so the days of cooperation between FrontPage and other operating systems may be numbered. SharePoint Services do, however, enable you to take advantage of the latest features in FrontPage, including XML-driven Web Parts, and integration with SharePoint document libraries.

If you decide to use a hosting provider that doesn't support any of these features, however, you can still use FrontPage to publish a Web site. Simply disable the use of features in your Web that your hosting provider doesn't support via the Page Options dialog box.

21

Putting Pages on the Internet

After your site is in working order, you're ready to publish it to the Internet. When you publish your site, you simply copy your pages, folders, and associated files from your local computer to a remote computer that provides Internet access.

This may sound like a daunting task with a lot of technical mumbo-jumbo, but if you designed your pages within a FrontPage-defined site rather than as individual pages, FrontPage makes it easy. In most cases, the remote computer is a server maintained by a Web hosting company, and all the information about how and where to copy, or upload, your site will be provided to you. It's simply a matter of entering that information into FrontPage and telling it what to do. This chapter explains the details of how to accomplish this.

Getting Ready to Publish

Before you begin publishing your Web site, you should complete any housekeeping tasks outstanding on the site. This may sound like the equivalent of being told by your mother to go clean your room. If you don't get your site's house in order before uploading, however, the whole world will see your dirty socks. After your site is live is the wrong time to discover that your hyperlinks don't work, your graphics have vanished, or that the navigation buttons send your visitors to the outer reaches of cyberspace. So before publishing your site, be sure to test and review your pages thoroughly.

To learn more about testing your site and preparing for publishing it, see Chapter 19, "Testing Your Web."

The next prepublishing step is to arrange to have your site hosted somewhere. Your Web host may be your company or university's Web server, the Web server of your Internet service provider, or a Web hosting company.

For instructions on using and finding a Web host for your site, see "Finding a Web Host," p. 323 .

Once you've set up an account with a Web host, they should provide you with the following information:

- Your user name and password
- The directory assigned to your site on the host's Web server (with few exceptions, this is also the URL for your finished site)

Configuring the Publishing Tools

If you built your Web site using FrontPage—especially if you added Web components, themes, and other FrontPage-specific elements—it's important to use FrontPage's publishing tools to upload your site to the Web. This is done using FrontPage's Remote Web Site view, shown in Figure 21.1. When you use Remote Web Site view, FrontPage not only enables you to upload the entire site or any portion thereof that you specify, but it also helps you keep track of your pages and folders so that you can synchronize the remote and local copies of your site.

FRONTPAGE UPLOAD TOOLS VERSUS FILE TRANSFER PROTOCOL

If you've done any previous Web development using other applications, you're probably familiar with FTP (File Transfer Protocol) to upload your files to a Web server. This method for uploading is explained later in this chapter, but it's not the preferred method for working with FrontPage sites. When you upload using FTP, FrontPage cannot accurately track your site and Web components. This may leave you with a corrupted site that's no longer easily edited in FrontPage. Some of the FrontPage elements that may become corrupted are as follows:

- **Hit counters**—These are used to keep track of the number of visitors your Web site receives.

- **Form handlers**—Form handlers send form results (like feedback forms) submitted by your visitors to a text file, e-mail address, or database.

- **Search forms**—Search forms enable your visitors to perform searches on your Web site.

FIGURE 21.1

FrontPage's Remote Web Site view enables you to transfer pages and related files between your local site and the Web server.

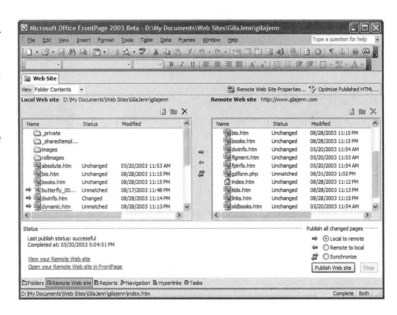

Remote Web Site View

The Remote Web Site view is publishing headquarters. To access this view, switch to Web Site view (either by opening a site in FrontPage or by clicking the Web Site tab at the top of the document window or selecting View, Folders from the menu if the site's already open), and then click the Remote Web Site button at the bottom of the screen. The first time you access the Remote Web Site view, you'll be prompted for information in the Remote Web Site Properties dialog box (shown in Figure 21.2).

The Remote Web Site Properties dialog box contains three tabs:

- The Remote Web Site tab
- The Optimize HTML tab
- The Publishing tab

FIGURE 21.2

So many choices! In most cases, the FrontPage or SharePoint Services option will best serve your needs.

The Remote Web Site Tab

The Remote Web Site tab enables you to establish the method by which you plan to publish your site and where you want your finished site to be uploaded. Fill in the fields on this tab as follows:

1. Click the FrontPage or SharePoint Services option to choose FrontPage or SharePoint Services as your Remote Web server type.

2. In the Remote Web Site Location box, type the URL provided by your Web host for your site (for example, http://www.gilajenn.com).

3. If you require a secure communications channel, click the Encrypted Connection Required (SSL) check box in order to select this. This feature is used when you need to prevent the interception of critical information, such as if you're accepting credit cards when selling goods through your site.

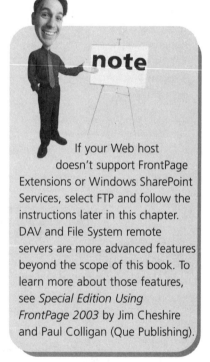

note

If your Web host doesn't support FrontPage Extensions or Windows SharePoint Services, select FTP and follow the instructions later in this chapter. DAV and File System remote servers are more advanced features beyond the scope of this book. To learn more about those features, see *Special Edition Using FrontPage 2003* by Jim Cheshire and Paul Colligan (Que Publishing).

The Optimize HTML Tab

The Optimize HTML tab, shown in Figure 21.3, contains settings to eliminate extraneous space and other elements in your code before publishing. By optimizing your code, you can reduce the size of your page files, thus decreasing the necessary download time when visitors view your site. There are varying pros and cons to optimization, depending on the element. Some of the elements you may remove include the following:

- **Comments**—Comments are notes that you can insert into your code to guide you during development. These notes aren't visible on the page, but because they're included in the page file, they can increase download time. The downside to eliminating comments is that they'll no longer be available if you somehow lose your local copy of the site and need to download the site from the remote server.

- **Whitespace**—The term whitespace in this context refers to indentation and blank lines that make your code more readable, thus helping you navigate through it. You can save on file size by eliminating this space—technically, HTML can be a single line containing all the tags and content for your page—but if you need to view the code later, it can be quite a job wading through it.

- **Word tags**—If you imported your page from Word, then that page will contain lots of extraneous tags and code that are used by Word to render the page both as a Word document and as HTML. Unless you plan to open this page in Word again later, this is one of those elements that can be optimized without any downside.

- **Vector markup and tracing images**— If you used FrontPage's drawing tools, those elements were created using Vector Markup Language (VML). This markup is included in the page code, along with a tag inserting a GIF or JPG file automatically created by the drawing tool. Unless you plan to edit the drawing later using

note

A *tracing image* is a graphic image that can serve as a prototype for your page's layout. When you apply a tracing image to a page, it guides you as you create layout tables and position images, but doesn't appear on the page when viewed with a browser. To learn more about tracing images, refer to Chapter 9, "Using Tables."

caution

The Optimize HTML tab of the Remote Web Site Properties dialog box enables you to optimize the code found on the remote server, but leaves the code on your local machine in its original state. If you want to optimize the code on your local machine, open a page and then open the Tools menu and choose Optimize HTML. Optimizing your local files, however, can lead to the elimination of comments and template links that are still of use to you.

FrontPage, this is another element that can be optimized right out of your code. Tracing images are also generally superfluous after the initial design stage of your pages.

FIGURE 21.3

The Optimize HTML tab enables you to reduce the size of Web site files.

The Publishing Tab

The Publishing tab (see Figure 21.4) enables you to choose from the following parameters for how you want FrontPage to publish your Web site:

- **Changed Pages Only**—Used to selectively publish your files. FrontPage compares the files on your local computer with those on the remote computer, and then publishes only the new or modified pages.

- **All Pages, overwriting pages already on destination**—Used to upload the entire local site to the remote server, regardless of which files are already on the server. This option should be used carefully, because if you overwrite files on the server that are more current than the ones you're uploading—say, if you uploaded from your office or laptop earlier in the day and are now uploading from your home computer—there's no way to recover them.

- **Include Subsites**—If you created subsites within your site, checking this box will instruct FrontPage to upload them when publishing the parent site.

- **Determine Changes by Comparing Source and Destination Sites**—Used to set the parameters for overwriting files based upon which is the source and which is the destination.

- **Use Source File Timestamps to Determine Changes Since Last Publish**—Used to set the parameters for overwriting files based on when the file was last saved. If you're working on multiple machines, this is usually your best option.
- **Log Changes During Publish**—Creates a log file detailing the names and dates when files were published.

Publishing a Site

After you configure the settings in the Remote Web Site Properties dialog box and click OK, the Name and Password dialog box opens. This is where you enter the user name and password provided to you by your Web host. You're then returned to the Remote Web Site view, which displays your local site on the left and the remote server on the right.

To publish your site, choose a transfer type from the bottom-right corner of the FrontPage window. You have the following three options:

- **Local to Remote**—Used to upload new or modified pages to your Web site.
- **Remote to Local**—Used to download Web pages from a remote computer to your local computer.
- **Synchronize**—Used to synchronize pages between your local computer and your remote computer, so both computers contain the same versions of each file and any pages that previously existed only on one computer are copied to the other. This is particularly useful if you work on multiple machines,

such as one at home and one at the office, so you can synchronize files that you modified and uploaded to the remote server from the office with your local computer at home before making further modifications.

After selecting the direction in which to transfer the files, click the Publish Web Site button. The Status area will track the progress of your transfer and inform you when it's complete.

Using the Remote Web Site View

After you've published your Web site, you can use the Remote Web Site view to perform a number of functions. You can upload new or modified pages to your Web site, using local-to-remote publishing. Using remote-to-local publishing, you can download Web pages from the Internet to your computer. Or, you can match local and remote files using synchronized publishing.

One really good feature of the Remote Web Site view is that it enables you to get a bird's-eye view of both your local Web site (on the left) and your remote Web site (on the right) at the same time, as shown in Figure 21.5. This lets you make side-by-side comparisons of the files residing on both Web sites.

FIGURE 21.5

When you synchronize files, the Name field displays icons noting which files will be updated, while the Status field provides insight into why the files are being updated— or not.

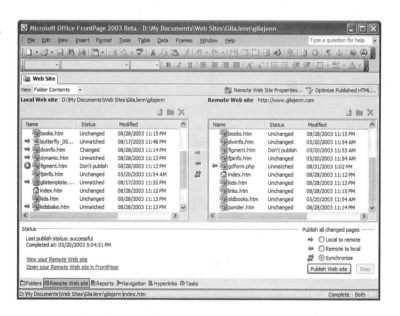

You'll notice, depending upon the publishing option chosen, that there are arrows adjacent to the file names. The direction of the arrow designates the publishing status of each file:

- **Right arrow**—Uploading from the local computer to the remote server.
- **Left arrow**—Downloading from the remote server to the local computer.
- **Double-sided arrow**—Synchronizing files.
- **X in a red circle**—File is set to Don't Publish status.
- **Blank**—File is the same in both locations.

The arrow icons in the Name field correlate with the status of each file. The Status field will display one of the following:

- **New**—The page was created after the last time you published.
- **Changed**—A previously published page has been edited.
- **Unchanged**—The page hasn't been edited since the last time it was published. When synchronizing files, these pages aren't transferred.
- **Unmatched**—The file exists only on either the local or remote server, and FrontPage can't match it to a similar file on the other server.
- **Conflict**—If a file's been modified in both the local and remote locations since you last published, FrontPage can't tell which version contains the proper content. Conflicts also can mean that a file was created or edited in an application other than FrontPage. To resolve the conflict, choose which version of the file should be published and publish the page individually, as shown in the next section.

> **note**
>
> There may be times when you want to update your site's files, but not a page that's still a work in progress. To set a file to Don't Publish status, right-click the filename and select Don't Publish from the context menu. The file will retain this status until you deselect this option using the same procedure.

Publishing Individual Files

At times, you'll want to publish individual files rather than publishing or synchronizing the entire site. If you're resolving conflicts between local and remote files, you'll want to use this option to transfer the proper version of the file so that both sites are current. This option also saves time if you're only publishing one file, such as a new page.

To publish individual files, simply select one or more files and use the arrows located between the Local Web Site and Remote Web Site listings to transfer the files in the direction you choose. Alternatively, you can click and drag the files to the other site listing with your mouse.

Publishing Your Web Site Using FTP

When the Internet was in its infancy, one of the first standards developed was a way to copy files from one computer to another. This process is known as *File Transfer Protocol (FTP)*. If your Web host doesn't have FrontPage Extensions or Windows SharePoint Services installed on the server—or if you're having trouble using the default FrontPage method to upload your files—try using FTP. FTP is the most common method of transferring files from a local computer to a remote server and can communicate with virtually any Web server.

When you publish your Web site using FTP, FrontPage still takes care of all the hard stuff. The key difference between FrontPage's proprietary upload protocol and FTP is how it handles FrontPage Extensions and Web components. If the site doesn't have the extensions installed, it stands to reason that not only can you not use the default publishing option, but any other features that require those extensions also won't work. Web components on your pages will crash or return pages stating that the extensions aren't available. If you must resort to using FTP, you should remove these features from your site before publishing.

To publish your Web site using FTP, do the following:

1. If you're not already in Remote Web Site view, click the Remote Web Site tab in the bottom-left corner of the FrontPage window.

2. Open the Remote Web Site Properties dialog box. If this is the first time you've configured the remote Web site for this site, the dialog box will open automatically when you switch to Remote Web Site view. Otherwise, click the Remote Web Site Properties button in the top-right portion of the screen.

3. In the Remote Web Site Properties dialog box's Remote Web Site tab, click the FTP option under Remote Web Server Type.

4. In the Remote Web Site Location field, enter the information given to you by your host. In some cases, the FTP location is different from your actual site URL, such as `ftp://ftp.example.com`.

5. In the FTP Directory box, type the name for the folder assigned to you by your Web host, as shown in Figure 21.6. If no FTP directory folder was assigned, leave this box blank.

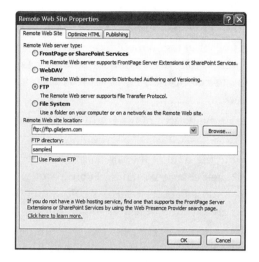

6. If your host requires the use of Passive FTP, click the Use Passive FTP check box to check it.

7. Use the Optimize HTML and Publishing tabs as needed.

8. Click OK. The Name and Password dialog box opens.

9. Type the required information in the applicable boxes, and then click OK.

10. The Remote Web Site view is again displayed, showing the local Web site on the left and the remote Web Site on the right. Click the Publish Web Site button in the bottom-right corner of the screen.

11. In the Status section of the Remote Web Site view, a green status bar indicates the progress of the publishing operation.

12. Upon completion, a message is displayed, indicating whether your Web site was published successfully, as shown in Figure 21.7.

Status	Publish all changed pages
Last publish status: successful Completed at: 05/20/2003 5:04:51 PM	⇒ ⦿ Local to remote ⇐ ○ Remote to local ⇄ ○ Synchronize [Publish Web site] [Stop]

Generating a Publishing Status Report

Organization is key when publishing to a remote server because everything you upload is immediately live and visible to the online community. One tool that can help you keep track of your site's publishing status is the Publish Status report. To view this report, do the following:

1. Click the Reports tab at the bottom of the FrontPage window to enter Reports view.

2. Click the down arrow to the right of the Site Summary heading at the top of the Reports view, and then choose Workflow, Publish Status. Alternatively, open the View menu, choose Reports, select Workflow, and then choose Publish Status; this enables you to access the report directly without first entering Reports view.

3. The Publish Status report opens, as shown in Figure 21.8.

FIGURE 21.8

The Publish Status report displays a list of every file in the site— including pages, graphics, and multimedia— and whether or not it's set to be included when the site is published.

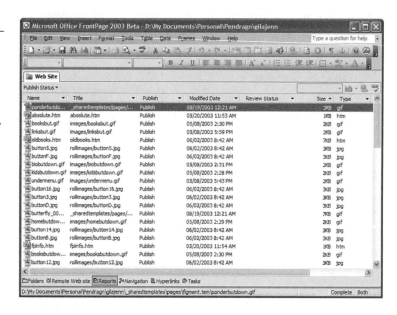

The publishing status of each file is different in this report than in the Remote Web Site view. Each file listed in the report is marked as either Don't Publish or Publish, along with the date the file was last modified. Files marked Don't Publish will automatically be flagged and listed at the top of the report. The Publish Status report will also list the status of all the other files in the site, where they're located in your local site folders, and the date they were last modified.

Understanding Search Engines and Your Site

One of the first things any site owner should do after launching a Web site is to get that site listed in a Web search engine. Registering with a search engine can be one of the best ways to enable people to find you.

That said, simply registering your site with a search engine is not necessarily going to drive a huge amount of traffic to your site. You also need to find a way to improve your site's rank in the list. For example, suppose there are 100,000 sites that cover the subject of home improvement. If your site is also devoted to home improvement, but your rank (or the number of entries that appear before yours in a search engine) is 85,001, even the most dedicated Web surfer is unlikely to wade through tens of thousands of other entries to find you.

Two terms you're going to encounter frequently in this chapter, and when you do more research into Web-site promotion, are *meta tag*, and *keyword*. These two words are often used interchangeably, although there is a difference. A *meta tag* is an HTML tag that describes the basic content of a Web page; *keywords* are one element of a meta tag and provide individual words that help to describe that content.

Although most of us can name at least a few search engines, such as Google and Yahoo, there are literally thousands out there. Many have very different policies about how a site gets listed, how it's ranked once it is listed, and so on. For example, some search engines

- Ignore or don't heavily rate included meta tags or keywords
- Ignore or don't heavily rate the actual site content
- Give extra weight to h1, h2, and h3 headings used on a home page

This has become such a major issue that it has spawned a whole new field called *search engine optimization (SEO)*, in which professionals study what works best for achieving a superior search-engine rank, and are often paid very good money to share that data with site owners and designers. Even a relative novice, however, can do his or her research, experiment with the possibilities, and manage to improve a site's search-engine ranking.

In order to improve your site's rank, it helps to understand that, using a process called *spidering*, search engines check a site's content by simply reading the text. Unfortunately, however, they typically don't read a lot of it—meaning they won't dig around to find your best content. Some only look at the first 200 text characters or the first 10–15 words.

One way to address this problem is to always include titles on your pages and to keep those titles highly descriptive—but short (12 words or fewer is best). If your home page consists primarily of images or long titles, your search-engine rank could be lower, making it harder for people to find you. Look at your design carefully.

Also, remember the tables and frames discussed in Chapters 9, "Using Tables," and 10, "Using Frames." The use of frames and tables, depending on how they're designed, can actually make it tougher for content on your site to get picked up and listed by a search engine.

Using frames and tables to lay out a page in such a way that it enables notice by search engines is an advanced topic that could warrant its own chapter. For the sake of clarity, however, this section looks at an easy example of how layout can affect how your site is seen by a search engine.

Figure 21.9 shows a layout with four different tables, numbered 1–4, with Table 1 acting as a sort of banner, Table 2 offering links to pages on the site, Table 3 serving as the meat and potatoes of the content of the page, and Table 4 housing a copyright message. A search engine will look at this layout sequentially, moving first through Table 1, then down to Table 2, and on to Tables 3 and 4. The contents don't appear, however, until Table 3, which means that the search engine could exhaust its quick peek at your site before it reaches what you may most want it to see.

FIGURE 21.9
This table layout doesn't begin to display the unique content of a page until Table 3, which may prevent a search engine from seeing it.

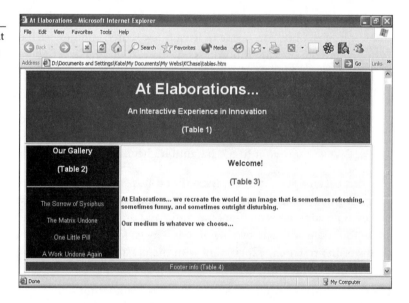

One simple way to address this is to shuffle your format around so that the actual page content appears in Table 2, as shown in Figure 21.10. This increases the likelihood that the search engine will find what it should.

If you are instead working with frames, you have a similar situation in that you must watch what frame becomes the main content frame. Some search engines always look at the right-most frame first, while others may simply look at the first frame they see and then move forward.

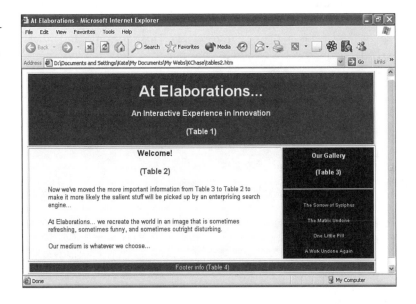

For this reason, you may want to think carefully about layout and whether a redesign may help you achieve better search-engine results.

Beyond that, you should add to your home page a good site description and keywords that, when chosen with extreme precision, can dramatically increase your site's rank. You'll learn about both later in this chapter.

Search Engine Tools

Pay no attention to e-mail solicitations from individuals and companies promising you—for a fee—to either list you in search engines or to ensure that you'll get top ranking in them. The truth is that no one can guarantee you a slot in a search engine's top 10 rank. If someone makes that promise, run!

Although some Web site promotion firms offer very legitimate services, some do nothing more than the kind of steps you can do for yourself—and a few have been known to pocket their customers' money while doing nothing at all.

That said, a host of tools exist—some for free, some for a fee—that help you generate the top keywords for promotion of a particular type of site, product, or service. Before you buy one, however, consider some of the online meta tag builders that you can use right from your Web browser, such as the one at `http://vancouver-webpages.com/META/mk-metas.html` (see Figure 21.11). This site can help you generate suitable HTML meta keywords to add to your page.

FIGURE 21.11

Vancouver-
Webpages Meta
Builder is one of
several sites that
enables you to
generate HTML
meta tags from
your browser by
providing just a
bit of informa-
tion.

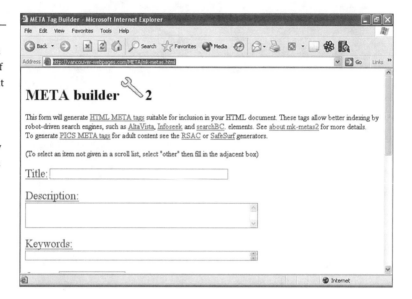

Also, rather than spend a large amount of time focusing on tools you can download, consider the one that exists between your ears. Do some advanced reading, talk to other people you know who run Web sites, and brainstorm to come up with your best ideas for the types of features, keywords, and promotional efforts that can help your cause.

Adding Keywords

Keywords are individual descriptive words that a person might use to search for a site like yours in a Web search engine. For example, a site created to provide a resource for nursing professionals might include keywords such as nurse, nursing, RN, LPN, VN, medical professional, hospital, and so on.

FrontPage includes no tool for adding keywords, also called meta keywords, to your pages. Instead, you must add them by hand using Code view. Although using this view isn't fully covered until Chapter 11, "Using Code in FrontPage," you get a preview here.

Before you begin, carefully consider which keywords may be best to use. Don't just come up with a short list of keywords off the top of your head. Research the type of keywords used by sites covering the same general topic(s) as yours.

After you have a list of at least 10 strong keywords, do the following:

1. Open your Web's home page and click the Code tab in the bottom-left area of the screen to switch to Code view.

2. On the line immediately beneath the title for your home page, press Enter to create a blank line.

3. In this blank line, type the following:

   <META NAME="keywords" CONTENT="

4. Immediately following the last quotation mark, type your keywords, each separated by a comma.

5. When you are finished adding keywords, type a closing quotation mark (") after the final keyword, followed by a closing (right) angle bracket (>).

note

You can modify and/or add keywords at any time. However, you must always follow this syntax.

The result should look similar to Figure 21.12. Double-check to be sure your syntax is correct and that you've made no typographical errors.

FIGURE 21.12

An example of a Web page in Code view where meta keywords have been added starting on line 9.

Writing Good Descriptions

Imagine how you would briefly but fully and richly describe the focus of your site to someone who had never visited it. As you do, consider how you can sell the site's content in perhaps 20 words or less in such a way that readers or listeners will run—not walk—to the nearest Web browser to check it out.

That's the task you face in creating a good site description, which will appear in a Web search engine listing when someone looks for sites fitting the topic you cover. While you work, think of yourself as part evangelist, part expert, and part marketing writer.

If it does not sound easy, don't worry. It's not supposed to be. You want to choose your words very carefully because they will present a major statement about what your site is about. Don't expect to get it perfect on the 1st, or even the 10th, attempt.

It's sometimes wise to come up with a short list of three to five of your best descriptions to test on an audience of friends or associates, especially ones who have some familiarity with your site already. Ask which one reads best.

After you have the description you want to use (you can always modify it later), you add it to your home page in Code view much as you added the keywords in the previous section.

To add a description to your home page, do the following:

1. Open your Web's home page and click the Code tab in the bottom-left area of the screen to switch to Code view.

2. On the line immediately beneath the title for your home page title (where you previously inserted your keywords), press Enter to create a blank line.

3. In this blank line, type the following:

   <META NAME="description" CONTENT="

4. After the last quotation mark, type your description, immediately followed by a closing quotation mark (") and a closing (right) angle bracket (>).

Figure 21.13 shows the home page seen in Figure 21.12, but with the description added on line 9. Again, verify that you have the syntax correct and that you haven't made any typing errors.

Listing with Search Engines

Although you can wait for a search engine to pick you up on its own—which does happen sometimes—it's much smarter to register with a search engine to expressly request that it include you in its listings. It can take 2–4 weeks from the time you register your site until its first listing appears, but this is usually still quite a bit faster than waiting for the search engine to find you.

FIGURE 21.13

A sample index.htm page with a description added on line 9, between the title and the keywords.

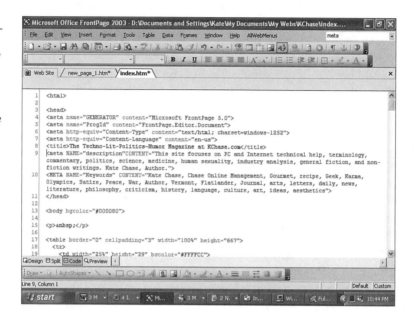

When you register with a search engine, consider these suggestions:

- Register your site with all the major search engines, including AOL, Alexa, AskJeeves, Google, HotBot, Inktomi, iWon, LookSmart, Lycos, MSN, and Yahoo.

- Before you register, check each search engine's Web-based pages offering recommendations on registering for best results; some may differ from others.

- Identify your competition and check their keywords and site descriptions (see the sidebar for more information).

ABOUT YOUR COMPETITION

Do you know other sites that cover the same basic topic that yours does? If so, see what keywords and descriptions they use and how they rank in search engines. You can usually find this by checking the site's code (in Internet Explorer, open the View menu and choose Source).

You also should use various search engines to look for additional sites that cover the same topic as yours and check those sites out. While you're looking, you would be wise to see what they have on their site that you think might bring you a wider audience. You don't want to just duplicate their efforts, however; you want to adopt their idea, but make it very much your own.

After your site has been registered with various search engines and begins to appear in search-engine listings, it's a good idea to monitor your ranking in each search engine on a regular basis. As you make changes to your site—adjusting keywords, changing the description, modifying and enhancing your content—try to determine which changes, if any, improve your ranking. If a particular set of keywords suddenly jumps your rank to number 5 or number 15 when you were previously listed at number 200, it likely indicates that you have found the right set of keywords. But if you change your keywords and notice your ranking drops sharply, you should pay attention to that as well.

THE ABSOLUTE MINIMUM

By now, you should feel you've got a pretty good handle on what it takes to get a site published. The absolute minimum you should know is that if you built your site with proprietary FrontPage elements—hit counters, feedback forms, and other Web components—it's best to publish on a host server that has FrontPage Extensions and/or Windows SharePoint Services installed.

Finally, you should know that a Web site is rarely static. Even after you've published the site, you'll likely want to add new pages and modify the existing ones. That's what keeps the Web—and your little corner of it—alive and vibrant. It also keeps people coming back to your site for more. Using the Remote Web Site view, you can easily transfer updates between your local and remote computers.

22

MAINTAINING A PUBLISHED WEB

Do you think your diligence and drive can take a breather now that your site is published and live? Unfortunately, the answer is no.

Even though you tested and checked your site rigorously before you published (as detailed in Chapter 19, "Testing Your Web"), it's vital that you reexamine it after it is live to be sure everything was published correctly. When that is done, you need to shift gears to focus on making certain that your site remains well maintained and up-to-date. You also need to clean up the clutter—such as pages and folders you no longer want or need—you may have left behind.

It's also time to think about what other content you want to add to your site, or have yet to finish. Often, most of us publish before everything we want to offer is ready to go, and post first publishing is a great time to take inventory of the situation.

Remember, FrontPage isn't just a Web-design package; its other job is to help you manage your site. It includes some features, such as site reporting and task assignment, that can help you keep track of the jobs still pending along with problems that may crop up on your site.

Creating and Deleting Folders

On your PC, every new Web you create is contained within a different folder, just as your individual applications usually install to separate folders, and your My Documents folder usually contains word-processing and other work-type files you create. The folder containing your Web is stored within a master folder, called the root or root Web, which holds all the Webs (often, this is the My Webs folder under My Documents). Any folders contained within an individual Web (such as the images folder) are actually subfolders because they're contained within a main folder holding that Web.

One of the jobs you may face when maintaining your site involves creating new (sub)folders in or removing existing (sub)folders from your FrontPage Web. Creating a new (sub)folder is wise when you begin to amass a number of files in your main or root folder and want to organize them into collections. The need to delete a (sub)folder may arise because you simply don't want or need a particular folder any longer.

To create a new subfolder within your root folder, do the following:

1. With your Web displayed in Folders view, right-click the folder in which you want to create a new subfolder, choose New, and then choose Folder.

2. A new folder is added to your Web. Type a label for the new folder, and then press Enter.

note

Do you want to create a subfolder that is normally hidden from view? This is often done when you want to store scripts or special images in a folder not normally visible to others who may work from your PC. If you do, in step 3 type an underscore (_) before the name of the folder like so, _old.

To delete a subfolder from your root folder, do the following:

1. With your Web displayed in Folders view, right-click the subfolder you want to remove and choose Delete.

2. When asked to confirm the removal, click Yes.

Removing Pages and Subfolders from a Published Site

What happens if you've removed a page or subfolder from your FrontPage Web, but you find that the page or subfolder still exists on your published Web site? In that case, you can remove them from your PC-based Web, republish your site, and when prompted whether you want to remove the files on the Web server that are no longer in your local Web, click Yes to delete them. You can also use FrontPage's Remote Web Site view to delete the page or subfolder from the Web server. Here's how you do it:

Normally, a subfolder should be empty of files before you try to remove it. To delete an individual file within a folder, click to select it, and then press the Delete key.

1. Access the Remote Web Site view by opening the View menu and choosing Remote Web Site.

2. In the Remote Web Site pane on the right-hand side of the screen, locate and select the file or subfolder you want to delete, as shown in Figure 22.1.

3. Click the Delete button (the one with an X on it) just above the Remote Web Site pane.

If you haven't already deleted the file or subfolder on your local Web when you perform this operation, you need to repeat the previous steps 2 and 3 for the left-hand Local Web Site pane. Doing so ensures that you won't develop conflicts created when your local Web and your remote Web contents no longer match up.

FIGURE 22.1

Locate the file or subfolder in the Remote Web Site pane, then click the Delete button just above the pane to remove it.

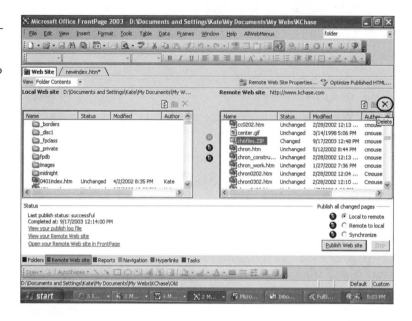

Creating Tasks

Task management in FrontPage is a way for you—especially when working with a group of people to develop and maintain a site—to keep track of who's responsible for what and what remains to be done. You can assign a task to virtually any type of work to be done on the site, from the creation of a specific Web page to individual elements like a graphic, sound file, or video.

The data available under each assigned task includes the following:

- **Status**—Notes whether the work is finished or is in progress.
- **Task**—Notes the specific task to be completed.
- **Assigned to**—Identifies who (a specific user or an entire workgroup) is responsible for completing the task.
- **Priority**—Displays the task's priority. You can assign either low, medium, or high priority to each task to help delineate which are most important.
- **Associated with**—Lists any files related to the task at hand.
- **Modified date**—Displays the most recent date on which the task details were modified.
- **Description**—Includes brief information about the exact nature of the task to be completed.

Follow these steps to create a task for your site:

1. With the Web you're working on open in FrontPage, open the View menu and choose Tasks.

2. Open the Edit menu, choose Tasks, then select Add Task.

3. The New Task dialog box opens (see Figure 22.2). Fill in the appropriate information and choose a task priority.

4. Click OK.

FIGURE 22.2

Don't forget to give the task a name and a description, and to assign a priority to it.

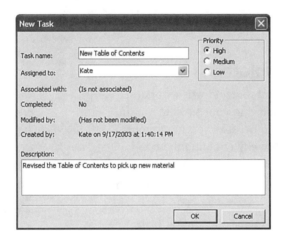

The instructions change slightly when you want to associate a file with a task. This is useful when you have a page under development or want to remind the person assigned to use a particular graphic or sound file with it.

Here's how to associate a file with a task:

1. Open your Web in Folder view.

2. Locate and select the file you want to associate with a particular task.

3. Click the down arrow just to the right of the New Page toolbar button and choose Task.

4. The New Task dialog box opens. Fill in the task information, including a priority setting.

5. Click OK.

After a task is assigned, you can jump right into working on that task from the Tasks screen. Here's how:

1. Open the View menu and choose Tasks.

2. For tasks not associated with a file, right-click on the task and choose Edit Task to open the Task Details window; then, select Start Task. For tasks associated with a file, right-click and choose Start Task.

Once Start Task is selected, FrontPage opens the task to be completed.

Marking a Task As Completed

One situation you want to avoid when working with a busy Web is allowing your tasks to mount. Often, this can happen because you fail to mark tasks as completed, thereby enabling them to be removed from the working assignment list.

Follow these steps to change a task's status to complete:

1. Open the View menu and choose Tasks.

2. Right-click the task to change and choose Mark Complete (see Figure 22.3).

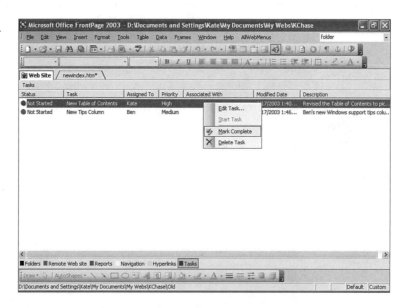

> **note**
>
> The procedure for marking a task as completed is a bit different when the task is associated with a file. In that case, anytime you work on a task and save your work, you'll be asked whether the task is complete. Choose Yes, and the task will be marked as finished.

FIGURE 22.3

A sample list under Tasks view, where you can right-click on a task to change its status.

Deleting a Task

After you (or someone else) finish a task, you should remove it from your task list. The same is true when, even if the task isn't finished, you decide not to complete the job involved (for example, you decide you no longer want to include a particular element, such as a site map, in your site).

Here's how to delete a task:

1. Open the View menu and choose Tasks.

2. In the Task list, right-click the task you want to remove and choose Delete.

STAYING FRESH

As you review your site, look for material that tends to date your site. Holiday content (text or pictures) or anything related to a time-specific event can look bad if left on your site more than a day or two past the event itself. Also, if you tend to put dates on all your pages but you don't expect to frequently update your site, you might want to reconsider; if many of your pages bear a date six months or more in the past, it tends to affect the freshness of your site.

If you don't have time to do a full site redesign but want to change the look of your site enough to make people recognize the difference, simply change your home page colors or try a different theme. This makes for a fast face-lift until you have the time to do more.

Finally, don't bite off more than you can realistically chew. Don't start several daily features (columns, news round-ups, and so on) that will require you to spend more time than you have trying to keep current.

Using Reports

FrontPage 2003's Reports option enables you to track and analyze specific information about your published site. For example, to see an overview of your site's vital statistics, you can view the Site Summary report (shown in Figure 22.4), which you access by opening the View menu, choosing Reports, and then selecting Site Summary.

Except for the Site Summary report, which is a category unto itself, FrontPage divides the remaining available reports into the following categories:

- **Files**—Use the reports in this category to check the files on your site, including their overall age, status, and task assignment. This can give you a good idea of how dated some of your files are and whether a major housecleaning or updating may be in order.

■ **Shared Content**—The reports in this category outline which features, such as themes and styles, are shared by more than one page. Use this to get an idea of what themes and such are in use on your site.

■ **Problems**—This is where to look for issues that affect usage, including pages that exceed satisfactory download times, broken hyperlinks, and nonworking components. Use these reports whenever you are performing regular maintenance.

■ **Workflow**—The reports in this category provide specifics about who is working on what pages. This is useful when a team of people is helping you with the site.

■ **Usage**—Check the reports in this category for details about site usage, including traffic, which sites are referring visitors to your site, and what browsers and operating systems are being used to access your site. This can help you decide how to tailor content to match the needs of the tools being used by your most frequent visitors.

FIGURE 22.4

A Site Summary report for a site where much of the content is older, but for which there are no other discernable problems.

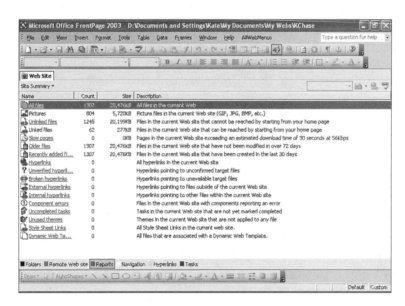

To access a report in FrontPage 2003, do the following:

1. Open the View menu and choose Reports.

2. In the Reports submenu, choose Site Summary, or choose the category that best describes the type of information you want to find.

3. If you chose a report category, a list of reports in that category is displayed. Choose the report you want to view, as shown in Figure 22.5.

4. Review the report when it appears in your FrontPage window.

FIGURE 22.5

The specific items available when you select the Problems category.

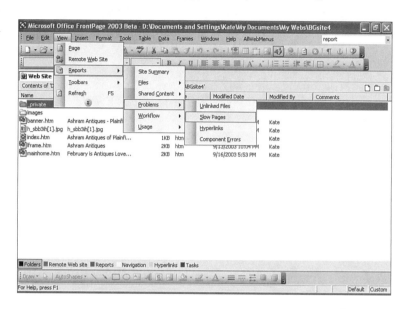

Unfortunately, reports don't work for everyone. For example, if your Web hosting service doesn't have FrontPage Server Extensions installed or it is not configured to enable you to receive report information, you'll receive a message that states "There is no usage data available for this Web site, because it has not been published to a server that supports usage analysis." If this happens to you, contact your Web hosting service; there may be something they can do to help you access report information.

note

If you find you can't access all components of FrontPage's Reports feature, your Web hosting service may have an alternative reporting mechanism—often presented via a special Web page—where you can check your site data. Check with your service provider for more information.

Setting Reports Filters

Not all data provided by FrontPage's various reports may be useful to you. To zero in on the information that is helpful in your analysis, you might want to set up filters that will block the data you don't need or want to see.

To apply a filter, do the following:

1. From your Web in FrontPage, open the View menu, choose Reports, and select the report you want to see.

2. Locate the column that contains the condition you want to filter by. For example, to filter by file type, displaying only pages of a particular type, locate the Type column.

3. Click the down arrow next to the column name, and choose the condition. For example, to display HTM pages only, choose htm from the list (see Figure 22.6).

FIGURE 22.6

In this Files report, you can set the filter so it only lists HTM pages, for example.

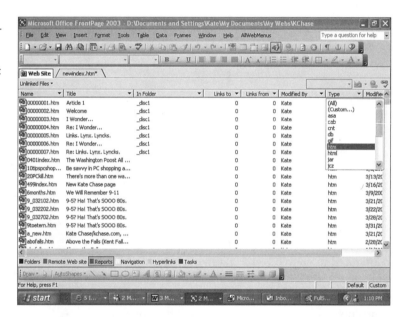

Any filter(s) you set will remain in place when you close and later reopen the site. However, if you later want to remove a filter you've added, you can do that, too.

To remove a filter, do the following:

1. From within an open report, right-click anywhere.

2. Choose Remove Filters.

Keeping a Copy of Reports

Some organized people like to keep a copy of individual site reports because they feel it helps them analyze changes and see where their repeat problems occur.

Although doing so is optional, you can easily keep a copy of your reports as well. That said, only some types of report data can be saved. This includes the following:

- Files
- Shared content
- Problems
- Workflow

To save a report, do the following:

1. With the Web open in FrontPage, open the View menu, choose Reports, and then select the report you want to run and save.

2. Open the File menu and choose Save As.

3. Type a name for your saved report and specify a location (try to keep your reports in the same folder for easier reference).

4. Click Save.

If you prefer to copy your report data into a spread-sheet program such as Microsoft Excel, do the following:

1. Open the spreadsheet in which you will copy your report data.

2. From FrontPage, with your Web open, open the View menu, choose Reports, and then select the report you want.

3. Right-click anywhere within the report and choose Copy Report.

4. Return to the spreadsheet, right-click anywhere within it, and choose Paste.

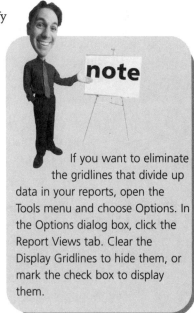

note

If you want to eliminate the gridlines that divide up data in your reports, open the Tools menu and choose Options. In the Options dialog box, click the Report Views tab. Clear the Display Gridlines to hide them, or mark the check box to display them.

Updating Links

Studies of Internet users report that few things irritate visitors more than a site that doesn't keep its hyperlinks up-to-date. When queried, many visitors complain that they're less inclined to revisit a site if they can't be sure its links work and feel that it's a strong indication of sloppy maintenance.

Dead or broken hyperlinks typically occur for one of two reasons:

- Because a page or site is no longer available—These should be removed.
- Because the exact URL for the page or site has changed—The hyperlink should be edited to reflect the change.

Such problematic links can be identified by checking the Problems report under Reports view. (Reports were discussed earlier in this chapter.)

To edit a hyperlink, do the following:

1. With your page open in Page Design view, right-click the hyperlink.

2. Right-click and choose Hyperlink Properties.

3. Specify the page you want to link to or edit the URL currently associated with the hyperlink in the Address box.

Here's how to remove a hyperlink:

1. Right-click the hyperlink in Design view and select Remove Hyperlink.

2. Press the Delete key on your keyboard.

Finally, you can keep the text related to a hyperlink, but remove the actual hyperlink itself. This is useful when you want to refer to a page or site but, because the link no longer works, you don't want visitors to be able to click on it and get bad results.

Follow these steps to accomplish this:

1. From Design view, select the hyperlink from your page(s).

2. Click the Insert Hyperlink toolbar button.

3. Click Remove Link.

THE ABSOLUTE MINIMUM

Once your Web site is published and traffic has begun to arrive, you want to be sure everything about the site is as close to perfect as it can possibly be. This means you need to perform some housekeeping and run some reports.

In this chapter, you learned how to remove unwanted pages and subfolders on your local Web, as well as create new folders to help organize your files. You also learned how to delete unused files and folders from your Web server, create task assignments and check their status or work on them to fulfill the task, understand and use the various report categories, keep a copy of your report information to maintain a historical profile of it, and fix/edit broken hyperlinks and remove dead hyperlinks.

Now that you have mastered some of the essential maintenance and information gathering you'll need to properly manage your site, you won't have to wait until a visitor complains to address a problem or need.

PART V

CODING YOUR WEB

A

INSTALLING FRONTPAGE

Because almost nothing in the computer world is more frustrating that software you want to use but can't install, this appendix is designed to address common situations that may lead to difficulty in installing FrontPage 2003.

Installation Problems

If you're having problems installing FrontPage 2003, you shouldn't automatically assume that the product just won't work on your system or that you got a bad copy. There are some small but frequently encountered issues that can make many types of applications hard to install.

The very first thing you should do is shut down and restart your PC. By doing this, you reduce the chances that some other issue on your desktop is responsible for hanging up your installation—which is highly possible.

After you restart your system, however, you might have programs that load automatically with Windows. One or more of these could affect your ability to start or complete a program installation. For this reason, you should close any open applications, as well as turn off utilities such as disk and virus checking, open Net communications programs, and anything meant to protect your PC from a crash. These are known to interfere with installations.

You can check what processes are currently running on your system by using the Windows Task Manager. To access Task Manager, press Ctrl+Alt+Del *once*. This opens a screen similar to the one shown in Figure A.1.

FIGURE A.1

Task Manager summarizes all processes running on your system.

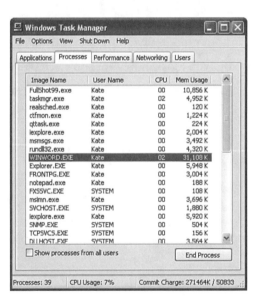

Unless you're very familiar with Windows, you may not understand all the processes listed here. If this is the case, click the Applications tab, which tells you exactly what programs are running at the time. If you see an automatically loaded program listed there, make a note of it, close Task Manager, and shut down that program.

Finally, if you used a beta copy of FrontPage 2003 and are attempting to install the final release of the program on your PC, you should remove the beta first (open the Control Panel and use Add and Remove Programs). Although FrontPage should try to remove the beta version itself as it installs, a problematically installed beta may prevent the final release installation.

If you still encounter problems installing FrontPage 2003, you can access the Microsoft Knowledgebase to search for known issues and possible solutions. Visit the site at `http://search.support.microsoft.com`.

Upgrading Windows

Unlike earlier versions of FrontPage, this release is very particular about which version of Windows it will install and operate on. That's because it was created in parallel with Microsoft Office 2003, which has similar restrictions.

To use FrontPage 2003, You must be running either of the following:

- Windows 2000
- Windows XP

If you're unsure of which version of Windows you have, here's a quick way to check:

1. Click the Start button and choose Control Panel (or click Start, Settings, Control Panel).
2. Double-click the System icon.
3. The System Properties dialog box opens. In the General tab, you will see your version number, as shown in Figure A.2.

FIGURE A.2

The System Properties dialog box's General tab provides your exact Windows version information.

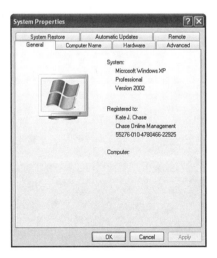

PART VI

CODING YOUR WEB

Index

NOTE: Page numbers preceded by "pdf:" are found in elements on the Web site.

F

How can we make this index more useful? Email us at indexes@quepublishing.com

How can we make this index more useful? Email us at indexes@quepublishing.com

X - Y - Z